Economic Modeling in the Post Great Recession Era

Incomplete Data, Imperfect Markets

John Silvia
Azhar Iqbal
Sarah Watt House

T0338409

WILEY

Cover image: © styleTTT/iStockphoto
Cover design: Wiley

Copyright © 2017 by John Silvia, Azhar Iqbal, and Sarah Watt House.
All rights reserved.

Published by John Wiley & Sons, Inc., Hoboken, New Jersey.
Published simultaneously in Canada.

No part of this publication may be reproduced, stored in a retrieval system,
or transmitted in any form or by any means, electronic, mechanical,
photocopying, recording, scanning, or otherwise, except as permitted under
Section 107 or 108 of the 1976 United States Copyright Act, without either the
prior written permission of the Publisher, or authorization through payment
of the appropriate per-copy fee to the Copyright Clearance Center, Inc., 222
Rosewood Drive, Danvers, MA 01923, (978) 750-8400, fax (978) 646-8600, or
on the Web at www.copyright.com. Requests to the Publisher for permission
should be addressed to the Permissions Department, John Wiley & Sons, Inc.,
111 River Street, Hoboken, NJ 07030, (201) 748-6011, fax (201) 748-6008, or
online at http://www.wiley.com/go/permissions.

Limit of Liability/Disclaimer of Warranty: While the publisher and author have
used their best efforts in preparing this book, they make no representations
or warranties with respect to the accuracy or completeness of the contents of
this book and specifically disclaim any implied warranties of merchantability
or fitness for a particular purpose. No warranty may be created or extended
by sales representatives or written sales materials. The advice and strategies
contained herein may not be suitable for your situation. You should consult
with a professional where appropriate. Neither the publisher nor author shall
be liable for any loss of profit or any other commercial damages, including but
not limited to special, incidental, consequential, or other damages.

For general information on our other products and services or for technical
support, please contact our Customer Care Department within the United
States at (800) 762-2974, outside the United States at (317) 572-3993 or fax
(317) 572-4002.

Wiley publishes in a variety of print and electronic formats and by print-on-
demand. Some material included with standard print versions of this book
may not be included in e-books or in print-on-demand. If this book refers to
media such as a CD or DVD that is not included in the version you purchased,
you may download this material at http://booksupport.wiley.com. For more
information about Wiley products, visit www.wiley.com.

ISBN 978-1-119-34983-9 (Hardcover)
ISBN 978-1-119-35082-8 (ePub)
ISBN 978-1-119-35086-6 (ePDF)

Printed in the United States of America

10 9 8 7 6 5 4 3 2 1

For more information on any of the above titles, please visit www .wiley.com.

To Jack, Ellery, William, Francis, Isaac, and Michael

Brutus, Caesar, and Diesel

Shahkora and Mohammad Iqbal, Nargis, Saeeda,
Shahid, and Noreen

Ken & Gingie and Mark & Millie

And to the family and friends who remain our
wellsprings of inspiration

In memoriam

To Lorrie DeGraffenreid Tubbs, teacher and principal, who was
one of the initial white teachers to go into Memphis's historically
black schools at the initiation of desegregation

Contents

Preface/Justification

For the entirety of the current economic expansion, outcomes have fallen short of expectations. Overall economic growth has been below perceived potential. Inflation remains persistently below the Fed's 2 percent target, while long-term unemployment remains higher and wage growth lower than anticipated. Why?

For decision makers, the deviation of actual outcomes from expected carries important lessons for how we model the actual economic environment we face rather than an idealized vision of the economic landscape that is often based on a view of the past.

Meanwhile, on the public policy front, neither fiscal nor monetary stimulus has delivered on their promised results in terms of real economic growth and jobs. For decision makers, there appears to be little guidance about the connections between idealized theoretical conditions of the economy and actual results of the current recovery.

Our challenge is to recognize that, as we saw with both the fiscal and monetary stimulus, the estimates of policy effectiveness vastly underweighted the impact of market imperfections at the time—looking at idealized conditions rather than the real economy. Broad verbal claims of economic policy effectiveness were disconnected from formal analysis of the actual economic conditions facing the economy and decision makers at the time. Hence, estimates of both fiscal and monetary multipliers were wildly overstated. Real-world conditions of very high credit and liquidity constraints, as well as high levels of policy uncertainty, were certainly present.

Unfortunately, we are now in the precarious situation of having readers of economic content and public policy pronouncements stop taking seriously any analysis of current economic conditions that purports to claim any degree of precision.

Our approach here is that we do not start with an idealized economy to draw lessons for decision makers; instead, we examine the economic world as it is—not as we imagine it. Stylized economic models are less useful for real-world decision makers. In this book, we focus on four market imperfections that persist in our economy in the current economic expansion—dynamic adjustment, imperfect information, lags in price movements, and policy uncertainty.

In contrast, idealized economic models often assume conditions of perfect competition. For example, it is often assumed that households and firms instantly react to an exogenous economic shock and move smoothly to a new equilibrium point. Second, the idealized model assumes full and complete information, but economic information is very imperfect and certainly economic policy intentions are anything but transparent. With respect to prices, it is obvious that many prices do not move instantaneously to a new equilibrium when faced with an exogenous economic shock. Moreover, there are many given, administered prices set by governments that interfere with price discovery. Finally, we are familiar with the experience of frequent changes in economic policy and, more fundamentally, uncertainty about what direction economic policy is actually taking.

FOUR CHARACTERISTICS OF A LESS-THAN-PERFECT ECONOMY

1. Economies Are Characterized by Dynamic Adjustments—Things Take Time

We are familiar with the proposition that monetary policy acts with lags, often long and variable lags. In theory, we have also begun to appreciate that the efficiency of countercyclical fiscal policy has been diminished by the recognition of significant policy implementation lags since the 1960s.

As for the private sector, alterations of consumer spending to a change in oil prices or tax incentives take place over time and with no consistent pace. This is also true of business investment, which we explore more thoroughly in Chapter 5.

2. Imperfect Information—What You See Is Not What You Get in an Imperfect Economy

During the past few years we have witnessed a series of examples where the information we see is not quite the reflection of reality.

In 2014, we had an instance where the Institute for Supply Management (ISM) manufacturing index, a key economic indicator, was released, re-released and then re-rereleased again in the same morning to correct a series of errors. This sequence created confusion in the markets, and no doubt, many missed trades and consequent capital gains and losses occurred that would not have been realized if the correct number had been initially released.

We are also very aware that, despite the monthly Bureau of Labor Statistics (BLS) releases and explanations, the public remains confused about the differences between the establishment and household surveys and how we can have job gains and a rise in the unemployment rate during the same month. Moreover, how come the number of jobs can be revised for prior months but not the unemployment rate? Additional series, such as retail sales, are also continuously revised—information remains imperfect.

3. Price Adjustment—Contracts—Hop, Skip, and Jump at the Local Gas Station

Price adjustments are not smooth in the real economy. Therefore, the economic system is in a constant state of disequilibrium, as prices do not reflect the full effect of market forces. Moreover, our forecasts seldom have time to play out, as there is often a regular sequence of market shocks over time. As all of our experience at the local gas station over the past year can attest, price changes are often not very smooth and frequently opposite in direction over short periods of time. Price adjustments reflect the judgments of sellers about the trade-off between customer satisfaction, maximizing profits, and fighting for market share.

Moreover, in the short run, price adjustments are limited by price fixing for many goods and services. Federal- and state-mandated prices are pervasive in areas such as labor (minimum wages), credit (interest rates and ATM fees), and other goods and services (utilities, rent controls, and health care). These pervasive fixed prices/federally mandated prices do not allow fully flexible prices—often in both directions.

4. Economic Policy Inconsistencies—The Parable of Strange Bedfellows

Policy inconsistencies reflect a frequent conflict between economic and political objectives and validate the volatility in the economic policy uncertainty index. Moreover, policy by polling is a growing phenomenon, and yet most of these polls are counterproductive.

Frequent political polls indicate that Congress is held in low esteem and yet most congressmen are reelected—quite a disconnect. Such polls contain little information about the actual economic value or effectiveness of policy since the polling sample so often reflects the self-selected viewing or listening audience itself. In addition, the actual policy put in place reflects the influence of an entire policy influence industry—lobbyists, D.C.-based news correspondents, Fed watchers, and D.C.-based political consultants.

Moreover, policy initiatives, such as the Affordable Care Act, are subject to frequent changes that limit the ability of private actors to respond to any tentative, but unclarified, elements of the original legislation. Fiscal tax policy is subject to perennial revisions every legislative session. Trade and environmental policies are altered by federal agencies such that the initial legislation is regularly revised in action, and this thereby increases the uncertainty of the impacts of legislation and thereby limits the willingness of the private sector to react to any initial legislation.

WHY THIS BOOK?

This book is well timed after the experience of the last six years. First, there has been a clear demarcation between the forecasts of policy makers and actual outcomes, and these persistent differences have required time for contemplation. Second, by letting the dust settle, we can better identify three key facets of economic behavior that distinguish the current economic recovery from an idealized recovery and, in addition, from recoveries in the past. Our approach is to provide both some explanation and statistical perspective on the actual economic workings of the economy during the current economic recovery. Waiting for the return to a "normal" economy has become like waiting for Godot.

Instead, given the evidence of structural breaks in the economy, real economic growth has been below prerecession rates. Labor force growth and its associated participation rate have been below the trends of prior economic recoveries. Inflation, despite quantitative easing, has been below 2 percent for all six years of the expansion.

Our value proposition is simple. We apply statistical techniques to economic factors of interest for private and public decision makers in the current expansion and characterize the evolving conditions of the U.S. economy relative to the idealized model of the workings of the economy. We address several statistical techniques to address critical character economic behavior in the context of the post 2007–2009 recession economy. We recognize structural change, not fight against it, and we do not engage in wishful hoping for a return to a simpler, idealized economic landscape.

Our book appeals to a broad audience. We address four economic characteristics that are central to the actual behaviors in the economy. These are dynamic adjustment, imperfect information, lags and disparities in price movements, and, finally, economic policy uncertainty. Then we examine six aspects of the economy, one of which is the labor market, and the implications of the four economic characteristics on the actual behavior in the labor market. We apply a number of statistical techniques to identify and quantify the behavior using SAS as our primary statistical tool. The book is aimed at practitioners and both advanced undergraduate and graduate students interested in techniques to understand and evaluate in an applied manner the current economic situation.

Chapters 1 through 4 identify the fundamental challenge to our economy today—the shift in the behavior of economic growth and the three characteristics that differentiate the current recovery from the idealized model of the economy that failed to provide the guidance necessary to forecast and understand current trends.

Dynamic adjustment, Chapter 2, reflects the reality that developments in the economy take time to adjust to what would be considered an equilibrium. This is certainly true of households and firms as they adjust to economic and political shocks. Here, the role of market frictions is paramount. For example, in the labor market, both employers and potential employees cannot move instantaneously to a new equilibrium in the labor market given these frictions. In many markets there are barriers to rapid adjustment that lead to excess inventories in production, structural and long-term unemployment, and credit rationing. As suggested by Reinhart and Rogoff, the current economic recovery has been limited by financial constraints and the implementation of new financial regulations. Uncertainty and expectations also play a key role in making decisions that determine the path of economic adjustment—the difference between what was expected and what is realized drives much of economic activity.

Chapter 3 focuses on the role of information and, more specifically, the reality of a world of decision making with imperfect information, incomplete information, and less-than-exact economic models. Imperfect information is well exemplified by the repetitive revisions of economic series such as employment, retail sales, and gross domestic product (GDP) that complicate decision making. Incomplete information follows from the missing variables problem we witness every day when we don't have measures for many economic behaviors that we believe are important to understanding the economy. Finally, decision making is subject to many biases but also the uncertainty of whether the precise model we are using for decision making actually matches the behavior of the economy. Current debates on the usefulness of the Philips Curve to forecast inflation are a prime example.

Finally, price adjustments are often portrayed as smooth, with quick and direct moves to the new equilibrium after an economic shock. Instead, as we examine in Chapter 4, price adjustments are not smooth and often reverse directions; "corrections, short-covering" are frequently cited in market commentary.

Moreover, price adjustments take time to play out—they are not instantaneous. Exchange rate misalignment in the late 1990s began to correct with Thailand in May 1997, when the central bank there failed to defend the Thai baht. In August, Indonesia adopted a free-floating regime—after which their currency immediately sunk. Price movements intensified in November as those corporations that had borrowed in dollars sold rupiah to get dollars, driving the rupiah down further. In November, values on the Seoul stock exchange dramatically declined. Economic weakness then led to a lower price of oil, which led to the 1998 Russian oil crisis, followed by the failure of Long-Term Capital Management in the United States and rapid Federal Reserve actions. Our lesson is that price adjustments take place over time and across numerous markets—credit, goods, foreign exchange, labor—generating real effects over time.

Our analysis extends the text into core economic factors that matter as inputs to effective decision making. In Chapter 5, we examine one aspect of aggregate demand—business investment. In this case we examine the role of dynamic adjustment and price movements. In addition, we examine the role of imperfect information as firms estimate the future path of real final sales, interest rates, and economic policy—especially tax policy on the planned investment horizon.

In Chapter 6, we examine the often overlooked role of corporate profits in the macroeconomy, both as a return to capital and as an input to growth. Profits are both an incentive and reward. Yet profits have very high cyclical variation relative to overall economic activity, thereby creating a difficulty in interpreting the information that profits provide to decision makers. Profits cannot be taken in isolation, as corporate profits play a role in the broader economy—representing returns to savers/investors and incentives for investment.

Labor markets set the tone as the second input to growth—and as a measure of the return to labor. In Chapter 7, we highlight the patterns of this economic expansion that has made the behavior this cycle in labor so different than in the past. The heterogeneity of workers, and employers' expectations has produced a significant amount of imperfect information between bid and offer in the labor market. Meanwhile, we have witnessed the drawn-out adjustment of both employment and the price of labor (wages) that reinforces the view that these adjustments are anything but consistent with the perfect competition model underlying most economic models.

In Chapter 8, we examine the behavior of inflation and focus on the change in price behavior over time, particularly the lack of accelerating inflation in the current expansion despite the declining labor market slack. Our work identifies the importance of structural breaks in the inflation series as a major barrier to developing a simple theory of inflation determination. Meanwhile, we put forward an early-warning system that provides for a distinct three-option outlook for inflation trends.

Combining the views on growth and inflation, our net result is to identify the structural breaks in the behavior of interest rates during the current cycle in Chapter 9. This provides us an excellent example of price discovery as the price of credit—interest rates—frequently overshoots, and then undershoots the expected equilibrium values. We also bring in the dynamic inconsistency character of a low-inflation policy by the central bank. This policy introduces another element of misinformation that increases the range of possible future values of interest rates and also adds to the forecast error.

In Chapter 10, we focus on the capital flows within the open economy model. This reflects the increasing globalization of capital markets as well as the unusual flight to safety incentive for global investors that has kept U.S. interest rates much lower than many forecasters had anticipated. What is also different during this expansion is that U.S. equity markets may also be influenced by the perception of flight to safety flows. We test this hypothesis in this chapter.

Finally, in Chapter 11, we highlight the implications of our three principles of the post–Great Recession economy and their importance for public- and private-sector decision makers. Our approach brings to decision makers three advantages when looking over the economic landscape. First, rather than an idealized approach to benchmarking economic activity, we recognize the character of the post–Great Recession economy that actually confronts decision makers. Second, we identify three aspects of economic behavior that influence the developments we actually see in product, credit, labor, and international capital markets. Third, we present statistical methods to identify the structural breaks and lags that characterize the information/adjustment issues faced by decision makers.

Acknowledgments

We would like to thank all of the people who have supported us through the writing and publication of this book. Special thanks to Alex Moehring and Michael Pugliese, for without their help this book would not be possible. We also wish to express our gratitude for the many people at Wells Fargo who have supported this project including Diane Schumaker-Krieg, Tim Sloan, and John Shrewsberry, as well as the technical support staff at Wells Fargo. Thank you Robert Crow, editor of *Business Economics* and the referees of that journal, as well as the referees of articles that have appeared in other journals, who have improved the quality of our research over the years. We are grateful for the instructors and students who have come through our lives and taught and inspired us (Nuzhat Ahmad, Kajal Lahiri, Asad Zaman, and Adil Siddique of SUNY-Albany).

CHAPTER 1

Setting
the Context

Returning from holiday on September 3, 1928, Alexander Fleming began to sort through petri dishes containing colonies of *Staphylococcus*, a bacterium that causes boils and sore throats.

Fleming noticed something unusual, imperfect, on one dish. The dish was dotted with colonies of bacteria, save for one area where a blob of mold was growing. The zone immediately around the mold—later identified as a rare strain of penicillin—was clear, as if the mold had secreted something that inhibited bacterial growth.

Fleming found that his "mold juice" was capable of killing a wide range of harmful bacteria. Such was the beginning of penicillin and a better life for all of us here.

In economics, it is the unusual, the imperfect, that provides the clues about the way forward—stagnation in the 1970s, tax policy and deregulation in the 1980s, and the financial crisis and subsequent reforms over the past 10 years.

THE PROBLEM WITH UNCRITICAL ASSUMPTIONS IN A LESS-THAN-PERFECT ECONOMY[1]

Yet in empirical work, economists are too frequently guided by a number of uncritical assumptions on how the world works. First, as economists, we must recognize and discourage straw man arguments that improperly identify the false choices in economic decisions or portray the outcomes of such decisions only in the context of an idealized economic model.

Second, we must be more critical of arguments that fail to recognize the assumption—or violation—of ceteris paribus when the outcomes of economic decisions are quite different when those ceteris paribus assumptions do not apply.

Third, we must be more critical of the simplistic view of the efficient market hypothesis—both information and foresight are not perfect.

Fourth, we must be more critical of the argument that economic markets discount all available current information, but fail to distinguish that markets are not clairvoyant for all future information.

---

[1] John E. Silvia, *Dynamic Economic Decision Making* (Hoboken, NJ: John Wiley & Sons, 2011) contains an extensive review of these challenging assumptions in Chapters 3, 4.

Fifth, we must be more critical to distinguish that private market failures do not automatically imply that government can do better or do something at all.[2]

Finally, following the line of reasoning of Captain Barbossa, economic rules are more like guidelines rather than rules.[3]

THE PROBLEM WITH MODELS IN AN IMPERFECT ECONOMY

Economic outcomes rarely come about as seamlessly as predicted by theories and models. As economists, we should be more critical on overly simplistic models that assume away the complexities of the modern economy.

As economists, we should be more critical of irrelevant models that solve problems that no one is seeking to address.

As economists, we should be more critical of models that assume away the essential problem to achieve precise mathematical results in an imprecise world.

As economists, we should be more critical of essays that claim—with surprise—that no one before has looked at this problem.

As economists, we should be more critical about models that assume supply and demand balance out rapidly and unfailingly and that perfect competition reigns in markets.

As economists, we should be more critical of models that cannot assign a probability to a critical event and then rule out that critical event when that event is crucial to a fair assessment of risks. Low-probability events, with high costs, are still very expensive.

As economists, we should be more critical about models that exclude almost all consequential diversity and uncertainty of households and firms—characteristics that in many ways are fundamental to the outcomes of the actual economy. This also includes the failure to include an extensive financial sector in many models.

---

[2] James Buchanan, *Democracy in Deficit* (Cleveland, OH: Academic Press, 1977). Government has its own pattern of rent seeking that is often not in the public interest of the broader society.

[3] *Pirates of the Caribbean*, Walt Disney Pictures, 2003.

As economists, we should be more critical of models that are useful only in a trend economy where they are estimated—when recessions, financial instability, and periods of the unusual are the real challenge to examine.

FOUR CHARACTERISTICS OF A LESS-THAN-PERFECT ECONOMY

Dynamic Adjustments—Things Take Time

First, we are familiar with the proposition that monetary policy acts with lags, often long and variable. In theory, we have also begun to appreciate that the efficiency of countercyclical fiscal policy has been diminished by the significant recognition of policy implementation lags since the 1960s. Unfortunately, however, the distinction between temporary and permanent policy changes has been continuously lost in policy making in recent years. Milton Friedman won his Nobel Prize for the permanent income hypothesis, but the failure of the 1968 tax surcharge appears to have been forgotten by today's policy makers. Temporary, lump-sum tax rebates are simply timing changes—not permanent action—and do not jump-start the economy. Cash for clunkers is a classic recent example. As a result, countercyclical fiscal policy has fallen by the wayside and now the focus of fiscal policy is more on long-run growth—incentives and disincentives for labor, capital, technology, and innovation.

Identifying permanent or temporary changes in economic policy has been made particularly difficult by the significant political election turnovers during the past 20 years. This has led to inconsistent economic policy and a significant shortening of time horizons for decision makers—especially for long-lived investment. In contrast to the Eisenhower vision on infrastructure—the interstate highway system—the focus today is on isolated, one-off, pork barrel projects to jump-start the economy; consider, then, the experience of Japan.

Moreover, one must think critically of the marginal cost/marginal benefit trade-off of individual infrastructure projects, not the blanket adoption of poorly specified spending programs. There must be a distinction between what we want and what we can afford, what is nice to have, and what can be justified by economic choices. Economists make choices—politicians make promises.

Second, dynamic adjustments are not symmetric across sectors of the economy. Capital moves faster than labor, cash moves faster than capital—a lesson in the current economic expansion. Asymmetric liquidity and credit constraints have limited consumption choices despite fiscal stimulus and monetary easing in the current recovery. A 10 percent increase in asset prices does not elicit an equal and opposite reaction as a 10 percent decline in asset prices within the economy. Going down stairs does not elicit the same amount of effort as going up stairs.

Third, adjustments occur not simply to new information, but when that information is different from what was expected. Markets are forward looking and discount expected future outcomes. Changes in asset prices are driven by the difference between expected and realized earnings, employment gains, inflation, and personal income patterns. Earnings, interest rates, oil prices, or regulatory actions by federal agencies or even the Supreme Court, for example, when different from market expectations, elicit significant reactions, and the movements are distinctly asymmetric.

Fourth, prices often overshoot—whether we are looking at exchange rates, interest rates, or commodity prices—oil prices in particular. Overshooting reflects the interaction between a complex of economic forces—not mere speculation. Expectations are not static; they evolve, reflecting the new information that is constantly appearing on our computer screens and the differentials between prices across markets.[4]

Therefore, our economy is seldom at equilibrium. Instead, there is a steady over/undershooting of prices, as illustrated in Figures 1.1 and 1.2 for inflation and 10-year U.S. Treasury rates since 1982.

However, in many cases, prices are not allowed to completely adjust due to public policy. This creates tension and persistent disequilibrium in the markets—most recently illustrated by Greece. Exchange rates are commonly not allowed to be free—they are often managed— see the recent experience in China. Since exchange rates do not completely adjust, interest rates, inflation, and growth do not completely adjust either—a continued disequilibrium—which often leads to a sudden break such as illustrated by the European Exchange Rate Mechanism (ERM)/British pound in 1992 and the Swiss franc/euro movements in 2015 (Figures 1.3 and 1.4).

---

[4] Rudiger Dornbusch, "Expectations and Exchange Rate Dynamics," *Journal of Political Economy* 84 (December 1976): 1161–1176.

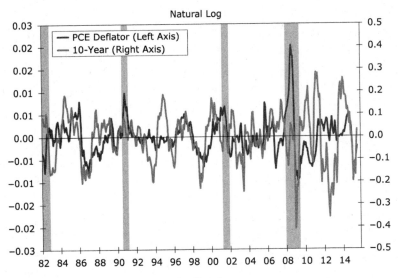

Figure 1.1 Deviation from the Long-Run Trend
Source: U.S. Department of Commerce and Federal Reserve Board

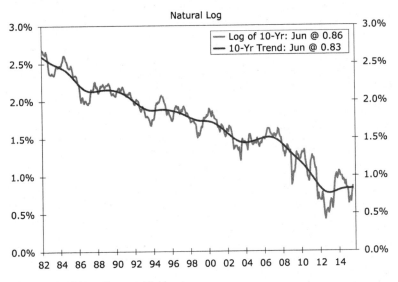

Figure 1.2 10-Year Treasury Yields
Source: Federal Reserve Board

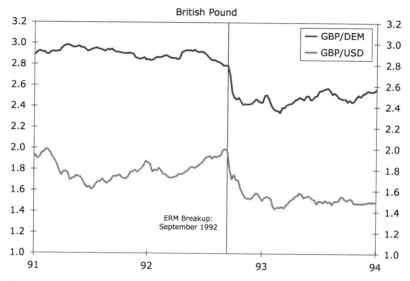

Figure 1.3 ERM Breakup
Source: Bloomberg LP

Figure 1.4 Swiss Exchange Rate
Source: Bloomberg LP

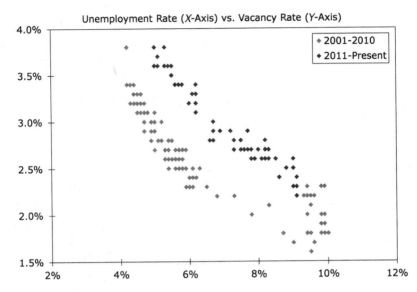

Figure 1.5 The Beveridge Curve
Source: U.S. Department of Labor

In addition, capital is not perfectly mobile—think of Japan in the 1980s and China today—and that limits the ability of interest rates, exchange rates, and the real return on physical capital to adjust and results in pent up demand/supply imbalances in capital flows over time.

Finally, we recognize that many economic series are not mean reverting, as illustrated by the outward shift in the Beveridge Curve more than six years after the labor market began to recover (Figure 1.5) and the U-6 unemployment rate (Figure 1.6).

Imperfect Information—What You See Is Not What You Get

In recent years, we have witnessed a series of examples where the information we see is not quite the reflection of reality. In mid-2014, there was an instance where the Institute for Supply Management (ISM), a key economic indicator, was released, re-released, and then re-rereleased again in the same morning to correct a series of errors. This sequence created confusion in the markets, and no doubt, many

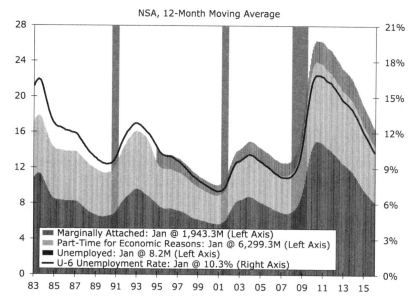

Figure 1.6 U-6 Unemployment
Source: U.S. Department of Labor

missed trades and consequent capital gains and losses that would not have occurred if the correct number had been initially released.

We are also very aware that, despite the monthly Bureau of Labor Statistics (BLS) releases and explanations, the public remains confused about the differences between the establishment and household surveys. How can there be more jobs and a rise in the unemployment rate in the same month? Moreover, how come the number of jobs can be revised for prior months but not the unemployment rate? Additional series, such as retail sales, are also continuously revised—information remains imperfect.

An Eagle That Chases Two Fish Catches Neither

In public policy and in public discussions, there is persistent confusion between relative and absolute prices. Media coverage does not make the distinction between real and nominal values—weak nominal retail sales can coexist with solid real consumer spending. As illustrated by Lucas in his 1972 paper, decision makers cannot distinguish if a price change reflects a relative price change or a change in the aggregate price level.[5]

Public and professional discussion continues the confusion between real and nominal prices—real wages, real interest rates, and real exchange rates drive real behavior in multiple markets, yet we continuously cite changes in nominal wages, nominal interest rates, and nominal exchange rates as drivers of economic activity.

Economic information is only one example of imperfect information. Tax and spending policy, and often nonpolicy in Washington, reflects a constant changing of the rules and rent-seeking behavior that reduces the efficiency of the economy. Tax and spending policy is constantly being changed. Uncertainties about highway funding make long-term decision making impossible. Tax cuts are phased-in and can easily be altered along the way. Obamacare, Dodd-Frank, and the many Basel Accords all generate rules—often vague and in bits and pieces—reducing the certainty of long-run credit and financial allocation decisions. Imperfect information generates imperfect decisions.

In monetary policy, the price we pay for committee-based policy making is imperfect information on the direction of monetary policy. There is a trade-off between more voices and greater transparency. There are practical trade-offs and weighing problems with multiple goals.

In labor markets, the search costs for information, as illustrated by research by Mortenson[6] and Phelps,[7] reflect reality in many economic sectors and the reality that nominal values can impact real economic variables—imperfect information is not neutral.

To illustrate, Figure 1.7 gives visual evidence about the ongoing debate about the persistently weak reported real gross domestic product (GDP) in the first quarter relative to the rest of the quarters since 1985. Figure 1.8 illustrates the mixed message of the discrepancy between GDP and gross domestic income (GDI).

---

[5] Robert E. Lucas, "Expectations and the Neutrality of Money," *Journal of Economic Theory* 4 (April 1972): 103–124.

[6] Dale T. Mortensen, "Job Search and Labor Market Analysis," in *Handbook of Labor Economics*, vol. 2 ed. Orley Ashenfelter and Richard Layard (Amsterdam: Elsevier, 1986), 849–919.

[7] Edmund S. Phelps, "Money-Wage Dynamics and Labor Market Equilibrium," *Journal of Political Economy* 76 (Part 2, July/August 1968): 678–711.

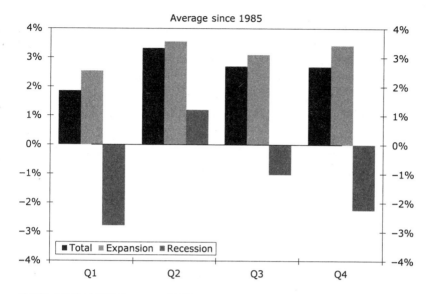

Figure 1.7 Real GDP Changes—CAGR
Source: U.S. Department of Commerce

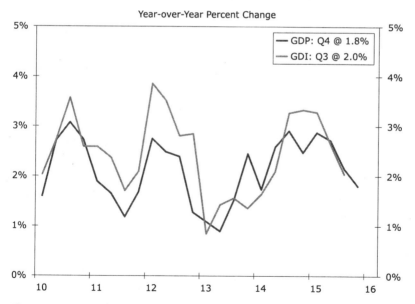

Figure 1.8 Gross Domestic Product vs. Income
Source: U.S. Department of Commerce

Imperfect information is obvious when we analyze the labor market. Which unemployment rate is the focus of monetary policy and financial markets? If the unemployment rate is the focus, then what added value is there to having a labor market index? Should we read the existence of a labor market index as suggesting that the unemployment rate is imperfect—as both the target of policy and a fair reading of the labor market? Our analysis indicates that the labor market index does provide some additional guidance on credit quality in the increasingly complex labor market of the twenty-first century.[8]

State-Dependent Pricing

Evidence suggests that economic agents follow a strategy of state-dependent pricing such that there is no simple pricing rule, but that pricing reflects the perceived state of the economy and is not simply dependent on time. What is interesting is that this is the type of pricing policy currently being followed by the Federal Reserve with respect to the federal funds rate.[9] Target pricing, rather than optimal pricing, appears to more often explain market behavior. This same pattern appears consistent with monetary policy and indicates that monetary policy, under certain conditions, can have real economic effects when price adjustments are not uniform and instantaneous.

Inflation inertia in price adjustments allows for monetary policy shocks to have long-lasting effects when some prices are predetermined. Once again, if prices are initially predetermined, but not all firms adjust prices in response to a monetary shock due to sticky information, then real economic effects are the result.[10] Sticky information results from the observation that it is costly to obtain and process information—so firms do not continually update prices—they choose a path for prices. This allows for the real effects of changes in monetary policy in the short run.

[8] John E. Silvia and Azhar Iqbal, "Measuring the State of the Labor Market: A New Index," Wells Fargo Special Commentary, October 28, 2013.

[9] Andrew S. Caplin and Daniel F. Spulber, "Menu Costs and the Neutrality of Money," *Quarterly Journal of Economics* 102 (November 1987): 703–725.

[10] N. Gregory Mankiw and Ricardo Reis, "Sticky Information versus Sticky Prices: A Proposal to Replace the New Keynesian Phillips Curve," *Quarterly Journal of Economics* 117 (June 2002): 358–374.

ECONOMIC POLICY INCONSISTENCIES—THE PARABLE OF STRANGE BEDFELLOWS

Policy inconsistencies reflect a frequent conflict between economic and political objectives and validate the volatility in the index of economic policy uncertainty (Figure 1.9). Moreover, policy by polling is a growing phenomenon, and yet we view many of these polls as counterproductive. Frequent political polls indicate that Congress is held in low esteem and yet most congressmen are reelected—a disconnect. Such polls tell us little about the actual economic value or effectiveness of policy since the polling sample so often reflects the self-selected viewing or listening audience itself.

Moreover, the actual policy put in place reflects the influence of an entire policy influence industry—lobbyists, D.C.-based news correspondents, Fed watchers, and D.C.-based political consultants—often involved in rent-seeking behavior that may have little positive influence on real economic growth.

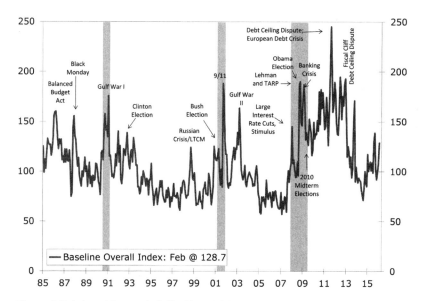

Figure 1.9 Index of Economic Policy Uncertainty
Source: Baker, Bloom and Davis[11]

---

[11] Scott Baker, Nicholas Bloom, and Steven Davis, Measuring Economic Policy Uncertainty, NBER working paper No. 21633, October 2015, www.policyuncertainty.com/.

Furthermore, policy initiatives, such as the Affordable Care Act, are subject to frequent changes that limit the ability of private actors to respond to any tentative but unclarified elements of the original legislation. Fiscal tax policy is subject to perennial revisions every legislative session. Trade and environmental policies are altered by federal agencies, and the initial legislation is regularly revised in action, thereby increasing the level of uncertainty of the impacts of legislation, limiting the willingness of the private sector to react to any initial legislation, and dragging out the response of economic actors. The long history of tariff policy in the United States has been a study of politics above economics.

Meanwhile, for fiscal policy, the continual alteration of tax laws undermines the ability of private actors to invest for the long term. Federal spending is often reflective of relative political power rather than economic rationale.

As for trade policy, Paul Krugman at a recent policy conference focused on the marginal costs/marginal benefit of an additional trade deal.[12] This reflects a more thoughtful approach to trade policy and a good benchmark for infrastructure spending rather than the absolute black-and-white approach to many policy issues. What is the balance between the marginal benefit/marginal cost of the next trade deal? What is the balance for the next infrastructure project?

---

[12] "TPP: No Big Deal?" NABE Policy Conference, March 10, 2015.

CHAPTER 2

Dynamic Adjustment in an Economy

Frictions Matter

Architecture starts when you carefully put two bricks together. There it begins.

—Ludwig Mies Van der Rohe

INTRODUCTION

For decision makers, theory provides useful guidelines. Almost every major central bank around the globe, along with international organizations such as the International Monetary Fund (IMF) and the World Bank, utilizes large-scale econometric models (also known as macro-models) based on theory to guide decision making. These models attempt to characterize the behavior of certain agents, including consumers, investors, and public policy makers. However, one of the central assumptions behind many of today's macro-models is that all agents in the model are in a state of equilibrium simultaneously or move seamlessly to such a state, which creates a general equilibrium and implies a frictionless model for the economy.

Yet the Great Recession, financial crisis, and the recent plunge in oil prices (along with several other events—debt and currency crises, for example) have forced economists to look beyond frictionless models and find alternatives. This chapter discusses some of these models with and without frictions. This first section of the chapter presents theoretical foundations of macro-models (adjustment) with frictions, and in the second section, we characterize the equilibrium states of different sectors and markets. The third and final section discusses guidelines to modeling equilibrium states with frictions.

In our view, frictions (barriers to smooth economic adjustment) exist, and in the presence of frictions, frictionless models do not provide an accurate assessment of the economy. As a result, policy recommendations based on frictionless models lead to misguided decisions and unanticipated outcomes.

In any economy, the short run goals of monetary and fiscal policy decisions change with the business cycle, and policy intervention is sometimes necessary to restore equilibrium in some sectors of the economy. By allowing for frictions in macro-models, policy makers would be more able to accurately assess the state of an economy, suggest appropriate policies, and anticipate the timing and magnitude of any policy change.

In the case of the U.S. economy, a number of policies fell short in the wake of the Great Recession due to a lack of acknowledgment of frictions. For example, while theory utilized in frictionless models suggested that significant fiscal stimulus in 2008–2009 and a zero-interest-rate policy would jump-start economic growth, uncertainty among consumers and businesses about financial regulation was an unforeseen friction, holding back credit markets and choking off the recovery.

"The Truth Is in the Details": Micro-Foundations of a Macro-Model

Standard macro-models consist of several blocks (sectors) and each block represents different aspects of the economy. Typical blocks of macro-models are (1) aggregate demand (AD), (2) aggregate supply (AS), and (3) economic policy.[1] The AD block consists of the spending versus saving decisions of economic agents (e.g., consumers, investors, and government), while the AS block evolves from the price-setting decisions of firms and the leisure/work decisions of households. Economic policy actions are included in the macro-models through the policy block. Some assumptions are crucial to understand the structure and output of a macro-model. For example, one assumption of the model is that microeconomics is the foundation of the AD and AS blocks. That is, decisions in the AD and AS blocks are based on a representative consumer and a representative firm. A second assumption states that different markets in the model are in equilibrium, or frictionless, in the long run.[2] These two assumptions are important, as they may be violated in the short run or in practice because of frictions. Furthermore, decision makers would need a different set of policy tools to address short-run frictions that would not otherwise exist in a frictionless economy.

How might you actually model these blocks of the economy? Households are typically assumed to be rational, which has a precise definition, although we can loosely define it as the existence of a utility function,

---

[1] For a survey of macro-models, see Jordi Gali and Mark Gertler, "Macroeconomic Modeling for Monetary Policy Evaluation," *Journal of Economic Perspectives* 21, no. 4 (Fall 2007): 25–45.
[2] There are several other assumptions of a macro-model—see Gali and Gertler (2007) for more details. In this chapter, we concentrate on these two assumptions and show why decision makers should include alternatives of these assumptions in decision making.

and their actions are consistent with maximizing expected utility subject to a budget constraint. Households generally maximize expected lifetime utility, and a simplified household maximization problem is given below, where household utility is assumed to depend only on consumption.

$$\max E_t \left(\sum_{s=t}^{\infty} \beta^{s-t} \log C_s \right)$$

Notice that the utility in any period is given by the natural logarithm of consumption ($u_t = \log C_t$). This is a convenient choice for a utility function because it is monotonically increasing (if $C_1 \leq C_2$ then $u(C_1) \leq u(C_2)$), easy to work with, and has another nice property: diminishing marginal returns. That is, the additional utility from and additional unit of consumption decreases as consumption rises ($\frac{\partial^2 u_t}{\partial C_t^2} < 0$). Combining this with a household budget constraint allows us to solve the household "problem" and obtain equilibrium conditions. Similarly for the production side of the economy, a representative firm is assumed to be a profit maximizer. Their problem is based on the available labor and capital, and they pay rents to the household to utilize these factors in production (assuming households own capital stock). This style of model is incredibly flexible and, although it can be complicated, can be extended in many ways. In addition, their micro-foundations provide a response to the Lucas Critique, as the agents in the economy will still attempt to maximize utility, profits, and so on, and yield a new equilibrium given a change in policy.[3]

The micro-foundations assumption, which states that a representative household/firm is the decision maker, implicitly assumes preferences such that expectations are identical within a group of economic agents.[4] The benefit of this assumption is that it makes determining equilibrium less complicated, as only one set of preferences for the household/firm is needed to represent the preferences of all agents in the model and thus determine the AD/AS blocks.

---

[3] Robert E. Lucas, "Econometric Policy Evaluation: A Critique," *Carnegie-Rochester Conference Series on Public Policy* 1 (1976).
[4] Another way of thinking would be to assume that average preferences between consumers (or investors) are identical. This would also create the same problem, however—frictionless models.

In reality, however, preferences and expectations are not identical within a group of economic agents (e.g., consumers and investors). These discrepancies, which Keynes originally called "animal spirits," may create frictions (disequilibrium or partial equilibrium) in the model, at least in the short run.[5] As a result of animal spirits, one segment of economic agents may be more optimistic (or pessimistic) about the economy than another segment of agents. This optimism (or pessimism) among certain agents may create a bubble (or bust) in that economy. Recessions provide us with undeniable evidence of frictions. Some recessions, such as the Great Recession of 2007–2009, might represent a structural break, in the sense that equilibrium may have shifted upward or downward for some sectors, or perhaps the entirety, of an economy.

For example, in response to the Great Recession, the Federal Open Market Committee (FOMC) brought down the federal funds target rate to an unprecedented 0.00 to 0.25 percent range, and kept the fed funds rate within that range for seven years (Figure 2.1). Similarly, the

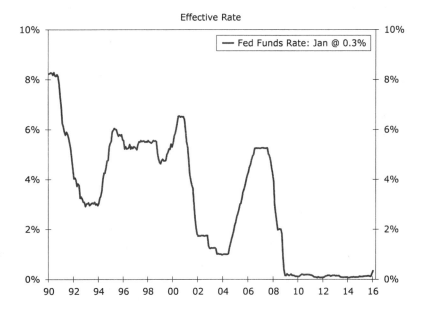

Figure 2.1 Fed Funds Rate
Source: Federal Reserve Board

---

[5] G. A. Akerlof and R. Shiller, *Animal Spirits: How Human Psychology Drives the Economy, and Why It Matters for Global Capitalism* (Princeton, NJ: Princeton University Press, 2009).

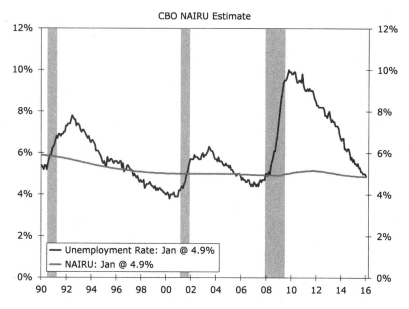

Figure 2.2 Unemployment Rate
Sources: U.S. Department of Labor and Congressional Budget Office

unemployment rate ran above the natural level, given by the nonaccelerating inflation rate of unemployment (NAIRU), for a longer period than in prior recoveries, another example of persistent disequilibrium (Figure 2.2).

Moreover, movements from one equilibrium to another are unlikely to be smooth, which further reiterates the importance of frictions. In sum, frictions are possible in the short run, and some short-run frictions even have the ability to shift the longer-run equilibrium. In the current cycle, an obvious piece of evidence of frictions and a shift in the longer-run equilibrium is the high number of employees who are working part-time for economic reasons and would desire a full-time job (Figure 2.3). Another illustration of market frictions is the outward shift in the Beveridge curve. This shift signals that at any given level of unemployed workers, there is a higher level of vacancies that firms cannot fill (Figure 2.4). Therefore, there is a persistent gap between the unemployed and job vacancies, which indicates an ongoing friction in the reestablishment of a new labor market equilibrium.

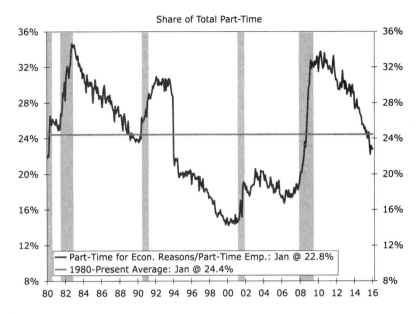

Figure 2.3 Part-Time Workers for Economic Reasons
Source: U.S. Department of Labor

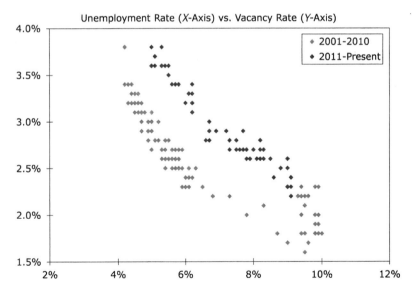

Figure 2.4 The Beveridge Curve
Source: U.S. Department of Labor

How Markets Function: Textbook Equilibrium

An economy consists of several markets (e.g., labor, housing, and money markets), and interactions between different economic agents determine equilibrium in these markets. Most economies are also open to international trade, thereby making the foreign exchange and trade markets also important. To understand how these markets function, we raise a few critical questions. What determines equilibrium in a market? What drives a market away from the equilibrium? How can equilibrium (or disequilibrium) in one market affect equilibrium in another market?

In the standard frictionless approach, a market (the labor market for example) is in equilibrium when the quantity demanded (demand) is equal to the quantity supplied (supply), ceteris paribus. Furthermore, this scenario of equilibrium supply and demand determines an equilibrium price (or wage rate, in the case of the labor market). Put differently, equilibrium in the labor market indicates that market participants (workers and employers) have obtained what they were seeking. That is, workers who are willing to work at the equilibrium wage rate (e.g., W*) would find work. By the same token, employers who are offering W* wage would find workers (Figure 2.5).

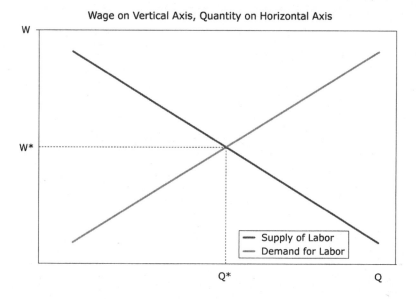

Figure 2.5 Labor Market Example

There are several crucial points we want to stress with this simple illustration, but let us review an intuitive example. First, we can typically divide participants of a market into two groups, which are demand (user) and supply (provider).[6] Second, decisions from these two groups determine equilibrium. Third, resources are optimally utilized in the market, as quantity demanded equals quantity supplied. Next, the equilibrium price (W*) does not imply a constant equilibrium value, as it may change over time. In addition, the equilibrium concept represents a stable path, and if one side of the market (e.g., demand) changes, then the equilibrium value (W*) would also change to equalize supply and demand.

Our final point divides changes in equilibrium states into two groups. If quantity supplied (supply) increases, then the equilibrium price would fall to equate supply and demand. In the frictionless sense, this scenario is known as "a movement along the curve." That is, if the equilibrium value changes due to the intramarket factors, then the economy moves along the supply-and-demand curves. However, if equilibrium changes due to external factors (outside the market), then it is a "shift in the curve." Both changes would require different policy actions from decision makers if policy makers desire a different outcome than that determined by the market. We shed light on this topic in the next section.

Dynamic Adjustments: "Creative Destruction" and Equilibrium States

A standard, frictionless, macro-model has good theoretical foundations; however, the model may be too simple for practical decision making. In practice, decision makers can design policies for the short run and long run. In the short run, markets experience shocks (internal and external), and those shocks create a state of disequilibrium. Frictions may be significant in preventing a smooth move to a new equilibrium and may

---

[6] For the sake of simplicity, we utilize the words *demand/user* and *supply/provider* interchangeably. In some cases, a user may also be a provider. In the case of the labor market, a worker is seeking a job but also providing supply of labor. Similarly, an employer is providing a job but also seeking a worker. The point we stress is that we need two sets of decisions to achieve equilibrium.

further alter the potential future path of the relationship between variables of interest in search of a new equilibrium, forcing us to rethink the model's existing theoretical foundations. A classic episode of such shocks and related market shocks (movements along the curve and shifts in the curve) has been observed recently. The Great Recession was a shock (a structural break) to the U.S. economy, and the effect of that shock was seen in every major sector of the economy. This begs the question: Can we quantify a market's distortions?

For some markets, there is more than one indicator to judge market disequilibrium. For instance, common measures to judge labor market performance are the unemployment rate, wage rate, monthly net change in nonfarm payrolls, and the labor force participation rate. For interest rates, short-term rates (the fed funds target rate), long-term rates (the 10-year Treasury yield), or a combination of both (yield spreads) can be utilized to evaluate the market's position relative to the equilibrium state.

There have been a number of sharp market adjustments in recent years. The first was the S&P 500 index, which dropped 51 percent between October 2007 and March 2009 (Figure 2.6). Another was the

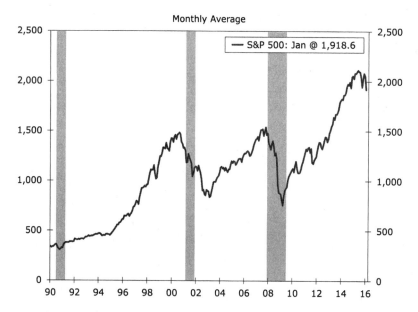

Figure 2.6 S&P 500 Index
Source: S&P

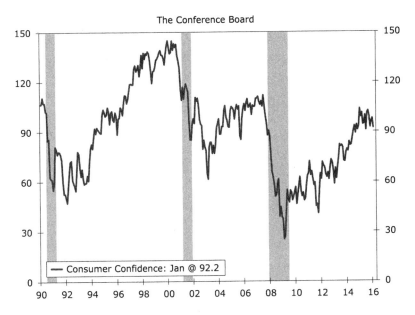

Figure 2.7 Consumer Confidence Index®
Source: The Conference Board, Inc. Reprinted with permission of The Conference Board. For more information, please see www.conference-board.org. Consumer Confidence Index is a registered trademark of The Conference Board, Inc.

consumer confidence index, which dropped 77 percent between July 2007 and February 2009 (Figure 2.7). A final example is the federal funds target rate, which was in the 0.00 to 0.25 percent range from December 2008 to December 2015. There are many more examples of such market movements, and each can be associated with large market disequilibria that require adjustments by market actors. Yet these actors are limited by frictions that alter the speed and completeness of adjustments relative to the assumption of a frictionless model.

Not all shocks create negative or sudden effects. Some shocks may shift equilibria upward, and the effect on the markets may be gradual. In 1942, Schumpeter developed the concept of "creative destruction," which suggests that new and improved technology not only replaces existing technology but also improves output, thus shifting equilibrium upward.[7] One example of creative destruction (positive, gradual

---

[7] For more detail about creative destruction, see Joseph Schumpeter, *Capitalism, Socialism and Democracy* (London: Routledge, 1942).

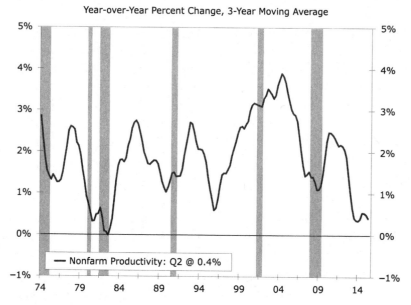

Figure 2.8 Productivity—Total Nonfarm
Source: U.S. Department of Labor

shock) is U.S. productivity growth since the mid-1990s (Figure 2.8). Some have used the term *productivity resurgence* to describe the post-1995 era, as U.S. productivity growth picked up between 1996 and 2006. The average productivity growth rate from 1996 to 2011 is 2.49 percent, higher than the average growth rate during 1974–1995 of 1.46 percent. Some analysts suggest information technology (e.g., the Internet and personal computers) is one of the major sources of productivity resurgence.[8] However, during the current economic recovery, productivity growth has slowed down considerably, averaging a weak 0.53 percent since 2011.

In sum, due to shocks and frictions, market disruptions can persist and the effects of a shock on a market's equilibrium can persist as well. In addition, a shock can shift a market's equilibrium upward or downward from the existing equilibrium state.

---

[8] For more detail about productivity resurgence see Ben Bernanke, "Productivity," 2005. Available at: www.federalreserve.gov/BoardDocs/speeches/2005/20050119/default.htm.

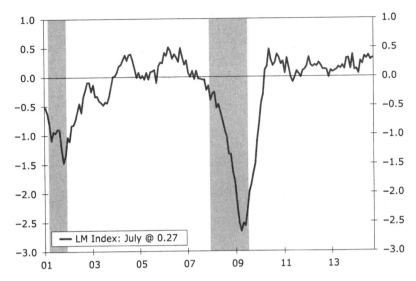

Figure 2.9 The Labor Market Index
Source: U.S. Department of Labor

Why Do We Care about Frictions?

After establishing that frictions exist, the question arises: Why do we care about frictions? For one, if a market is in disequilibrium, then it may imply that resources in the market are not being fully utilized. The Labor Market Index below zero during the Great Recession is an example of the labor market disequilibrium (Figure 2.9). For example, labor market disequilibrium suggests that some workers are unable to find jobs, some employers are unable to find workers, or perhaps both parties are unable to find matches. Another aspect of frictions is that sometimes distortions need to be "fixed." That is, policy intervention (e.g., monetary and/or fiscal policy) is required to bring the market back to a state of equilibrium.

A key point that is crucial for decision makers is that distortions in one market can affect other markets. For example, the Taylor rule suggests a relationship between interest rates, inflation, and output. Money neutrality implies a relationship between money supply and inflation (Figure 2.10), and the Phillips curve describes a link between the unemployment rate and inflation.

Our takeaway from this review is that there are relationships between different markets, and therefore disequilibrium in one market will

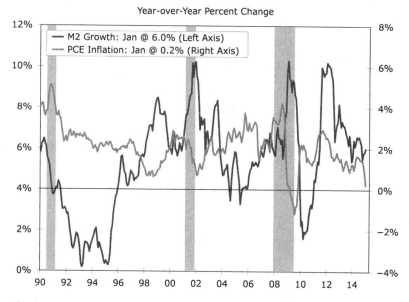

Figure 2.10 M2 Money Supply Growth vs. PCE Inflation
Sources: U.S. Department of Commerce and Federal Reserve Board

likely lead to further adjustments in other markets.[9] We have also seen this in practice, as the housing sector was the epicenter of the Great Recession, but the labor market experienced the largest job loss in the post-WWII era (Figure 2.11). The unemployment rate stayed elevated for several years even after the official ending of the Great Recession. Furthermore, the fed funds target rate was held at an unprecedentedly low 0.00 to 0.25 percent range for seven years, far below what many consider normal. Finally, average inflation rates remain far below the Fed's target of 2 percent. Since 1994, the annual change in the personal consumption expenditures (PCE) deflator has averaged 1.9 percent, while that average has fallen to 1.4 percent since 2009. Therefore, distortions in one market (interest rates) can spread to others (asset prices) and also require policy interventions to restore equilibrium states in markets.

A final point we want to stress is the possibility of a partial equilibrium, instead of general equilibrium, in an economy. That is, it may be possible that some markets are in disequilibrium and others

---

[9] R. Barro and H. Grossman, *Money, Employment and Inflation* (Cambridge, UK: Cambridge University Press, 1976).

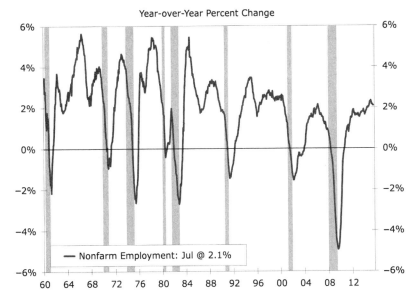

Figure 2.11 Nonfarm Employment Growth
Source: U.S. Department of Labor

are simultaneously in a temporary, unstable equilibrium, within an economy. For instance, inflation rates, interest rates, and the labor market experienced distortions, but output and equity markets appear to be functioning without frictions currently. Yet economic growth is considered subpar, while financial asset prices are considered exceedingly high by some. Industrial production and the Institute for Supply Management (ISM) manufacturing index are suggesting normal functioning in the manufacturing sector (Figure 2.12) while labor markets exhibit a persistent excess supply of labor.

Industrial production crossed its prerecession peak in November 2014 and the ISM manufacturing index entered expansionary territory (above 50) in August 2009 and has been above 50 most of the time since then. The Standard & Poor's (S&P) 500 index, a proxy for the equity market, crossed its prerecession peak in March 2013 and has climbed to new all-time highs. Therefore, the output/financial sectors of the U.S. economy appear to be functioning normally over the past few years, while the labor market remains in significant disequilibrium, as illustrated by the structural shift in the Beveridge curve and the persistence of long-term unemployment (Figure 2.13).

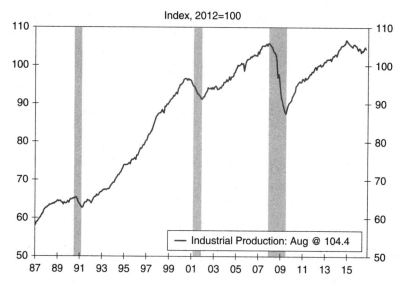

Figure 2.12 Industrial Production
Source: Federal Reserve Board

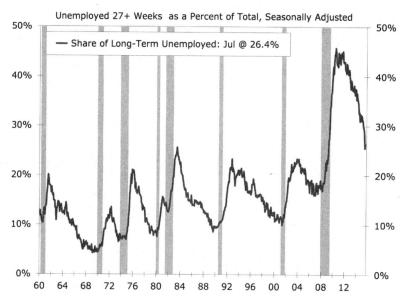

Figure 2.13 Long-Term Unemployment
Source: U.S. Department of Labor

For decision makers, the concepts of frictions and partial equilibrium are crucial since decision makers need to assess (or forecast) the chances of an impending crisis and may need to design appropriate policy tools to address that crisis. Predicting a crisis is often extremely difficult, as suggested by Rudi Dornbusch, who said that a crisis "takes a much longer time coming than you think, and then it happens much faster than you would have thought."[10] However, by allowing for the possibility of frictions and partial equilibria in models, decision makers can improve the decision-making process.

A Frictionless Assumption Is Not a Harmless Assumption

Decision makers utilize many tools to analyze an economy, in particular, when estimating the impact of an impending crisis or the effect of a policy change on different sectors of an economy. One widely employed tool in today's decision-making world is known as a macro-model. One of the key assumptions of a standard macro-model is the frictionless movement of prices and production. However, frictions exist, and in the presence of frictions, frictionless models do not provide an accurate assessment of the economy. Certainly, this was true in the wake of the Great Recession. Furthermore, policy recommendations based on an incorrect assessment of the functioning of the economy would lead to poor decisions and disappointing results.

In sum, private and public policy decisions change with the business cycle and policy intervention is sometimes necessary to restore equilibrium in some markets of an economy. However, by allowing frictions in the macro-model, we can provide more accurate assessments of the state of the economy and suggest appropriate policy actions. In the case of the United States, during the past eight years, sector-specific policies have been hit and miss in their ability to restore equilibrium in their respective sectors due to the misreading of the actual functioning of the economy.

---

[10] Sometimes this is referred to as "Dornbusch's Law." For more detail about Dornbusch's law, see www.pbs.org/wgbh/pages/frontline/shows/mexico/interviews/dornbusch.html.

QUANTIFYING FRICTIONS: IS THE LONG-RUN AVERAGE A USEFUL GUIDE FOR THE FUTURE?

It is the mark of an educated mind to be able to entertain a thought without accepting it.

—Aristotle

Keynes said, "This long run is a misleading guide to current affairs. In the long run, we are all dead." Still, many analysts utilize the "long-run average" concept as a guideline without regard to possible changing circumstances. Such average projections reflect the presence of the anchoring bias. In addition, some analysts extend past trends to predict the future. Is the past trend useful to predict the future? Is there a long-run average that decision makers can utilize for future guidance? In truth, the answer depends on the individual situation of each sector—there is no a priori answer.

In other words, we must determine the behavior of a data series before we make a prediction or assume a long-run average as a benchmark for our models. When we utilize past information, or long-run averages, the implicit assumption is that the future will be similar to the past. The assumption that the future would be consistent (similar) with the past has serious consequences, if incorrect, for econometric analysis and forecasting. As mentioned earlier, standard econometric models, which assume frictionless (future is similar to the past), may provide misleading analysis in the presence of frictions. This section presents methods to identify frictions in an economy that would impact our forecasting accuracy.

Several econometric methods are utilized to identify frictions in the U.S. economy.[11] Some of the major sectors of the economy, including the labor market, interest rates, financial sector, output, exchange rates and others, are characterized by such breaks. Many economic series (e.g., employment, productivity, dollar-index, S&P 500, 10-year Treasury, and money supply) are not mean reverting and experience structural breaks. These findings imply that the assumption that these series move around a stable average value (mean reverting) over time

---

[11] For a broader explanation of these techniques and a number of applications, see John E. Silvia, Azhar Iqbal, Kaylyn Swankoski, Sarah Watt, and Sam Bullard, *Economic and Business Forecasting* (John Wiley & Sons, 2014), 98–101.

is incorrect. Furthermore, evidence of structural breaks provides caution to analysts that future behavior of these series may be different than the past. In addition, econometric analysis using traditional tools (ordinary least squares, for example) would provide misleading results and inaccurate forecasts as well as forecast bands (confidence intervals). Decision makers should not put heavy weight on the past average behavior of the series and expect the future will be the same.

Picturing Adjustments in Motion

The first method to identify frictions (a different behavior than the past) in a variable (or a sector) is the estimation of a long-run trend using the Hodrick-Prescott (H-P) filter.[12] Major benefits of estimating a long-run trend are (1) determining whether a series has a cyclical pattern and (2) at any point in time, we can evaluate whether a series experiences an acceleration/boom (above trend) or deceleration/bust (below trend) around that cyclical pattern. In addition, the presence of a time trend or cyclical feature would be an indication of dynamic adjustment. How?

Figure 2.14 shows the log of nonfarm payrolls (employment) and its long-run trend (H-P filter–based trend). The employment series' trend moves upward, most of the time, and since 2000, the series also showed cyclical behavior. The upward long-run trend of employment, on average, has some notable points as well as a strong indication of structural breaks. First, the trend experienced several shifts (breaks) and every break reduced the pace of employment growth (trend becomes flatter). Second, between early 2000 and 2015, the trend has flattened and became more like a horizontal line, which indicates a loss of the pre-2000 momentum. Finally, since 2011, the trend resumes along the pattern of a cyclical recovery. That trend, however, is at a different pace than the pre-2000 behavior. In sum, the H-P filter–based trend shows different behaviors for the various time periods for employment growth. The long-run average of employment growth may

---

[12] The H-P filter analysis utilizes the log form of a variable to estimate the long-run trend. The log-difference of a series approximates the growth rate and also most likely removes any nonstationarity. We cannot apply the H-P filter on negative values. For comparison, we plot the log of the actual series along with the long-run trend. For more detail see Silvia et al., 2014.

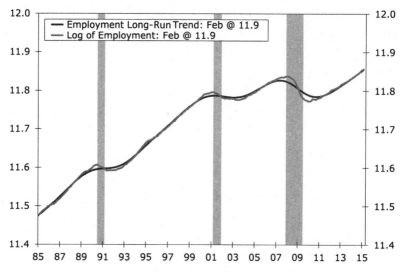

Figure 2.14 H-P Filter–Based Long-Run Trend of Employment
Source: U.S. Department of Labor

not be a useful guide for the future and moreover, the long-run average is actually the result of several distinct short-run cyclical trends.

The H-P filter–based unemployment rate trend shows strong cyclical patterns (Figure 2.15). The cyclical behavior of the unemployment rate trend is expected, as unemployment tends to move up during recessions and decline during the expansionary phase of a business cycle. The fed funds rate trend, on average, has declined over time (Figure 2.16). The long-run trend of productivity (Figure 2.17) has moved upward over time.[13] The rate of growth accelerated during the mid-1990s, although productivity has slowed since the late 2000s.

In sum, these four graphs show that underlying economic series have different behavior during various time periods. That is an indication of dynamic economic adjustment in contrast to a frictionless series, which would show a more consistent behavior over time.

---

[13] Note: We apply the H-P filter on the level form of employment and productivity because growth rates of both series contain negative numbers. We cannot apply the H-P filter on a negative number.

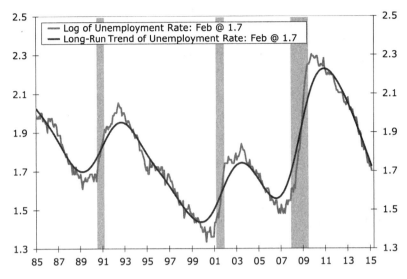

Figure 2.15 H-P Filter–Based Long-Run Trend of Unemployment Rate
Source: U.S. Department of Labor

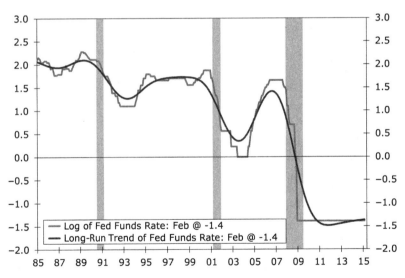

Figure 2.16 H-P Filter–Based Long-Run Trend of Fed Funds Rate
Source: Federal Reserve Board

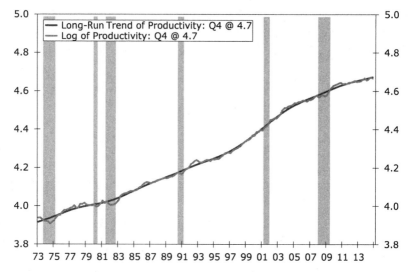

Figure 2.17 H-P Filter–Based Long-Run Trend of Productivity
Source: U.S. Department of Labor

Let's Put Statistics to Work: Does Volatility Differ Over Time?

If a series experienced different behavior for different subsamples, then that series shows evidence of dynamic adjustment. How can we measure the behavior of a series for subsamples? When we say behavior has changed over time, it implies the average growth rate and/or volatility (stability ratio) has changed over time. We can calculate standard statistics (mean, standard deviation, and stability ratios) to examine the behavior of a series over time (Table 2.1). The average growth rate of employment during 1990–2015 was 1.0 percent, the standard deviation was 1.7 percent, and the stability ratio (standard deviation as a percentage of the mean) was 162.7. A stability ratio above 100 indicates a volatile series, as the standard deviation is greater than the mean. Put differently, for some periods, deviations from the average growth (which is 1.0 percent) were higher than the mean and vice versa. We can then divide employment growth into subsamples including the pre–Great Recession (2000–2007) and post-recession (2009–2015) eras. The 1990s experienced high and stable employment growth, as the highest mean and lowest stability ratio were seen in the 1990s period. The average growth rates for the 2000–2007 and 2009–2015 periods were similar, but the post-recession era (2009–2015) showed higher volatility, as the stability ratio was 271.1. The 2000–2015 period saw the slowest employment growth, on average, and the highest stability ratio (most volatile employment growth). Overall, employment growth showed different behavior in terms of the mean and stability ratio in the various subsamples.

Two other key indicators of the U.S. labor market, the unemployment rate and average hourly earnings, also showed signs of dynamic change over time (Table 2.1). The post–Great Recession period observed the highest unemployment rate along with the lowest wage growth, on average. For all three measures of the labor market, the 2000–2015 period was most volatile as stability ratios are highest for that time period. In sum, all three variables show different behavior for different subsamples.

We also calculate the mean, standard deviation and stability ratio for productivity growth to analyze its behavior (Table 2.2). The post–Great Recession era (2009–2014) showed the smallest productivity growth, on average, and the pre-recession period (1996–2007) saw the highest average growth rate. The highest stability ratio was recorded for the 1973–1995 period, which marked the most volatile period for productivity growth. Overall, our findings in the analysis of productivity growth are consistent with the three labor market variables and show signs of dynamic adjustment that may reflect frictions in the real economy that would upset the smooth move to a new market equilibrium as assumed in many traditional economic models.

Are Markets' Behaviors Frictionless in the Long Run? Mean Reversion

Does dynamic adjustment in the economy indicate a return to a steady equilibrium or is there evidence of market frictions that prevent such a return? Keynes said that the long-run concept is a misleading guide to current affairs. We can rephrase the question: Is there a long-run average growth rate? Does the series move around that average and return to that average over the long run? Basically, we can test whether a variable is mean reverting (frictionless) in the sense that the variable

Table 2.1 Change Over Time in Unemployment Rate and Average Hourly Earnings

Variable	1990-2015			1990-1999			2000-2007			2009-2015			2000-2015		
	Mean	S.D.	Stability Ratio	Mean	S.D.	Stability Ratio	Mean	S.D.	Stability Ratio	Mean	S.D.	Stability Ratio	Mean	S.D.	Stability Ratio
Nonfarm Payrolls (YoY)	1.0	1.7	162.7	1.8	1.3	69.4	0.8	1.1	139.3	0.7	2.0	271.1	0.5	1.7	328.6
Unemployment Rate	6.1	1.6	25.7	5.8	1.0	18.2	5.0	0.7	13.6	8.1	1.4	17.0	6.4	1.8	28.3
Averg. Hrly Earn. (YoY)	3.0	0.8	26.2	3.2	0.6	19.4	3.2	0.7	22.8	2.1	0.4	18.5	2.9	0.8	29.5

Table 2.2 Mean, Standard Deviation, and Stability Ratio

Variable	1973-2014			1973-95			1996-2007			2009-2014			1996-2014		
	Mean	S.D.	Stability Ratio	Mean	S.D.	Stability Ratio	Mean	S.D.	Stability Ratio	Mean	S.D.	Stability Ratio	Mean	S.D.	Stability Ratio
Productivity (YoY)	1.85	1.66	89.86	1.53	1.75	114.67	2.70	1.22	45.30	1.51	1.57	103.94	2.23	1.46	65.40

moves around its mean growth rate and deviations from that average are temporary in the long run. In the next step, we test whether measures of the labor market exhibit mean-reverting behavior. That is, for example, does employment growth move around an average value over time and are deviations from the average values temporary?

Two tests are utilized to determine whether a series is mean reverting. First, we test for a structural break in a series and the second approach is the application of a unit root test.[14] If we find evidence of a structural break in a series, then that series is not mean reverting because the series' behavior (mean and/or standard deviation) is different for the pre- and post-break eras. If there is not a break in a series and the Augmented Dickey-Fuller (ADF) unit root test indicates the series is stationary, then that would suggest the series is mean reverting. The structural break and ADF test results are presented in Table 2.3.

Our results indicate that employment growth experienced structural breaks during the 1990–2015 period (identified in Table 2.3 as a level shift in the middle column) and that indicates employment growth is not mean reverting. In addition, this result also indicates that the dynamic adjustment in the labor market faces a set of frictions such that the pace of employment growth does not return to the same trend over time in our sample period. A similar conclusion is found for wage growth, the unemployment rate, and productivity growth. Overall, the four variables show evidence of structural breaks (they are not mean reverting), and therefore these variables do not move around an average value over time. This finding is consistent with Keynes's notion that the long-run average concept is a misleading guide for current affairs.

Moving Beyond the Labor Market: Not All Frictions Are Equal

An economy consists of several sectors (markets) and the various markets may perform differently over time. In addition, individual markets may react to a shock (or to a recession) differently. Here, we apply

---

[14] We utilize the State-Space approach to detect a structural break and Augmented Dickey-Fuller test to determine mean reversion. Both approaches are explained in detail in Silvia et al., 2014.

Table 2.3 Identifying a Structural Break Using the State-Space Approach

Employment (Not Mean Reverting)		
Break Date	**Type of Break**	**Coefficient**
Mar-94	Level Shift	0.47
Feb-00	Additive Outlier	–0.28
Mar-10	Level Shift	0.47
Average Hourly Earnings (Not Mean Reverting)		
Break Date	**Type of Break**	**Coefficient**
Apr-90	Additive Outlier	–0.49
Jan-89	Level Shift	0.52
Jul-85	Additive Outlier	–0.40
The Unemployment Rate (Not Mean Reverting)		
Break Date	**Type of Break**	**Coefficient**
Nov-10	Additive Outlier	0.45
Jan-86	Additive Outlier	–0.4
Dec-08	Level Shift	0.45
Productivity Growth (Not Mean Reverting)		
Break Date	**Type of Break**	**Coefficient**
Jan-02	Additive Outlier	2.14
Jan-82	Additive Outlier	–1.80
Jan-93	Level Shift	–2.54

the H-P filter on several variables representing several major sectors of the U.S. economy. The long-run trend along with the log of housing starts, a proxy for the housing sector, is plotted in Figure 2.18. The housing starts trend bottomed out in 2010, well after the official end date of the Great Recession. Furthermore, the current level of the trend is significantly below the pre-recession peak, which confirms a slower recovery in the housing sector compared to its prior history.

The long-run trend of the trade-weighted broad dollar index (Figure 2.19), a proxy for the foreign exchange market, shows a completely different behavior than the housing starts series. That is, the dollar's long-run trend peaked in 2001 and continued its downward trend through 2012. Basically, the dollar trend did not show any significant change during the Great Recession.

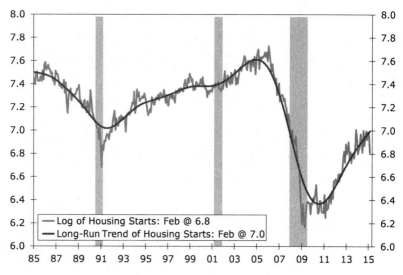

Figure 2.18 H-P Filter–Based Long-Run Trend of Housing Starts
Source: U.S. Department of Commerce

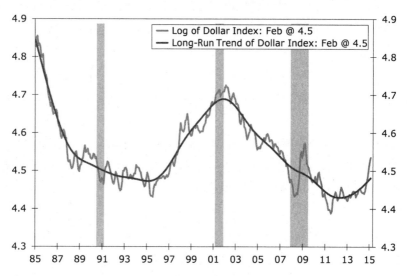

Figure 2.19 H-P Filter–Based Long-Run Trend of Broad Dollar Index
Source: Federal Reserve Board

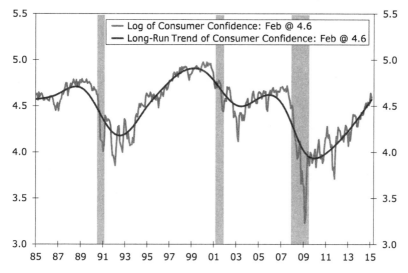

Figure 2.20 H-P Filter–Based Long-Run Trend of Consumer Confidence®
Source: The Conference Board, Inc. Reprinted with permission of The Conference Board. For more information, please see www.conference-board.org. Consumer Confidence Index is a registered trademark of The Conference Board, Inc.

The Great Recession did affect consumer sentiment, as the long-run trend of the consumer confidence index (Figure 2.20) dropped to its lowest level since 1985. However, the current level of the trend is fairly close to the pre-recession peak, which suggests a solid recovery in consumer sentiment. The recovery in the production side was not the same as the housing sector and consumer sentiment recoveries. The long-run trend of industrial production (Figure 2.21), a proxy for real output, is presently at the highest level in our sample period, which starts in 1985. In sum, these variables, representing major sectors of the economy, showed different behavior and reactions to the Great Recession. This finding does shed light on the different types of frictions that will influence dynamic adjustment over time and that not all economic sectors of the economy reacted the same to the Great Recession.

How Volatile Are Some Major Sectors of the U.S. Economy?

To measure volatility, we provide the mean, standard deviation, and stability ratio for some of the major sectors of the U.S. economy in

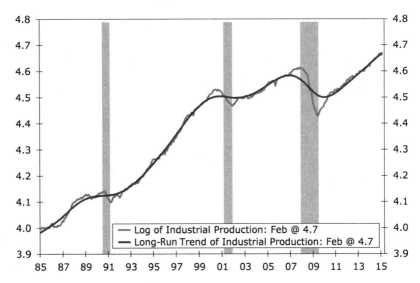

Figure 2.21 H-P Filter–Based Long-Run Trend of Industrial Production
Source: Federal Reserve Board

Tables 2.4 and 2.5. To represent the credit/U.S. Treasury market, the U.S. 10-year Treasury yield and federal funds target rate are examined. The lowest 10-year average yields along with the fed funds rate are in the post–Great Recession era (2009–2015). For the 2000–2015 period, the stability ratio for the fed funds rate was above 100, indicating this was a very volatile period for the fed funds rate, despite the appearances of a low level of the policy rate. The growth rate of the dollar index was very volatile for the complete period as well as for the subsamples, as the smallest stability ratio is 442.7. Housing starts and the consumer confidence index series were also very volatile, as the lowest stability ratios were 182.9 and 136.2, respectively. S&P 500 returns, in contrast, were very stable during the 1990s, where the stability ratio was 74.2.

The pre–Great Recession era (2000–2007) was the most volatile period for S&P 500 returns, as the stability ratio was 596.6. The 2000–2015 period reported the highest stability ratios for industrial production and the ISM manufacturing index. The post–Great Recession era observed the highest average growth rate of the money supply and the highest stability ratio for the PCE deflator. Overall, consistent with the labor market analysis, these major sectors also experienced

Table 2.4 Mean, Standard Deviation, and Stability Ratio for Major Sectors

Variable	1990-2015			1990-1999			2000-2007			2009-2015			2000-2015		
	Mean	S.D.	Stability Ratio	Mean	S.D.	Stability Ratio	Mean	S.D.	Stability Ratio	Mean	S.D.	Stability Ratio	Mean	S.D.	Stability Ratio
10-Year	4.9	1.8	36.7	6.7	1.1	15.8	4.7	0.7	14.1	2.6	0.7	25.3	3.8	1.2	31.4
Fed Funds	3.2	2.4	72.7	5.1	1.4	26.7	3.4	1.9	55.1	0.25	0.0	0.0	2.0	2.1	101.7
Dollar (YoY)	-0.1	5.0	-4,069.0	0.8	4.5	578.3	-1.0	4.5	-442.7	-0.7	4.7	-711.5	-0.7	5.2	-731.2
Housing Starts (YoY)	0.6	18.4	2,830.9	2.8	14.3	504.4	-1.6	13.7	-871.5	10.2	18.6	182.9	-0.8	20.6	-2,638.1
Consumer Conf(YoY)	2.1	23.9	1,130.6	3.9	22.0	560.9	-1.9	16.5	-853.9	16.2	22.0	136.2	0.9	25.1	2,690.0

Table 2.5 Mean, Standard Deviation, and Stability Ratio for Major Sectors

Variable	1990-2015			1990-1999			2000-2007			2009-2015			2000-2015		
	Mean	S.D.	Stability Ratio	Mean	S.D.	Stability Ratio	Mean	S.D.	Stability Ratio	Mean	S.D.	Stability Ratio	Mean	S.D.	Stability Ratio
S&P 500 (YoY)	8.9	16.5	185.5	15.8	11.7	74.2	2.5	14.8	596.6	14.3	11.9	83.4	4.3	17.5	404.0
Industrial Production (YoY)	2.2	4.1	184.0	3.7	2.6	70.9	1.5	2.6	164.7	2.9	3.9	134.4	1.2	4.5	370.9
ISM-M	51.9	5.0	9.7	51.6	4.5	8.8	52.0	4.8	9.2	54.6	2.7	5.0	52.1	5.3	10.2
M2 Money Supply	3.3	2.9	87.6	1.6	2.8	169.0	3.8	2.0	52.1	4.7	2.4	50.7	4.3	2.4	54.8
PCE Def. (YoY)	2.1	1.0	46.9	2.3	1.0	43.2	2.3	0.6	28.2	1.5	0.8	53.6	2.0	1.0	48.8

different behavior in different subsamples, thereby indicating that frictions acted upon the behavior of each of these variables in different ways and at different times.

Are These Sectors Mean Reverting?

In the next step, we test whether these major series were mean reverting. We found that the U.S. 10-year Treasury, fed funds rate, and dollar index were not mean reverting (Table 2.6).

Table 2.6 Identifying a Structural Break Using the State-Space Approach

10-Year Treasury (Not Mean Reverting)		
Break Date	Type of Break	Coefficient
Dec-08	Level Shift	–0.95
May-00	Additive Outlier	0.44
Nov-87	Level Shift	–0.68
Fed Funds Rate (Not Mean Reverting)		
Break Date	Type of Break	Coefficient
Jan-08	Level Shift	–1.23
Jan-01	Level Shift	–1.02
Dec-08	Level Shift	–0.75
Dollar (Not Mean Reverting)		
Break Date	Type of Break	Coefficient
Oct-08	Level Shift	4.22
Oct-09	Level Shift	–4.72
Oct-85	Additive Outlier	–2.26
Consumer Confidence (Mean Reverting)		
Break Date	Type of Break	Coefficient
Oct-12	Additive Outlier	39.20
Feb-11	Additive Outlier	36.78
Mar-10	Additive Outlier	30.12
Housing Starts (Mean Reverting)		
Break Date	Type of Break	Coefficient
Apr-10	Additive Outlier	34.46
Mar-94	Additive Outlier	30.78
Jan-92	Additive Outlier	30.50

The growth rates of consumer confidence and housing starts were mean reverting in our sample period (Table 2.6). However, these two series were volatile and our econometric analysis found several outliers in each series. The ISM manufacturing index was also mean reverting, with possible volatile behavior (Table 2.7). The growth rates of money supply and the PCE deflator, along with S&P 500 returns, are not mean reverting (Table 2.7).

Summing up, we have characterized 14 different variables, representing major sectors of the U.S. economy, and only 3 of them (consumer confidence, housing starts, and the ISM manufacturing index)

Table 2.7 Identifying a Structural Break Using the State-Space Approach

The S&P 500 (Not Mean Reverting)		
Break Date	Type of Break	Coefficient
Oct-09	Level Shift	18.61
Jan-92	Additive Outlier	11.73
Mar-10	Additive Outlier	11.29
Industrial Production (Not Mean Reverting)		
Break Date	Type of Break	Coefficient
Sep-09	Level Shift	4.30
Sep-08	Level Shift	−4.27
ISM-Manufacturing (Mean Reverting)		
Break Date	Type of Break	Coefficient
Oct-01	Additive Outlier	−4.33
May-11	Additive Outlier	−4.26
Jun-96	Additive Outlier	4.23
Money Supply-M2 (Not Mean Reverting)		
Break Date	Type of Break	Coefficient
Sep-01	Additive Outlier	1.73
Dec-08	Level Shift	1.89
PCE Deflator (Not Mean Reverting)		
Break Date	Type of Break	Coefficient
Nov-08	Level Shift	−1.11
Sep-06	Level Shift	−1.03
Sep-11	Additive Outlier	−0.55

turned out to be mean reverting. The remaining 11 variables were not mean reverting. That indicates the long-run average of many economic series, as a guideline for future estimates and decision making, can be misleading when projecting future values of these economic indices.

Are There Benefits to Identifying the Existence of Possible Frictions in the Dynamic Adjustment of Economic Series?

Several major sectors of the U.S. economy were analyzed to verify the notion that the long-run average is a misleading guide for the future. Our econometric analysis found that many series (e.g., employment, productivity, dollar index, S&P 500, 10-year Treasury, and money supply) were not mean reverting and experienced structural breaks, evidence of frictions in the dynamic adjustment process.

The findings imply that if decision makers assume that these series move around an average value over time (follow a frictionless behavior over time), they assume incorrectly. Furthermore, evidence of structural breaks provides caution that future behavior of these series may be different than in the past. In addition, econometric analysis using traditional tools (e.g., ordinary least squares [OLS]) would provide misleading analysis and forecasts. In sum, decision makers should not put heavy weight on the past average behavior of these variables as predictors of future values without further testing.

MODELING DYNAMIC ADJUSTMENT DUE TO ECONOMIC FRICTIONS: DECISION MAKING IN AN EVOLVING WORLD

The art of economics consists in looking not merely at the immediate but at the longer effects of any act or policy; it consists in tracing the consequences of that policy not merely for one group but for all groups.

—Henry Hazlitt

Christina Romer once said, "There's a joke in economics about the drunk who loses his keys in the street but only looks for them under the light posts. When asked why, he says, 'because that's where the light is.'" Hazlitt's statement and Romer's (insightful) joke shed light on issues related to the limits of conventional econometric tools and hence the opportunity to improve decision making.

First, for instance, the total effect of a policy change is typically distributed over a prolonged period and we should not estimate or expect the impact of a policy change to appear within just one period. Second, a policy change may produce heterogeneous effects among the markets (sectors) of an economy. Globally, sometimes the effect of a policy change in one country may spill over into other economies (countries), as would be a characteristic of U.S. monetary policy. Third, a policy change may produce short- and long-run effects, which may be different from one another. Fourth, we want to stress that the effect of a policy change on markets (e.g., raising the fed funds target rate) may be different during different time periods because relationships between economic/financial variables evolve over time. The fifth and final point we want to highlight in this section is that the frictionless assumption (finding keys only under the light post) could pose serious issues for effective decision making and evaluation.

In previous sections, we have discussed issues related to the frictionless assumption in the dynamic adjustment process and how to identify the existence of possible frictions. This final section provides a guide to identifying a change in economic variables that allow for the existence of economic frictions that influence effective decision making. In particular, we estimate the effect of a policy change on a sector (market) and then determine whether the effect is heterogeneous for multiple markets. In effect, we describe how to search beyond the "light posts."

To anticipate our results, in our first case study we estimate the effect of a one percentage point increase in employment growth on key labor market indicators. One result we find is that the largest effect was noted for the unemployment rate (a drop of 0.2 percentage points). Second, the change in the fed funds rate produced a heterogeneous effect for multiple markets, ranging from the largest change of 0.12 percentage points in the PCE deflator to no meaningful change in the S&P 500 and the growth rate of housing starts. Third, the effect of a change in interest rates is different during different time periods, which suggests that past benchmarks of policy effectiveness need to be reevaluatcd.

Finally, our econometric analysis found that the conventional relationship between gross domestic product (GDP) and the unemployment rate (Okun's Law) is not stable—therefore, the relationship cannot be utilized as a guide (without further investigation). For decision makers in an ever-evolving world, one must go beyond the light posts to search for "keys" (reliable results) to effective decision making.

Estimating the Distributed Effect of a Policy Change: Impulse Response Functions

How might we estimate the effect of a change in the fed funds rate on different real sectors of the economy—for example, the labor and output markets and housing? To answer this question, we turn to the vector autoregression (VAR) modeling methodology.[15] The beauty of VARs is that they are simple statistical representations of economic systems, as they rely only on the variables that comprise the system and a few lagged values of those variables. In addition, VARs can be "shocked" to show how all the variables respond to a change in one of the other variables. The way the variables respond over time to a change in the "shocked" variable are called impulse response functions (IRFs).[16]

Furthermore, we can approximate the total effect of a change in the funds rate on the other real variables of interest where the impact may be distributed over a prolonged period of time. Therefore, we estimate the effect of a change in the fed funds rate in the current month on the unemployment rate, inflation, output, and the housing market over the next 12 months.

---

[15] See Christopher Sims, "Macroeconomics and Reality," *Econometrica* 48 (1980): 1–48.
[16] For a broader explanation of these techniques and a number of applications, see Silvia et al., 2014.

What Would Be the Reaction to a Change?
A Single-Market Case

Our first application focuses on just one sector, which is the labor market. We estimate the effect of a 1 percentage point increase in employment growth on the unemployment rate, labor force participation rate, and average hourly earnings. This example is a simple one, as it only shows the effect for the labor market and not for other markets. The increase in employment growth is associated with a reduction in the unemployment rate, with the largest drop appearing during the second month, a drop of 0.2 percentage points (Figure 2.22). The rise in employment growth boosts the growth rate in labor force participation by 0.09 percentage points in the first month, and that is the largest change in the participation rate (Figure 2.23). So there is some evidence for the view that employment gains are associated with a rise in participation rates. Average hourly earnings show a negative growth rate (with the largest drop of 0.1 percentage point for the first month) in response to the employment growth increase (Figure 2.24). The drop in the earnings growth rate may suggest that a rise in the

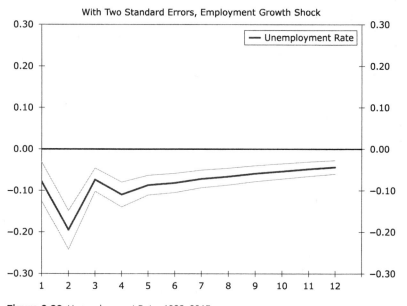

Figure 2.22 Unemployment Rate: 1983–2015

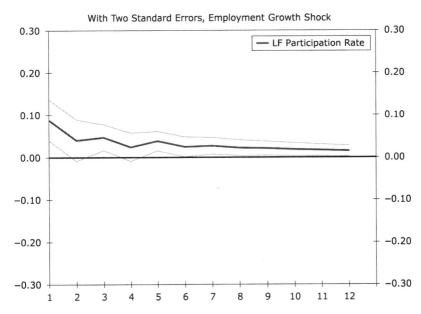

Figure 2.23 Labor Force Participation Rate: 1983–2015

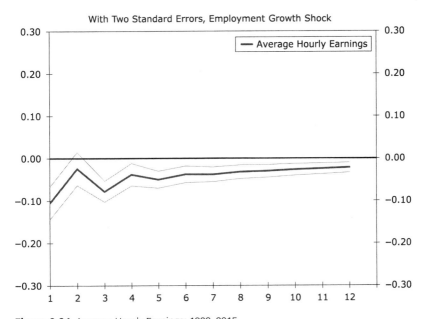

Figure 2.24 Average Hourly Earnings: 1983–2015

employment growth rate boosts participation rates, which put downward pressure on earnings growth as new, less skilled or experienced workers are drawn into the labor force at lower wages. Typically, during the first year of job expansions, workers with less experience and training reenter the job market.

In sum, an increase in the employment growth rate affects other key elements of the labor market and the largest response to the employment growth change is noted for the unemployment rate. In addition, the total effect of an increase in employment on the unemployment rate is 0.97 percentage points (sum of total declines in the unemployment rate over the 12-month period), 0.38 percentage points for the labor force participation rate, and 0.51 percentage points for the average hourly earnings series. This indicates that the total impact on the unemployment rate is more than the combined effect of the labor force and earnings series, another way of saying there is a heterogeneous effect. Therefore, decision makers should estimate the possible impact of a change in one variable on each of the interested variables because the impact could be heterogeneous for different variables in contrast to the common assumption that the adjustment process to any exogenous change would be uniform within a single market.

Does a Change in the Fed Funds Rate Matter? Heterogeneous Reaction among Markets

An economy is comprised of many major markets and, therefore, the reactions to any policy change may be different in timing and size for different markets. Here we build a model that includes information from six major sectors of the U.S. economy. The six sectors are: interest rate/credit markets (fed funds target rate as proxy), prices/inflation (PCE deflator), labor market (unemployment rate), financial/equity market (S&P 500 index), housing sector (housing starts), and output (industrial production).

During midsummer 2015, most commentators expected that the FOMC would raise the target for the fed funds rate in the near future. An important question for analysts is what is the likely effect of a fed funds rate hike on the major sectors of the economy? Using a data set spanning 1983–2015, we estimate the effect of a 1 percentage point

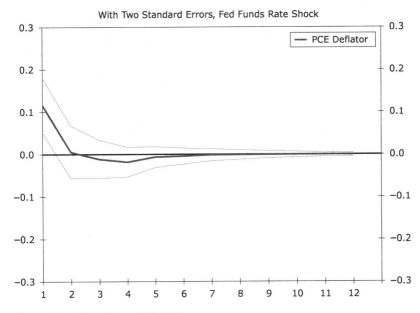

Figure 2.25 PCE Deflator: 1983–2015

increase in the fed funds rate on the remaining five indicators of the chosen major sectors of the economy.[17]

First, the hike in the fed funds rate is not associated with a drop in inflation, at least for the first couple of months (Figure 2.25). However, the PCE deflator does show nonpositive numbers for the remaining 3 to 12 months of our study. One major reason for the positive relationship with the PCE deflator is that the FOMC usually raises the fed fund target rate during expansions (later part of the recovery/expansion cycle) and that phase of the business cycle is usually associated with rising inflation. Second, a rise in the fed funds rate is also associated with falling unemployment (Figure 2.26). This result is not so surprising given that the FOMC typically raises rates during expansions, and the unemployment rate also tends to fall during those same expansions.

---

[17] We utilize growth rates of PCE deflator, S&P 500 index, housing starts, and industrial production in our econometric models. Typically, growth rates (differenced form) of many variables are stationary. In addition, level form may be nonstationary and econometric results using a nonstationary data set would produce unreliable (spurious) results.

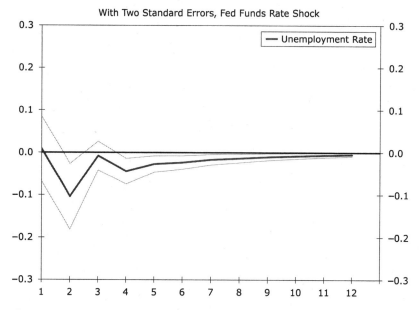

Figure 2.26 Unemployment Rate: 1983–2015

Third, the change in the fed funds rate does not produce a meaningful effect on S&P 500 returns (Figure 2.27) or on housing starts (Figure 2.28). The changes in both sectors are approximately zero for all 12 months. Finally, the change in the growth rate of industrial production is positive for all 12 months in response to a fed funds rate hike (Figure 2.29). Overall, a fed funds rate hike is associated with a heterogeneous effect among different markets, ranging from the largest change of +0.12 percentage points for the PCE deflator to no change at all for the S&P 500 and housing starts.

Is It All about the Base Period? The Lucas Critique

For effective decision making, we must make sure the results/conclusions are consistent between subsamples, which is the essence of the so-called Lucas Critique.[18] Put differently, the implied conclusion should not change with a change in the sample period base (starting

---

[18] Lucas, 1976.

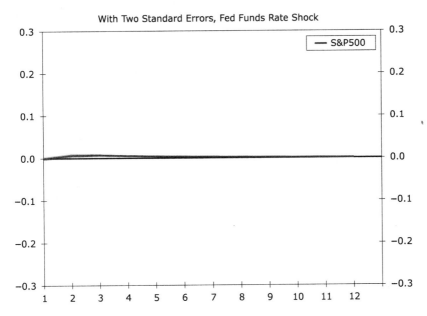

Figure 2.27 S&P 500: 1983–2015

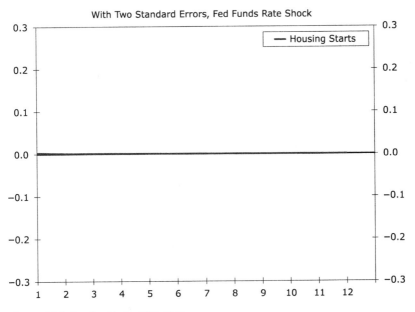

Figure 2.28 Housing Starts: 1983–2015

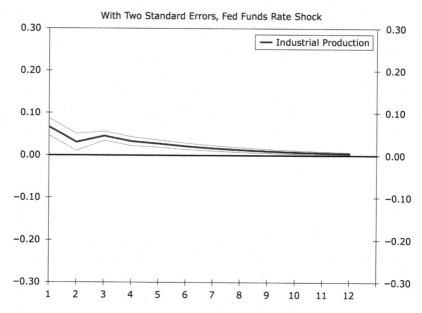

Figure 2.29 Industrial Production: 1983–2015

or ending point of the sample). To test for the robustness of our results, we estimate the effect of the fed funds rate hikes on the five major series identified earlier using the 1983–2005 period. We choose an ending point in 2005 because it is approximately in the middle of the previous expansion. Results are reported in Figures 2.30 through Figure 2.34. We do note a change in the magnitude for the PCE deflator (Figure 2.30) and the unemployment rate (Figure 2.31). The largest change was for the PCE deflator, which jumped to 0.19 percentage points from 0.12 percentage points based on the 1983–2015 period. The 1983–2005 period showed the largest drop in unemployment (0.17 percentage points) compared to a drop of 0.10 percentage points for the 1983–2015 period. The response of industrial production was stronger, at least for the first several months, for the 1983–2005 period compared to the 1983–2015 period reaction (Figure 2.34). The overall conclusions, however, are similar for both time periods. The response of inflation, the labor market, and output sectors to a fed funds hike are meaningful. The fed funds hike was unable to make a noticeable effect on the growth rate of housing starts and S&P 500 returns (Figures 2.32 and 2.33).

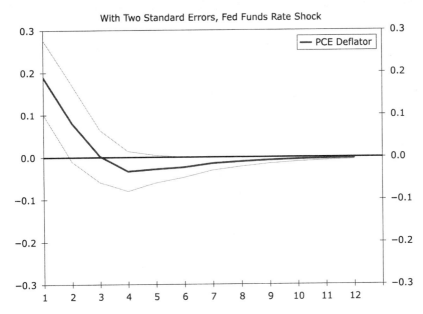

Figure 2.30 PCE Deflator: 1983–2005

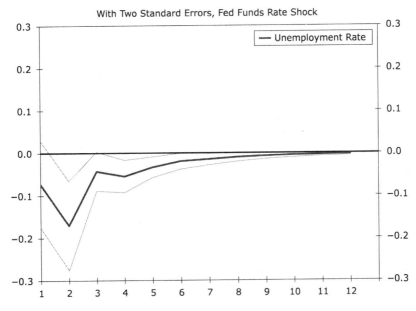

Figure 2.31 Unemployment Rate: 1983–2005

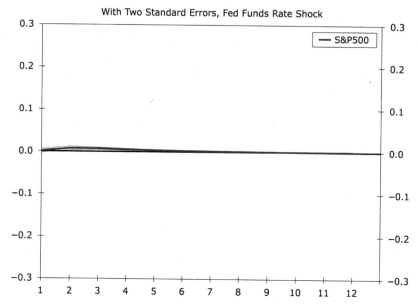

Figure 2.32 S&P 500: 1983–2005

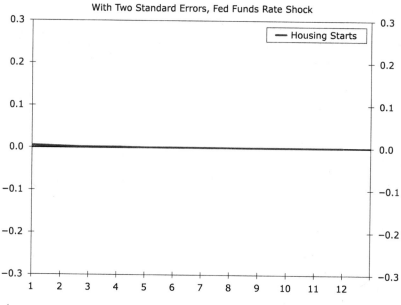

Figure 2.33 Housing Starts: 1983–2005

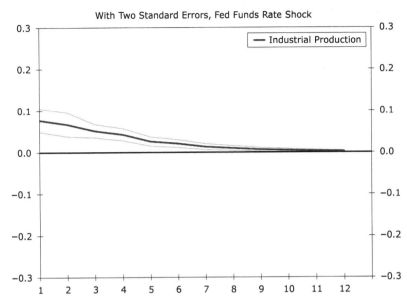

Figure 2.34 Industrial Production: 1983–2005

In addition, we conduct another analysis using the 1983–2008 time span. The logic behind this subsample is that the ending points of our previous two analyses were in expansions and ending the sample period in 2008 gives us an opportunity to estimate the effect of a change in the fed funds rate on the variables during a recession. Since the impulse response functions (IRFs) are linear, the interpretation can be done for a drop in the fed funds rate by changing the sign of the estimated coefficient. For example, a 1 percentage point increase in the fed funds rate is associated with a 0.12 percentage points increase in the PCE deflator growth rate. We can also interpret that a 1 percentage point drop in the fed funds rate would reduce PCE inflation by 0.12 percentage points. Therefore, we can interpret the 1983–2008 period results for a drop in the fed funds rates as, typically, the FOMC reduces the target for the fed funds rate to combat recessions. Results are shown in the appendix of this chapter. The conclusions from the other two samples were valid for this time period as well.

Therefore, there is no change in the conclusions using three different sample periods, which indicates that our results are robust. Furthermore, we end our sample for both expansionary and contractionary phases of a business cycle, and our conclusions still hold, which may fulfill the Lucas Critique requirement for a policy recommendation.

Does the Base Period Matter for the Labor Market Analysis?

We also test the robustness of the labor market analysis and estimate the effect of a one percentage point increase in employment growth on the unemployment rate, labor force participation rate, and average hourly earnings using the 1983–2005 subsample. Results are shown in Figures 2.35 through 2.37. The results lead to similar conclusions with the 1983–2015:Q4 period. A positive shock to employment growth leads to a decline in the unemployment rate, a pickup in labor force participation, and a slight decline in average hourly earnings. In addition, we rerun our model using the 1983–2008 period to see if our conclusions hold when ending in a recessionary period and we find this is true; see appendix for results.

It is important to note that, although results in both case studies are consistent among these subsamples, this does not necessarily hold for all cases/subsamples. Therefore, before we make policy recommendations, we should test and reconfirm our results using different samples/subsample periods.

Is Okun's Law Still Valid? Searching beyond the Light Posts

Unfortunately, some decision makers utilize economic/financial heuristic guidelines as benchmarks without reconfirming the validity of these theories with the data. In our view, they are searching for "keys under the light posts." Economies evolve over time and the relationships between variables also evolve. Therefore, for effective decision making, it is crucial to retest/reconfirm the underlying relationship suggested by a theory before using that theory as a guide. In other words, we must search beyond the light posts to find the "keys." One

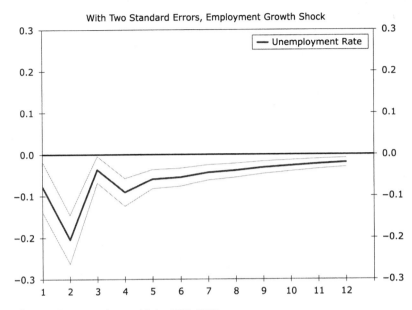

Figure 2.35 Unemployment Rate: 1983–2005

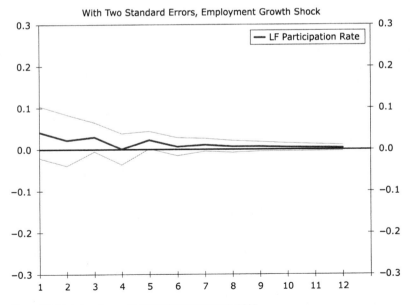

Figure 2.36 Labor Force Participation Rate: 1983–2005

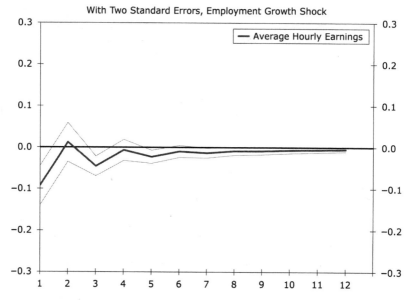

Figure 2.37 Average Hourly Earnings: 1983–2005

important application could be Okun's Law, which suggests a relationship between GDP and the unemployment rate.[19] That is, a boost in GDP growth rates would help to reduce the unemployment rate. In our view, before decision makers utilize Okun's Law as a guide, they must test the causal relationship. What is the direction of the relationship? Is GDP growth causing (leading) unemployment or vice versa?[20]

The Granger causality test is a useful tool to determine causal relationship between variables of interest. Results based on the Granger causality test are reported in Table 2.8. The GDP growth rate Granger-causes the unemployment rate using the 1983–2015:Q1 data set (Table 2.8, Box A). That is, the GDP growth rate is a useful predictor for the unemployment rate. However, the unemployment rate is not a useful predictor for the GDP growth rate in our sample period.

---

[19] Arthur M. Okun, "Potential GNP: Its Measurement and Significance." American Statistical Association, Proceedings of the Business and Economic Section, 1962, pp. 98–104.
[20] We utilize the Granger causality test to determine the causal relationship between GDP and unemployment. The Granger causality test and its application are explained in detail in Silvia et al., 2014.

Table 2.8 Testing the Causal Relationship: The Granger Causality Test

Time Period		Regressor	Dependent Variable	
			Unemployment Rate	Real GDP
A	1983-2015:Q1	Unemployment Rate	NA	0.34
		Real GDP	0.00*	NA
B	1983-2007:Q3	Unemployment Rate	NA	0.07***
		Real GDP	0.00*	NA
C	1990-2015:Q1	Unemployment Rate	NA	0.78
		Real GDP	0.00*	NA
D	1990-2007:Q3	Unemployment Rate	NA	0.23
		Real GDP	0.00*	NA
E	2000-2015:Q1	Unemployment Rate	NA	0.27
		Real GDP	0.00*	NA
F	2009:Q3-	Unemployment Rate	NA	0.68
	2015:Q1	Real GDP	0.79	NA

* Significant at 1 percent, ** Significant at 5 percent, *** Significant at 10 percent

Before we jump to a conclusion, we need to test the robustness of the results. We rerun the Granger causality analysis between GDP growth and the unemployment rate using the 1983–2007:Q3 period (pre–Great recession era, results in Box B). We find a two-way Granger causality relationship, which implies GDP is Granger-causing the unemployment rate and the unemployment rate is also Granger-causing GDP. Certainly a different result than the one based on the 1983–2015:Q1 period (Table 2.8, Box A). These different results lead us to two different conclusions for the different samples and raises questions about the reliability of Okun's Law over time.

To retest our results, we run another analysis using the 1990–2015:Q1 period. We utilize this alternate sample period because the last three economic recoveries are considered "jobless" recoveries and that may have posed a structural break in the unemployment rate/GDP relationship. Therefore, testing the relationship between the two variables using the post-1990s period would be crucial for effective decision making. The results (Box C) suggest that GDP growth Granger-causes unemployment but that unemployment does not Granger-cause GDP.

We also run the Granger causality test using 1990–2007:Q3 (pre-Great Recession era) and results suggest Granger causality runş from GDP to the unemployment rate only. To find what happens to Okun's Law in the post–Great Recession world, we utilize the 2009:Q3–2015:Q1 period.[21] Results (Box F) indicate there is no Granger causality between GDP and the unemployment rate during the latest period.

Summing up, using several different samples/subsample periods, our analysis suggests that Okun's Law needs to be reevaluated and may not be utilized (without further investigation) as a guide in decision making. This is a good example of a heuristic guideline in forecasting and policy that does not stand up to standard statistical analysis.

Economies Evolve—So Must Our Evaluation

Often, economic and financial theories are utilized as a guide for decision making. In our view, theories may be utilized as a first step but must be reevaluated over time before implementation in practice. The reason is that economies evolve over time, as do relationships between economic variables. That is, the impact of a change in policy or a variable could be different across sectors as well as between time periods.

Our econometric results suggest that the effect of a 1 percentage point increase in employment growth on key labor market variables is indeed different between variables and over time. Second, the change in the fed funds rate produces a heterogeneous effect for multiple markets, ranging from the largest change of 0.12 percentage points in the PCE deflator to no meaningful change in S&P 500 returns and the growth rate of housing starts. Furthermore, the effect of a change in the fed funds rate is different for different time periods, which suggests that past benchmarks on policy impacts need to be reevaluated. Finally, our econometric analysis found that the conventional relationship between GDP and the unemployment rate (Okun's Law) is not stable—it cannot be utilized as a guide (without further investigation) for public policy decision making. For decision makers in an ever-evolving world, one must go beyond the light posts to search for "keys" (reliable results) to effective decision making.

---

[21] It is important to note that this sample period is too short for the Granger causality test and results may not be reliable.

DYNAMIC ECONOMIC ADJUSTMENT: AN EVOLUTION UNTO ITSELF

Economic adjustment is different for the various sectors/markets of an economy and over time. The key takeaways of our discussion are, first, the process and speed of adjustment is different for different sectors. Second, the speed of adjustment may change and become faster/slower over time for some markets. Third, changes in one market may affect other markets. Fourth, the relationship between different markets and variables changes over time. Fifth, some markets may be in equilibrium while others are simultaneously not in equilibrium, suggesting the possibility of a partial equilibrium. The sixth and final point is that, due to the evolving nature of economies, the relationship between variables changes over time and decision makers should estimate the actual current relationship between variables of interest using recent data instead of believing historical trends/averages.

Appendix

A CASE FOR THE MULTIPLE MARKETS: 1983–2008

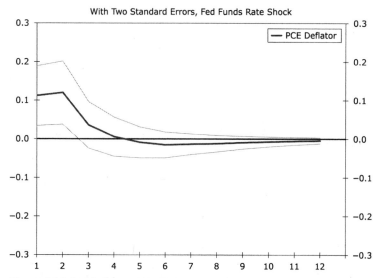

Figure 2.38 PCE Deflator: 1983–2008

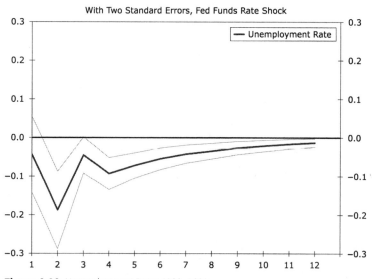

Figure 2.39 Unemployment Rate: 1983–2008

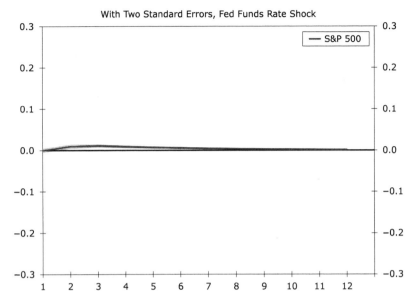

Figure 2.40 S&P 500: 1983–2008

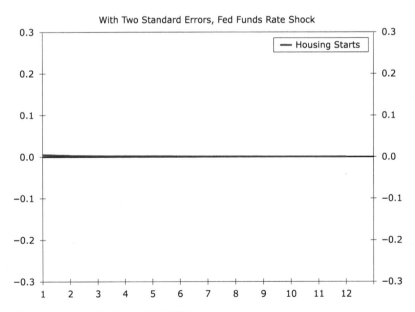

Figure 2.41 Housing Starts: 1983–2008

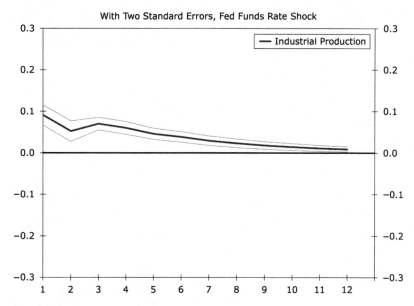

Figure 2.42 Industrial Production: 1983–2008

THE LABOR MARKET: 1983–2008

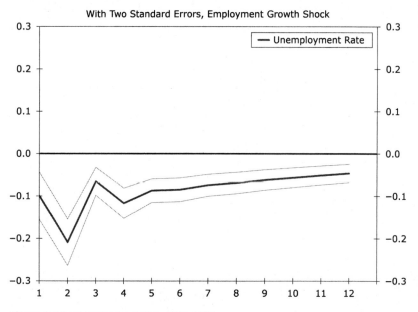

Figure 2.43 Unemployment Rate: 1983–2008

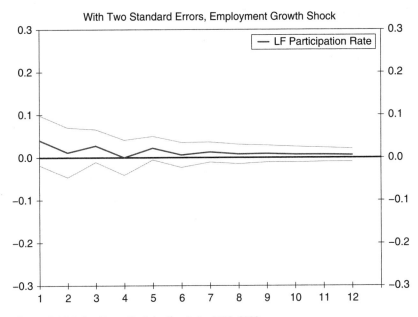

Figure 2.44 Labor Force Participation Rate: 1983–2008

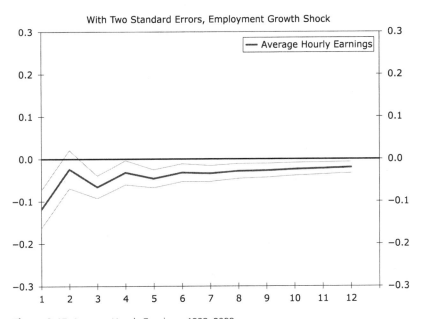

Figure 2.45 Average Hourly Earnings: 1983–2008

CHAPTER 3

Information

Past Imperfect, Present Incomplete, Future Uncertain

Capt. Bart Mancuso: How did you know that his next turn would be to starboard?

Jack Ryan: I didn't. I had a 50/50 chance. I needed a break. Sorry.

Capt. Bart Mancuso: That's all right, Mr. Ryan. My Morse is so rusty; I could be sending him dimensions on Playmate of the Month.

This simple exchange from the movie *The Hunt for Red October* illustrates the need to make decisions without complete, perfect information and the need to communicate what we think is the correct message under uncertainty.

The reality of the world we live in is that there are many possible outcomes with less-than-perfect information in decision making. This is the focus of this chapter.[1] Three regularities in decision theory add to the richness, or some would say complications, to economic decision making. First, decision makers tend to focus more on losses than gains. Second, persons focus more on changes in their utility states than they focus on absolute utilities. Finally, the estimation of subjective probabilities is severely biased by anchoring, recency, and other decision-making patterns.

Two stories from WWII highlight the role of information and its importance. At the start of WWII, both Great Britain and Germany had functioning radar systems. For Great Britain the use of radar was the key to victory in the air battles we term the Battle of Britain, as radar allowed the British to deploy their limited fighter force in direct proportion to incoming German fighters and bombers. In contrast, Germany did not use all tools, such as radar, due to leadership prejudice against defensive measures.[2] Second, the Germans also failed to coherently incorporate

---

[1] Patrick Leach, "Why Can't You Just Give Me the Number? An Executive's Guide to Using Probabilistic Thinking to Manage Risk and to Make Better Decisions," 2006; and Raiffa Howard, "Decision Analysis: Introductory Lectures on Choices Under Uncertainty," 2007.

[2] Raymond C. Watson Jr., *Radar Origins Worldwide: History of its Evolution in 13 Nations through World War II* (Bloomington, IN: Trafford Publishing, 2009).

new technology to upgrade and secure their Enigma coding and this failure to improve information processing led to the British breaking of the codes and, once again, better allocation of forces in the war.[3]

To illustrate the importance of information in decision making, especially bad information, one can simply turn to the events of the first business day in June 2014 and the release of the Institute for Supply Management (ISM) manufacturing survey. At 10 A.M. on June 2, the organization reported that their factory index fell to 53.2 in May from 54.9 in the prior month. This was weaker than the consensus had expected and, in economics and financial markets, the difference between expectations and what is realized is what drives markets and the economy.

The 10-year Treasury yield declined immediately following the weaker-than-expected read on the manufacturing sector, as the index indicated to investors a weaker economy ahead. The yield declined from 2.51 percent to a touch below 2.5 percent (see Figure 3.1). Yet

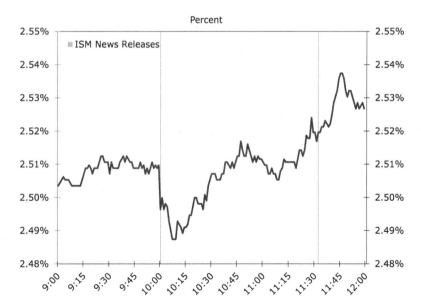

Figure 3.1 10-Year Yield on June 2, 2014
Source: Institute for Supply Management and Bloomberg LP

---

[3] Simon Singh, *The Code Book: The Science of Secrecy from Ancient Egypt to Quantum Cryptography* (New York: Knopf Doubleday Publishing, January 2011).

shortly after the release there were questions about the headline number. By 11:15 A.M., a *Bloomberg* story appeared quoting the research firm Stone & McCarthy that their calculations suggested a stronger number due to the use of what they considered a correct set of seasonal adjustment factors. By 11:32 A.M., the ISM had corrected its initial report to read 56.0 from 53.2 and, in response, the 10-year yield rose to 2.54 percent at around 11:45 A.M.

Yet, the story continues. Suspicions in the marketplace persisted that the second release was not quite correct either and that the second release number, at 56, was too high. By 12:09 P.M., *Bloomberg* reported that a second correction was to be released within the hour. At 12:32 P.M. the second correction was issued and the final number came in at 55.4—above the original release and yet below the second release. The markets had been whipsawed on both the long and short side of the release. This episode highlights the importance of accurate information in determining market actions.

STORY BEHIND THE NUMBERS

Imperfect information for decision makers requires caution—as if driving in a fog, you adjust and slow down. Imperfect information leads to incomplete and partial adjustments. The source of the fog is found everywhere—oil price collapses in the mid-1980s and more recently in 2014–2015, policy shocks and major currency devaluations, or fiscal policy changes abroad. The existence of incomplete adjustments opens up the possibility that changes in nominal money growth will give rise to incomplete adjustment of nominal prices and thereby real changes in employment and output. More broadly, the existence of uncertainty—imperfect information, contracts, and renegotiation costs—all provide a basis for partial adjustment and thereby changes in the real economy.

One channel through which this works is when producers and workers know their individual prices/wages but not the aggregate price level.[4] Therefore, they will make decisions without full knowledge of

---

[4] Robert E. Lucas Jr. "Expectations and the Neutrality of Money," *Journal of Economic Theory* 4 (April 1972): 103–124.

the relative prices they receive for goods/labor. When prices change, the producers/workers are not sure if the aggregate prices have changed, and therefore they are likely to attribute part to change in the aggregate price level and part to change in relative prices. In the United States, this was quite manifest in the housing price rise in the mid-2000s. Recall that the observed price of a good is the sum of the aggregate price level and the good's relative price expressed as:

$$P_g = P * \left(\frac{P_g}{P} \right)$$

That is, the price of the good g equals the product of the aggregate price level and the good's relative price. The insight that economic agents observe their own price—but not the aggregate price—is certainly true in credit markets where there is oftentimes no aggregate index of the specific product being traded as many financial products are imperfect substitutes and there is no aggregate measurement for the sector.

Since agents have imperfect information on the price change, both the producers and workers exhibit a partial response to any change and, as a result, aggregate output and labor will exhibit a partial response such that a rise in prices would be associated with a rise in output/labor giving rise to a positively sloped short-run aggregate supply curve. A recent example of this was the rise in both prices and output in the oil sector from 2012 to 2014.

Policy shocks are just one source of change that can cause real economic changes. For example, random changes in preferences—fur fashions in pre-revolutionary America—led to a rise in fur production and prices and, just as quickly, prices collapsed as European fashion preferences changed. Unobserved changes in money supply, credit supply, and money multipliers in many sectors give rise to real economic changes as imperfect information permeates the economy in all sectors.

For the individual agents, the relative price provides a signal to action whereas the aggregate price level is noise. As a result, the departure of output from its long-run potential level is positively correlated with the price level. When oil prices surprised to the upside in 2012–2014, oil production rose. When oil prices surprised on the downside in 2014–2016, however, oil production fell. The departure of output/labor from its normal level is an increasing function of the surprise in the price level. As the relative price of oil rose, output rose. When relative oil prices fell, output declined.

Imperfect information on price movements is an essential part of business cycle fluctuations. When changes in the money supply are observed accurately and there are no frictions preventing price adjustment, then changes in the money supply are neutral and output does not shift. Aggregate prices change, but output remains unchanged. However, when money supply shifts are not observed accurately or frictions are introduced as in the previous chapter, then output will change.

The positive link between prices and output once again reflects the experience of 2014–2016. As the unexpected decline in oil prices is associated with a decline in output, the price change is clearly not neutral. The positive relationship between output and prices gives rise to the Phillips curve.

Expectations matter and any changes in policy or exogenous shock alter those expectations. As a result, shifts in policy will change aggregate relationships. In contrast, temporary changes in policy do not alter economic activity, as evidenced by the 1986 temporary tax increase. In general, only unobserved shocks to aggregate demand or supply give rise to real economic effects.

The precise conduct of monetary policy is not available to private agents, evidenced by the surprise move by former Fed Chairman Ben Bernanke when he discussed reducing the pace of asset purchases that gave rise to the taper tantrum in mid-2013 as well as the surprise move by the Swiss National Bank to drop the Swiss franc/euro floor in 2015. In contrast, the response to publicly available information is minuscule at best and helps explain why publicly announced monetary actions, when anticipated in advance, often generate little response. Unanticipated policy announcements do generate a response in interest rates and exchange rates.

Moreover, the Fed has imperfect information on inflation. Consider the numerous measures of inflation and labor market slack utilized by decision makers and it is clear that there is no clear measure of aggregate inflation or labor market conditions. Moreover, there is little consensus on accurate measures of growth or inflation in many emerging economies, China being only one instance.

What is often unappreciated is that inventories are also quite present in financial markets in the form of assets on trading desks and in investment portfolios. When a surprise policy announcement is made, these inventories are either in or out of the money and significant sharp adjustments are often seen. This was evident again in response to Chair Yellen's comment on high-yield bonds that led to an immediate repricing of high yield debt as illustrated in Figure 3.2. As with the inventory of real goods, an inventory adjustment of financial instruments creates its own cycle.

Economic shocks from nominal disturbances can also have real economic effects and significant distributional impacts. This is possible given the asymmetric information that is present in many debt contracts. During the 2014–2016 period, a nominal decline in the price of crude oil had significant negative economic effects on equipment and structures spending due to two features of financial contracts. First, many debt contracts were not indexed to the value of a barrel of crude oil. Second, loan agreements are made in nominal terms where the borrower may have better information on the operation of the energy

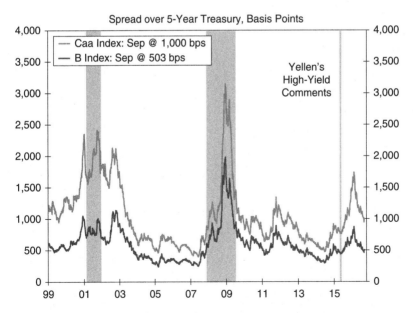

Figure 3.2 High-Yield Spreads
Source: Bloomberg LP

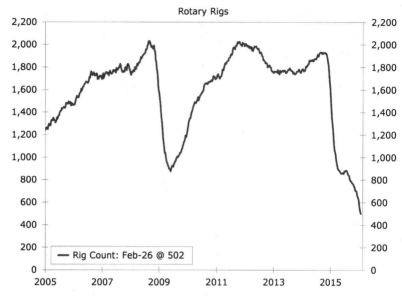

Figure 3.3 Baker-Hughes Rig Count
Source: Baker-Hughes

business they are conducting than the lender. This asymmetric information may give rise to greater risk taking on the part of the borrower than what was priced into the contract by the lender.

Given the market experience with the oil price decline from 2014 to 2016, the subsequent bankruptcies and depreciation of the value of high-yield energy-related bonds certainly gives evidence of asymmetric information. The subsequent decline in energy-related equipment and structures investment (Figure 3.3) lends support to the view that nominal shocks give rise to real economic effects.

The Underlying, Implicit Assumptions in Economic Decision Making

Many economic models begin with the assumption of an ideal decision maker, fully informed, fully rational, and able to compute with perfect accuracy all options. Yet in the real world, we deal with imperfect information, imperfect rules and models as well as a number of biases in decision making. This idealized decision maker acts in the way people ought to make decisions. Given the reality of actual decision making, however, how do consumers and firms behave with the limits of information in their decision-making process? What is the actual decision-making process—not the normative, idealistic aspect of decision making? Unlike playing the game of chess or tic-tac-toe, all rules are not obvious and all possible moves are not known.

When the assumptions of perfect competition, rational agents, and perfect information are made, it often allows the precise mathematical derivation of desirable results. In addition, the assumptions underlying many economic models dictate that each economic agent possesses knowledge about other market participants, and that knowledge is available to all participants. Each participant knows the payoffs and strategies available to other players. But we must ask what happens when these pristine assumptions are unrealistic and not reflective of reality. When examining the economy in action, it is unrealistic to expect perfect desired results.

The Limits of Public Policy in Society[5]

Given the limits of information in society, we immediately recognize the restraints on decision making in the face of imperfect information. Central planning cannot match the efficiency of the open market because any single decision maker knows only a small fraction of all that is known collectively by society.

Therefore, decentralized decision making in an economy complements the dispersed nature of information spread throughout society. This principle of dispersed information, that no single agent has information as to all the factors that influence prices and production throughout the economic system, intimates that markets search for an equilibrium of buyers and sellers, which gives a dynamic to economic activity that influences the pattern of behavior in product, labor, and credit markets.

---

[5] Friedrich A. Hayek, "The Use of Knowledge in Society," 1945. Library of Economics and Liberty, June 10, 2014, www.econlib.org/library/Essays/hykKnw1.html.

Decision Theory: The Importance of Imperfect, Incomplete, and Dynamically Incorrect Information

Unlike in tic-tac-toe, each player's cards are hidden from other players in a game of poker—an example of incomplete information. The challenge for each player is to identify available information, uncertainties with respect to that information, and other issues relevant in a given decision. This is in contrast to the idealized decision maker, who is fully informed with perfect information and able to compute with perfect accuracy the possible outcomes and is fully rational in each decision (bias-free decision making).

Instead, we face choices under conditions of imperfect information along with all the computational problems and personal biases in our decision making. The result is that we calculate, either heuristically or with some simple model, the expected value of possible outcomes by identifying outcomes, determining their values and associated probabilities.

Limited Information Limits Results: Why Perfect Models Fall Short

At first glance we often model the behavior of economic variables over time with an assumption of perfect competition and flexible prices (wages, commodity prices, interest rates, and exchange rates). However, once we take these models into the real world and examine the data, we find that the patterns of the data do not represent smooth adjustments from one equilibrium point to another. In cases where information is imperfect, the results differ from the predictions of simple models with overly restrictive assumptions. Therefore, we should expect a different result from that predicted from many policy initiatives that are hatched in perfect model incubators. Instead, we face a wider range of outcomes and lower probability of any individual outcome than what perfect models predict.

Moreover, as time passes, we get new information that leads to new equilibria that were unanticipated when initial policy actions were implemented. Fiscal stimulus in 2009 did not give us the rapid economic and employment growth that was predicted by Keynesian models. Rapid growth in the Fed's balance sheet did not generate the inflation feared by those who use monetarist models (Figures 3.4 and 3.5).

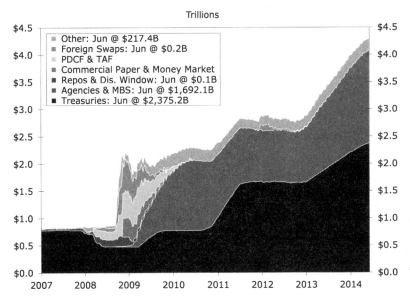

Figure 3.4 Federal Reserve Balance Sheet
Source: Federal Reserve Board

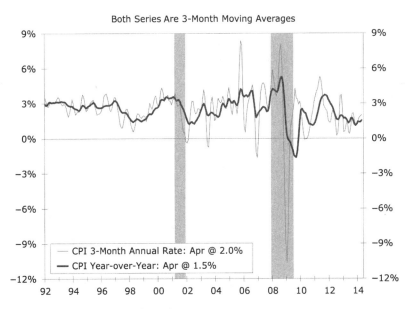

Figure 3.5 U.S. Consumer Price Index
Source: U.S. Department of Labor

Credit markets often do not adjust smoothly to changes of policy actions or changes in expected policy, as illustrated by the jump in market interest rates and credit availability following the hint of Fed tapering beginning in May 2013. In addition, wholly unanticipated was the sharp reaction to this same hint of policy change in the exchange rate markets for emerging market countries.

In economic forecasts, and in many models, the pattern forecasted for the data is smooth. Yet in the reality of markets, movements can be very sharp and often unexpected. Moreover, these movements can lead to further changes that are not anticipated and provide new information and therefore lead to further economic developments that were not expected.

Furthermore, imperfect information, such as inherent sampling problems when constructing many economic statistics, may also lead economic agents to make decisions that would not have been made with perfect information. Samples for retail sales, employment, and durable goods orders, series critical to making effective decisions, are all subject to large revisions as more complete information is developed.

In addition, gross domestic product (GDP) can be influenced by weather, as we saw in the first quarter of both 2014 and 2015, which can give a misleading impression of the pace of economic growth. Estimates of first-quarter GDP for these years were negative, and this information is clearly not representative of the underlying pace of growth, but the initial estimates of GDP have led some analysts to conclude the economy is weak and these analysts are making decisions under that assumption.

Building the Model: Barriers to an Effective Idealized Economic Model in the Real World

For effective econometric modeling, an analyst must consider the issue of incomplete information. As in the case of incomplete and imperfect information, a model would produce unreliable results.[6] Here,

---

[6] If the information is incomplete/imperfect then the model has an autocorrelation problem. In the case of an autocorrelation problem the variance is inefficient (no minimum) and hence results are unreliable. For more detail about autocorrelation, see John E. Silvia, Azhar Iqbal, Kaylyn Swankoski. Sarah Watt, and Sam Bullard, *Economic and Business Forecasting: Analyzing and Interpreting Econometric Results* (Hoboken, NJ: John Wiley & Sons, 2014), 319–321.

we list potential sources of incomplete/imperfect information along with possible remedial steps.

We begin by outlining three types of real-world information problems that interfere with our perfect models of economic information. First, there is the issue of incomplete information—economic agents do not know all the facts and therefore economic agents may delay decisions or make different decisions than what would have been made if all information had been available. This incomplete information is apparent when the president and Congress are moving ahead with major legislation and yet the details of such information is not yet available, or legislation has been passed but federal agencies have not yet put in place the rules implementing that legislation.

Incomplete Information

Incomplete information emphasizes the observation that in the real world, in contrast to perfectly competitive model assumptions, no agent has full information as to other agents' budgets, preferences, resources, or technologies, not to mention their plans for the future and numerous other factors that affect prices in markets.

Real business investment is one area where incomplete information is most obvious. A firm may find that it needs to adjust its capital stock to achieve a level of capital consistent with a new level of expected output. Since the costs of a full adjustment and the cost of making a mistake may be very high, a firm will pursue a policy of partial adjustments. In our analysis, this may give rise to a distributed lag process in a series such as capital investment. Incomplete information also leads to a bias in thinking called the hindsight bias. Sometimes called the "I-knew-it-all-along" effect, the tendency is to see past events as being predictable at the time those events happened.

Currently, there are two other fields where incomplete information is having a significant impact on current economic activity. First, in labor markets, both potential workers and potential employers face incomplete information barriers regarding job opportunities and the location of skilled workers to fill those jobs. One sign of these information barriers is exhibited in the sharp peaks and valleys of the unemployment rate in Figure 3.6. Both potential employers and employees

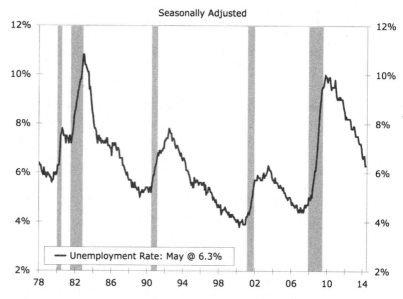

Figure 3.6 Unemployment Rate
Source: U.S. Department of Labor

face significant search costs to find a match.[7] The gap between job searchers and employers looking to fill a vacancy is illustrated in Figure 3.7. For a given vacancy rate on the *y*-axis, there has been a clear outward shift in the unemployment rate during the current cycle.

A classic example of incomplete information is when an important variable is missing from the model. For example, the Taylor (1993) rule suggests inflation and the unemployment rate (or output) are two key determinants of the federal funds rate, or short-term interest rates.[8] If we were to model the fed funds rates and include only the inflation rate as a determinant, we would likely see an autocorrelation problem. The estimated results including the confidence interval would be unreliable.[9] That said, the missing variable is often unknown

---

[7] For an original exposition on search costs see Dale T. Mortenson, "Job Search, the Duration of Unemployment, and the Phillips Curve," *American Economic Review* 60 (December 1970): 846–862.

[8] John B. Taylor, "Discretion versus Policy Rules in Practice," *Carnegie-Rochester Conference Series on Public Policy* 39 (1993): 195–214.

[9] For more detail, see Jan Kmenta, *Elements of Econometrics* (New York: Macmillan, 1971), Chapter 8.

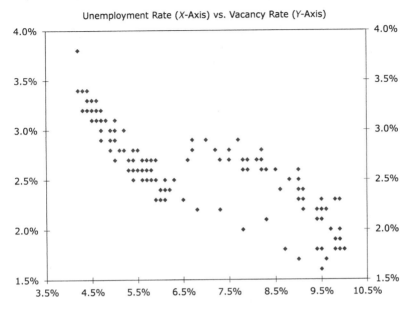

Figure 3.7 The Beveridge Curve
Source: U.S. Department of Labor

or unobserved. That is, in the above example, we know the unemployment rate is missing from the model and that would be considered a known unknown. Known unknowns are not the only case of missing variables and the other, more complicated, example would be an unknown unknown case—a variable is missing and we do not know what is missing. One major reason of this unknown unknown scenario is that economies are complex and evolve over time and the relationships between variables also evolve. A good example of this is the Phillips curve relationship between unemployment and inflation.[10] If we model inflation using the Phillips curve and utilize the unemployment rate as predictor, then that model may produce autocorrelation. In this case, we are following the economic theory, no known unknowns, but economies also evolve and introduce the problem of unknown unknowns. For example, between May 2012 and January 2016, the

---

[10] A. W. H. Phillips, "The Relationship between Unemployment and the Rate of Change of Money Wage Rates in the United Kingdom, 1861–1957." *Economica* 25, no. 2 (1958): 283–299.

unemployment rate dropped from 8.2 percent to 4.9 percent, but the personal consumption expenditures (PCE) deflator stayed below the Federal Open Market Committee's (FOMC) target of 2 percent for the entire period—the longest period of below 2 percent inflation in several decades. That suggests we need to include more variables (e.g., interest rates, oil prices, a measure of overall economic activity) to improve model fit in an attempt to address the unknown unknown problem.

Another possible source of incomplete information is the missing observations problem, where a data set contains missing values. The missing observations problem may lead to measurement errors and inconsistent results—see Chapter 9 of Kmenta (1971) for more detail. Another source of missing observations, typically for time series data, is due to the selection of the time span. That is, if we were to estimate the Taylor rule using the post-1990s era only, we would get different results from the pre-1990s era. The past three recoveries are considered "jobless" by some observers and the inflation rate, on average, was much lower compared to the pre-1990s—again economies evolve over time. Furthermore, we are not sure whether the future will be like the 1990s or closer to the 1980s. Therefore, to avoid incomplete information we should use the entire data set.

Incomplete information is also a problem when decision makers attempt to assess the state of the economy and the behavior of other economic agents in response to economic events. For example, we note the sometimes surprising reactions of financial markets to an economic data release that would appear very positive for the economy, but the market reaction is negative. One only has to experience a few releases of the Employment Situation report and the subsequent market reaction to appreciate the problem. In this case, what we are witnessing is the release of an economic number, such as employment, that is positive but that is not as positive as the market had expected. The difference between expected and actual will generate the market response. In addition, implications for inflation from a rapidly expanding economy and the revisions to expectations for monetary policy moving forward can weigh on financial markets.

Incomplete Information: Dealing with Missing Variables in Our Empirical Work

When forecasting economic series there are frequently pieces of data we would like to have but do not. In this example for interest, we utilize a modified Taylor rule that includes the fed funds rate, unemployment rate, and PCE deflator to show the missing variable (incomplete information) case. The unemployment and inflation rates are two potential determinants of the fed funds rate. We estimate three different regressions or models; (1) the fed funds rate and unemployment rate (inflation is missing); (2) the fed funds rate and PCE deflator (unemployment rate is missing) and (3) the fed funds rate, unemployment rate, and PCE deflator (complete model).

Two measures of a model's fit are the root mean square error (RMSE) and the Schwarz Bayesian Criterion[11] (SBC). The model with a smaller RMSE/SBC value has a better fit (and contains more useful information), although one must be wary of overfitting the model. The third model, which includes the fed funds rate, the unemployment rate, and PCE deflator, produces the smallest values for both RMSE and SBC.[12] Note, by including a relevant variable, we increase the usefulness of our estimates. In other words, if we use the first or second models to explain movements in the fed funds rate, then the error in estimation is larger than that of the third model. In the present case, the larger error is because a relevant variable is missing from the model. Therefore, a missing relevant variable in the model or incomplete information can lead to a larger error and hinder the decision-making process.

Imperfect Information: Data Revisions and Data Quality

Second, the case of imperfect information—information that does not precisely reflect reality—is often faced by decision makers. The challenge is faced all the time because so much economic information comes via initial surveys of activity that are frequently revised,

---

[11] Gideon E. Schwarz, "Estimating the Dimension of a Model," *Annals of Statistics* 6, no. 2 (1978): 461–464.

[12] The SBC and RMSE values for Model 1 are 1,858.26 and 2.82, for Model 2 values are 1,677.8 and 2.23, and the Model 3 values are 1,637.6 and 2.1.

sometimes significantly, as further information is gathered. Initial estimates of retail sales, GDP, employment, and capital goods orders are more often than not revised from their initial released number.

For many, house hunting is daunting because of the uncertainty on pricing. In fact, many of us will sometimes ask—why is this house so cheap? In credit, there are the issues of adverse selection and moral hazard as well as questions on the quality of bank capital in the United States, Europe, and China. Finally, there are always questions on the quality of corporate profits and analysts are always asking for more details, suggesting that there is still information that remains to be found that could improve the quality of earnings estimates.

What about the cost of labor? In recent years, decision makers have had many different measures of labor costs, as illustrated in Figure 3.8. First, there is the traditional average hourly earnings series that is released along with the nonfarm payroll report at the start of each month. A second release is the wages and salaries series that is part of the personal income report. Finally, there is the employment

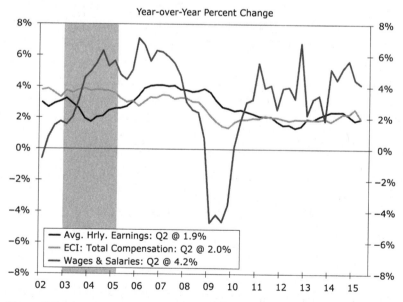

Figure 3.8 Labor Costs
Sources: U.S. Department of Labor and U.S. Department of Commerce

cost index, which provides a summary of the wages, salaries, and benefit changes that accrue to workers.

Economic variables that we model are presumed to influence, or at least represent, the actual economy. However, we often receive new information (note the revision of GDP estimates we witnessed for the first quarter of GDP in 2014 and 2015) such that the initial information imperfectly represents the real economic situation. Lucas has made the case for imperfect information on prices, whether a relative price change compared to other competitors or an absolute change for all competitors.[13] If a firm perceives that the price change is relative (greater demand for its products), then that firm may alter its production schedules. Although a firm may actually be misreading the data, the firm will pursue a departure from previous output schedules. For any decision maker the critical question becomes: how much of our macro data reflect actual activity as opposed to our perceptions of what activity we believe to be happening?

Imperfect information: Dealing with the Problem of Measurement Error

There are several potential sources of imperfect information resulting in unreliable conclusions. In most cases, imperfect information would lead to autocorrelation or nonstationary problems, and results are unreliable in either case; see Silvia et al. (2014) for more detail.

Here, we examine the problem of imperfect information by comparing the Standard & Poor's (S&P) 500 index and nonfarm payrolls. A common measurement error is that an analyst may utilize the level form of the variables in regression/correlation analysis. Many time series variables are nonstationary at their level form. The common estimation method utilized by analysts is the ordinary least squares (OLS) model, which assumes the underlying data set is stationary.[14] If the data are nonstationary at the level form, then using OLS on

---

[13] Robert E. Lucas Jr., "Expectations and the Neutrality of Money," *Journal of Economic Theory* 4 (April 1972): 103–124.

[14] For a detailed discussion about the unit root concept, see G. S. Maddala and In-Moo Kim, *Unit Roots, Cointegration and Structural Change* (Cambridge, UK: Cambridge University Press, 1998).

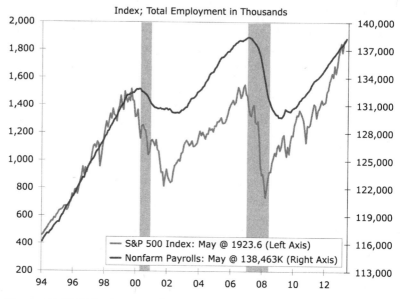

Figure 3.9 S&P 500 Index vs. Nonfarm Payrolls
Sources: S&P and U.S. Department of Labor

that data set would produce spurious results; that is, it would tend to suggest a very strong relationship (denoted by a very high R-squared value), even though there is no meaningful relationship between the variables. In our example, both the S&P 500 index and nonfarm payrolls are nonstationary at level form and using that form of the variables, we obtain a very high R-squared value of 0.89 (Figure 3.9). The difference form (month-over-month percent change in this case) of a series, however, is usually stationary and, therefore, is better suited for regression analysis. Using the difference form of the S&P 500 index and nonfarm payrolls, we obtained a lower, but more reliable R-squared of 0.01 (Figure 3.10). Therefore, measurement error (wrong functional form) can lead to a completely wrong conclusion.

The OLS regression is a simple and widely utilized method of estimation and forecasting. A typical OLS model consists of a dependent variable (left-hand side variable) and one or more independent variables (right-hand side variables). The OLS method is simple because of several limitations. First, OLS only estimates a statistical association between the variables of the model and does not identify the statistical

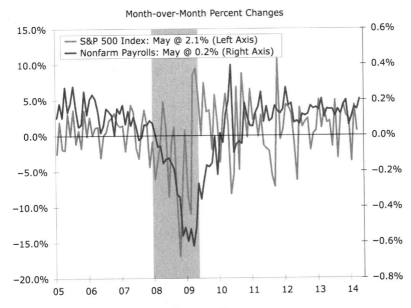

Figure 3.10 S&P 500 Index vs. Nonfarm Payrolls
Sources: S&P and U.S. Department of Labor

causal relationship. Second, to generate out-of-sample forecasts of the dependent variable, we need out-of-sample values of the right-hand side (independent) variables. Third, we cannot include too many variables because we would reduce our degrees of freedom and/or introduce multicollinearity problems. Fourth and finally, since the OLS is a single equation (only one dependent variable), it is unable to capture the underlying structure of an economy and may suffer model specification issues and provide unreliable results.

The Bayesian Vector Autoregression (BVAR) model, on the other hand, addresses the issues mentioned above. The BVAR approach can be utilized to test causal relationships between variables of interest (Granger causality). The BVAR model does not require future values of the right-hand side variables to generate out-of-sample forecasts for target variables. In addition, the BVAR approach allows us to include many variables in the model and hence permits us to include more information than the OLS model. Finally, the BVAR method improves upon the single-equation approach into a system of equations (several dependent variables) and can better capture the underlying structure of an economy. In general, the BVAR approach is more flexible and should be utilized to test causal relationships as well as generate forecasts.

Information Dynamics: Information Can Change in the Future—Out-of-Sample Forecast Errors

Third, information is also dynamic over time. For example, information on the pace of economic growth and job creation over time is revised and this changed perspective leads to alternative decisions or decisions that are regretted and would have been different if economic agents did indeed have perfect foresight. In war, it is said that battle plans change after the first shot. In business, the introduction of New Coke was met with an immediate negative reaction that marketing executives completely failed to anticipate.[15] Many times, government rules on land use or flood plains can change after a developer or homeowner has bought a piece of real estate.[16]

Credit decisions can be turned on their head by court decisions on municipal bankruptcies, rule of law in corporate bankruptcies and federal mandates, or simply a rewriting of federal/state laws that upset the previously understood relationship between creditors and debtors. Finally, recent years have witnessed significant shifts in sovereign government commitments to exchange rate regimes and trading agreements, as a new political leadership assumes leadership after an election.

Forecast errors tend to increase with the forecast horizon—the longer the forecast horizon, the larger the forecast error. This can be illustrated by the forecast variance of the canonical autoregressive model of order one (AR[1] model). For tractability, we assume there is no drift term (constant). An AR(1) model is given as follows[17]:

$$X_t = \beta X_{t-1} + \varepsilon_t \text{ where } \varepsilon_t \sim N(0, \sigma^2)$$

---

[15] New Coke was the unofficial popular name for the reformulation of Coca-Cola, introduced in the spring of 1985. The public reaction was negative to the new formula and the new formula was replaced with the original formula a few months later. This episode remains a warning to developers to be careful about altering an established brand.

[16] See, for example, the eminent domain case of *Kelo v. City of London*, 545 U.S. 469 (2005).

[17] For more detail, see Maddala and Kim, 1998.

Where X_t is the time series being studied and ε_t is the independent and identically distributed error term with mean zero and variance of σ^2. The l-step ahead value of our series is given by recursively stepping forward in the model as follows:

$$X_{T+l} = \beta^l X_T + \sum_{i=1}^{l} \beta^{l-i} \varepsilon_{T+i}$$

The expected value of this series is given below, as the error terms drop out.

$$E\left[X_{T+l}\right] = \beta^l X_t$$

The variance of this forecast, however, is fully dependent on the variance of the error terms. Note that the error of our forecast will be given as the difference of the actual value (X_{T+l}) and the expected value, which simplifies to the cumulative error:

$$e_T(l) = \sum_{i=1}^{l} \beta^{l-i} \varepsilon_{T+i}$$

$$var\,[e_T(l)] = E\left[\left(\sum_{i=1}^{l} \beta^{l-i} \varepsilon_{T+i}\right)^2\right]$$

Now this seems like an ugly equation to work with. This is why the assumption of i.i.d. error terms is useful. This means that $E\,[\varepsilon_a \varepsilon_b] = 0$ whenever $a \ne b$. Therefore, most terms in the above equation drop out. We can simplify further to:

$$var\,[e_T(l)] = (1 + \beta^2 + \cdots + \beta^{2(l-1)})\,E[\varepsilon^2]$$

$$var\,[e_T(l)] = (1 + \beta^2 + \cdots + \beta^{2(l-1)})\,\sigma^2 = \frac{1 - \beta^{2l}}{1 - \beta^2}\,\sigma^2$$

Note that, as one would expect, variance is monotonically increasing the further out into the future we are forecasting. That said, the concavity of the error is dependent on the value of β. If $\beta < 1$, the series is mean reverting, and the standard deviation of the forecast is concave down. If the series is not mean reverting, however, and $\beta > 1$, then the standard deviation is concave up, and therefore our forecasts will be poor.

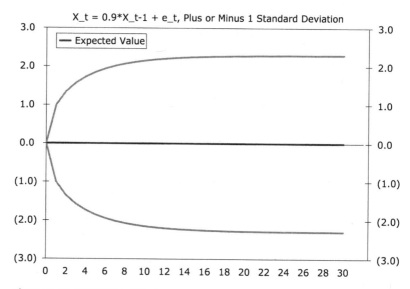

Figure 3.11 AR(1) Forecast Variance

There are several reasons behind the larger forecast errors for longer forecast horizons (Figure 3.11). For instance, the cumulative chance of a shock (in policies or consumer/investor behavior for example) increases with time. In addition, the objective function of other players may change over time, thereby complicating economic decisions. European governments can quickly shift to tighter fiscal policy—as we saw post-2009. Foreign governments can quickly shift exchange rate policy. Domestically, regulators can alter the direction of policy and rules over time. This problem is compounded with changes in political party leadership. At the state/local level, changes in land use policy after property has been bought for development affects the planned development and therefore limits economic development in many local areas. As a result, in contrast to the model that assumes that the objective functions of economic agents do not change over time, the reality is that change is constant on the part of decision makers and the rules they promote. New information and rules alter the payoffs and the expected rates of return on investment in equipment and workers. This uncertainty regarding future policy changes will tend to reduce long-term investment in equipment and the hiring of workers. The time horizon for all economic decisions is shortened given the risk/uncertainty of future political/policy change.

Processing Bad Information Poorly: Imperfect Rules and Models

Thus far, we have outlined how the quality of information influences the effectiveness of economic modeling and forecasting efforts. However, with imperfect decision making, there are additional problems that further complicate the ability to estimate the impact of economic activity and policy changes. Information is often processed in inefficient ways that further drive economic results away from the idealized forecasts. Market prices are the result of price discovery—from both the supply and demand sides—and how agents gather, process, and distribute information affects this process. Price discovery faces numerous challenges. Here we highlight eight issues: analysis paralysis, bounded rationality, information asymmetry, imperfect decision making, cognitive bias, rational ignorance, heuristics, and prospect theory.

Analysis Paralysis

Too much information can be a problem. For both public and private decision makers, too many guidelines and economic indicators can actually stifle decision making. The perceived cost of making a decision exceeds the benefits that could be gained by enacting some decision. Decision makers often seek the optimal or perfect solution to a problem as they rightly fear the costs of a wrong decision, leading to over analysis. That said, no action is often more costly than many suboptimal actions. This is a problem today in several areas. First, in monetary policy, as we have cited before, there are several economic guidelines (multiple measures of labor slack and inflation) such that so much information may stymie any future decision making by often suggesting contradictory assessments of the economic situation. This uncertainty often prompts cautious responses—overly cautious policy may be too late. In addition, financial institutions face numerous regulators (Federal Reserve, Securities and Exchange Commission, Federal Deposit Insurance Corporation, and the Comptroller of the U.S. Treasury), each with their own set of priorities. In the face of many possible disparate regulatory signals, in the private sector, both financial institutions and nonfinancial corporations, rather than moving forward by putting cash to use, these institutions simply sit on the cash waiting for further information. In a similar way, private nonfinancial firms face similar problems with the multiple information guideposts on taxes and public spending decisions. In each case the quantity of information and analysis overwhelms the decision-making process and thereby inhibits an economic agent from making a decision.

In addition, when public policy makers do act, their decisions may create the impression that there is some special piece of information available to them, not available to the private sector, such that the private sector asks itself—what are we missing?[18]

Bounded Rationality

Herbert A. Simon commented that the rationality of individuals is limited by the information they have, the cognitive limitations of their minds, and the finite amount of time they have to make a decision.[19] This is the reality of making decisions on production, hiring, and allocating credit in real time. This leads many decision makers to be satisficers—not optimizers with complex mathematical models. Households apply their rationality only after having greatly simplified the choices available. Households, firms, and even public policy makers lack the ability and resources to arrive at the optimal solution.

Decision makers pick a stopping point—they do not seek all the information that might be available. However, the particular stopping point differs among individuals. As a result, the perfectly rational decisions assumed in economic models are often not feasible in practice even with perfect information because of the finite computational resources and time available for making them.

Our evaluation of economic activity and the impact of public or private sector actions must begin with the recognition that the costs of gathering, processing and disseminating information provides an incentive to limit the time spent in these efforts. In fact, the complexity of the situation may limit, rather than expand, the information process. In real time, actions must be taken despite the complexity,

---

[18] See Robert J. Barro, "Rational Expectations and the Role of Monetary Policy," *Journal of Monetary Economics* 2 (January1976): 1–32; Thomas J. Sargent and Neil Wallace, "Rational Expectations, the Optimal Monetary Instrument, and the Optimal Money Supply Rule," *Journal of Political Economy* 83 (April 1975): 241–254.

[19] Herbert A. Simon, *Models of Man: Social and Rational* (New York: John Wiley & Sons, 1957).

as in Captain Mancuso's need to send a message without gathering information and checking his Morse code. Decision makers simply are unable to process and compute the expected utility of every alternative action. Deliberation costs might be high, and they are often concurrent with economic activities also requiring attention so decision makers have limits on time and the ability to process information.

Information Asymmetry

Here, we focus on decisions in transactions where one party has more, or better, information than the other. There are three situations that produce results that are contrary to the idealized results of the perfectly competitive market model: adverse selection, moral hazard, and the principal-agent problem.[20]

Adverse selection arises when one party to the agreement lacks critical information while negotiating an agreed contract. This problem often arises in financial services when a loan is being made and complete information about the credit history and the motivations of the borrower are unknown. Other situations of adverse selection include used cars and home purchases—consider the canonical market for lemons.[21]

Moral hazard arises when one party lacks critical information about performance of the agreed-upon transaction or lacks the ability to retaliate for a breach of the agreement. Households/firms may behave more recklessly after becoming insured, but the insurer cannot effectively retaliate against the insured in the short run during the term of the current contract. Only in the long run can the insurer deny to renew—but even here that ability is sometimes prohibited. Furthermore, the riskiest individuals are more likely to buy insurance and insurance companies often cannot discriminate due to the force of law. We can see this in the market for health insurance where younger, healthier people are less likely to buy medical insurance compared to older, less healthy people.[22]

---

[20] Sherwin Rosen, "Prices and Incentives in Elimination Tournaments," *American Economic Review* 76, no. 4 (1986): 701–715.

[21] George A. Akerlof, "The Market for Lemons: Quality Uncertainty and the Market Mechanism," *Quarterly Journal of Economics* 84, no. 3 (1970): 488–500.

[22] Kenneth Arrow, "Uncertainty and the Welfare Economics of Medical Care," *American Economic Review* 53 (1963): 941–973.

In the case of the principal-agent problem, there is an information asymmetry where agents have more information and the principal cannot directly ensure that the agent is always acting in the principal's best interests. In the most common situation, corporate management acts as agent and shareholders are the principal.[23] In another case, politicians are the agent and voters are the principal. The information asymmetry therefore has significant private-sector implications with respect to the incentives for corporate management, where maximizing shareholder value may not be the driving principle for management, and it is therefore difficult to determine if management is truly maximizing profits—a basic tenet of microeconomic theory about the firm. In public policy, do politicians support policy actions to actually maximize economic growth or are decisions on policy, such as a fiscal stimulus, directed more toward ensuring their own reelection rather than public benefit?

Imperfect Decision Making

In policy making, the problem of imperfect information arises in two distinct paths. First, while there is one monetary policy, we often hear from several different members of the FOMC that create different impressions for the direction of policy. Second, currently the FOMC is following a broad set of labor market indicators to determine the direction of policy. Although this may enhance policy, the information problem is that a central bank that follows multiple labor market indicators sends a confusing signal to the private-sector investor. As the adage goes, a man with one clock will know what time it is, but a man who has two clocks is never sure. This policy-making problem is further complicated by the initial unemployment rate guidepost of 6.5 percent being replaced by the emphasis on a wider range of labor market indicators. This problem is also present when several different inflation guidelines shift between core and overall inflation, consumer price index (CPI), and PCE inflation—once again, too many clocks.

---

[23] Lucian Bebchuk and Jesse Fried, *Pay without Performance* (Boston: Harvard University Press, 2004).

Cognitive Bias

Even with the proper information, the decision maker has biases that will often not produce an optimal solution. The decision maker employs his or her own subjective social reality, not the objective input of relevant information that would lead most other people to pursue a different decision path. Judgments deviate from the optimum, so it becomes increasingly difficult to judge the range of outcomes and their possibilities. This situation often arises when investors seek to evaluate the strategy of corporate leadership and that strategy of introducing new products/prices or acquisitions appears confused and without a clear path forward. These cognitive biases include the confirmation bias, framing, and the sunk cost bias.[24]

All of these biases introduce challenges to the assumption of rationality. The price one paid for a good or asset should not be relevant when it comes to selling the good or asset. That said, one must not look far to find someone who is reluctant to sell an asset for less than what they paid for it, even though this is an arbitrary delineation because the purchase prices is a sunk cost. Anchoring biases are also present throughout economics. While the ratio of home prices to income was roughly constant for several decades, this relationship was forgotten during the run-up to the Great Recession, where home prices grew rapidly (Figure 3.12). People began to believe that the recent trend would continue indefinitely. Analysts failed to consider the implications for a decline in home prices and largely ignored that possibility.

Rational Ignorance

Rational ignorance occurs when the cost of educating oneself on an issue exceeds the potential benefit of that education.[25] In this case, the decision maker comes to a rational decision that the cost of educating oneself on an issue outweighs any potential benefits; therefore, it is irrational for a decision maker to waste time pursuing additional information. That is, once the marginal cost of searching for information exceeds the marginal benefit of obtaining that information,

---

[24] John E. Silvia, *Dynamic Economic Decision Making* (Hoboken, NJ: John Wiley & Sons, 2011).
[25] Anthony Downs, *An Economic Theory of Democracy* (New York: Harper & Brothers, 1957), 244–246, 266–271.

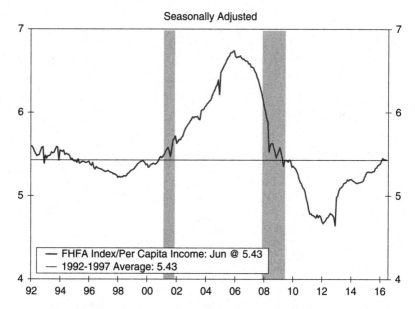

Figure 3.12 FHFAHPI/Per Capita Income
Sources: FHFA and U.S. Department of Commerce

it would be irrational to continue searching. For example, consumers have limited time, so visiting another store to possibly find a better price may not be worth the time. Now, of course, consumers will use the Internet to search for better prices or product information to lower the marginal cost of information.

This can also be seen in politics. Small groups who derive substantial benefits from a policy are incentivized to lobby hard for that policy. Policy makers may implement the policy, even if it is costly to the public, because the cost would be spread among a large group of people and be relatively small. It would often be irrational for voters to learn the specifics of each issue in an election from a purely economic standpoint, as the expected benefit of this is minuscule. The probability that an individual vote will matter is small and even if that vote is persuasive, the policies the voters advocate are not necessarily what will be made into law.

Heuristics

Heuristics are often employed by economic agents, where households and firms employ experience-based techniques for problem solving, learning, and discovery, which gives a solution that is not guaranteed to be optimal. Here, exhaustive searching for, and processing of, information is impractical. Heuristic methods are employed to speed up the process of finding a satisfactory solution via mental shortcuts to ease the cognitive load of making a decision. In other contexts, we can refer to rules of thumb, educated guesses, intuition, working backward, or trial and error. With rational ignorance, where it is impractical to gain all the information, heuristics are often employed.

Prospect Theory

Under prospect theory, households make decisions based on the potential value of losses and gains rather than the final expected outcome, and then people evaluate their prospects (these losses and gains) using certain heuristics rather than precise economic models.[26] Our focus here is the way people choose between probabilistic alternatives that involve risk, where the probabilities of outcomes are known. This involves a two-step process. First, households order outcomes and match outcomes that are perceived to be equivalent. Then households set a reference point and then consider lesser outcomes as losses and greater ones as gains. This involves considering the entire distribution of outcomes from a decision rather than simply looking at the expected value. Because agents in an economy are typically risk averse, we must consider all possible outcomes, not solely the mean. In the traditional capital asset pricing model, notice how the undiversifiable risk influences the expected return of a stock. That is, investors require a higher expected return because of the increased risk to the downside.

CONCLUSION

Recent experience with the ISM release and GDP revisions reinforce the basic message that decision makers do not make critical decisions in an environment of perfect information. Critical to our decision making is that we often must treat the data with an element of caution.

---

[26] Daniel Kahneman and Amos Tversky, "Prospect Theory: An Analysis of Decision under Risk," *Econometrica* 47 (1979): 263–291.

Because of the uncertainty surrounding the quality of information we have today, we also realize that public and private decision makers face a wide range of possible outcomes for any decision despite the precision that we attribute to the sophisticated models and simulations we run. We must recognize that we do not have complete information in making a decision, as there are costs to obtaining all available information. Second, information is often imperfect and does not perfectly reflect the current state of the economy. Once again, the frequent revisions to economic data emphasize this point. Finally, the information we have today may not be reflective of information in the future about the economy. Unfortunately, many economic projections assume a smooth path of growth or straight line projections of recent behavior (recency bias). As a result, decision makers often rely on heuristic tools to make decisions within the universe containing significant amounts of information—even as the information is less than we often assume in our models.

CHAPTER 4

Price Adjustment and Search for Equilibrium

Many stylized models of economic behavior that decision makers utilize assume that prices instantaneously adjust to new equilibriums following external shocks or changes to policy. This, however, is clearly not reflective of the real world, as price adjustments are not smooth. In reality, the economy is in a constant state of disequilibrium as prices take time to fully reflect market forces while additional shocks may also influence price movements in the economy. This presents a challenge to decision makers and economic forecasters, as forecasts seldom have time to play out because of the slow adjustment of prices and constant stream of economic shocks.

Take the recent housing boom and bust illustrated in Figure 4.1. Once home sales began to roll over, it took time for prices to adjust and begin their decline. In addition, once prices fell back to historically affordable levels, home sales were slow to show much improvement. The many other factors affecting the economy and subsequent shocks increased the duration of the adjustment process—frictions in the foreclosure process and a slow recovery in personal income in addition to global shocks emanating from Europe and China have all dragged out the process. The term *ceteris paribus* is common in economic analysis,

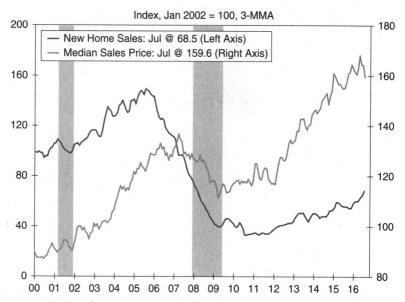

Figure 4.1 New Home Sales and Prices
Source: U.S. Department of Commerce

which means all else equal—that is, studying the impact of a shock assuming only one variable changes in response. Analysts must be careful when assuming ceteris paribus and recognize that other variables that could impact the series under study are rarely constant in the economy—look at how historically low inventories held back home sales following in the recent economic expansion despite improving incomes and still-low interest rates.

In the short run, price adjustments are often limited by price fixing for goods and services. Federal- and state-mandated prices are pervasive in areas such as labor, credit, exchange rates, and other goods and services, which we will explore further later in this chapter (utilities, rent controls, and health care). These pervasive fixed prices inhibit the adjustment of prices to their new equilibrium following a shock—often leading to the buildup of imbalances, such that markets retain a bias to react in sharp, frequent, and often different directions over time.

WHAT BARRIERS ARE THERE TO PERFECTLY FLEXIBLE PRICES?

Economic theory gives myriad explanations for why prices are not perfectly flexible. We will outline several of the traditionally cited causes of price stickiness before discussing the implications imperfect price adjustment has for the economy, especially in the post–Great Recession world.

Menu Costs[1,2]

One reason that prices take time to adjust in an economy is due to menu costs. The basic idea behind menu costs, as stated in the seminal work of Sheshinski and Weiss, is that "price adjustments are not costless" for firms. These costs can come in many forms. Menu costs could be the costs associated with a restaurant physically designing and printing a new menu every time prices change, a supermarket

---

[1] George Akerlof and Janet Yellen, "Can Small Deviations from Rationality Make Significant Differences to Economic Equilibria?" www.aeaweb.org/yellen_articles/aer.75.4.708.pdf.

[2] Eytan Sheshinski and Yoram Weiss, "Inflation and Costs of Price Adjustment," *Review of Economic Studies* 44, no. 2 (1977): 287–303.

paying an employee to relabel goods, or even the cost associated with disgruntled customers who may be unhappy when they realize a different customer received a different price for the same good purchased only slightly before or after they did.

The result of such costs to a firm for changing prices is that, even with perfect knowledge and foresight of future inflation, firms will hold nominal prices constant for a period of time before changing prices in discrete increments despite continuously changing prices for inputs. That is, firms will adjust prices only if the marginal benefit of doing so outweighs the marginal cost. While certainly an oversimplification of the phenomenon, it is clear that menu costs can prevent the rapid response of prices to shocks. As a shock hits the economy, firms must weigh the costs of changing their prices and the benefits that occur from doing so. The perceived permanence of the shock and impact on expected prices and demand into the future certainly play into the decision-making process.

Anecdotal evidence suggests that technology may be reducing menu costs in some industries. The trend toward e-commerce clearly makes changing prices easier and less costly for firms (Figure 4.2). That

Figure 4.2 Rise of E-Commerce
Source: U.S. Department of Commerce

said, we do not feel that e-commerce can fully eliminate menu costs. As mentioned earlier, customers likely will become agitated if there is a significant increase in volatility of the prices for goods and services. Take, for example, the challenges faced by companies such as the ride-hailing service Uber, which has the ability to constantly adjust the price for its services through surge pricing. During times of peak demand, fares can rise to multiple times the normal fare, to which the company has received blowback, particularly around crisis situations.[3] This has led the firm to limit surge pricing at times, preventing them from maximizing their profits because they deemed the cost of changing prices too expensive—a form of menu costs. Despite these issues, technology has certainly enabled firms to adjust prices faster in response to changing economic environments.

Contracts—Labor/Suppliers/Hedging

Contracts can also contribute to the inflexibility of prices in the economy. A large share of economic contracts—whether they are for inputs to the production of final goods, contracts to sell products to consumers, debt contracts or labor contracts—are priced in nominal terms. That is, they are not typically indexed to the price level. This means that the price of the good or service being exchanged between the involved parties during the life of the contract is fixed in nominal terms, which can lead to lags in adjustments to shocks. Because of the fixed nominal price, expectations are critical in forming the contract. Again, as we have seen before, how economic news and the economy evolve relative to what was expected is relevant to economic decision making. Consider the aviation industry, where the activity of hedging energy costs is commonplace. If an airline hedged some portion of their fuel needs in late 2014, they would likely be slower to lower their fares compared to airlines with no hedging. That is, because they would still be paying the elevated fuel costs for at least a portion of their fuel

---

[3] Utpal Dholakia, "Everyone Hates Uber's Surge Pricing—Here's How to Fix It," *Harvard Business Review*, 2015, https://hbr.org/2015/12/everyone-hates-ubers-surge-pricing-heres-how-to-fix-it.

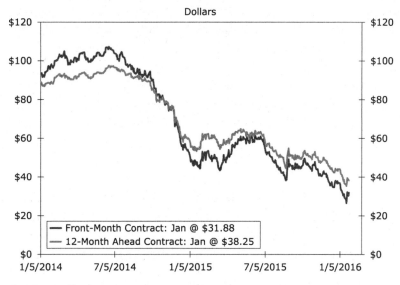

Figure 4.3 Oil Futures Contracts
Source: Bloomberg LP

needs, it would be difficult to lower prices (Figure 4.3). Contracts, such as hedging contracts at the firm level, contribute to slow price adjustment in the economy as a whole.

In addition, labor contracts make it difficult to adjust wages and the level of employment in response to shocks to aggregate demand, which may in turn lead to a slow adjustment process. We will discuss nominal wage rigidities in greater detail shortly, although contracts can certainly contribute to nominal rigidities in the labor market.

Mandated Prices

Examples of mandated prices can be found in many sectors of the economy. Many regulated industries such as utilities and health care have limits on what they can charge for their goods and services. In addition, the price of labor for all firms in the economy is often mandated via minimum wage laws and required benefits. These topics are highly controversial, and there are many stakeholders involved in determining the optimal policies, meaning that a thorough review would not be possible in this text. We simply highlight the impact these policies have on the economy's adjustment to shocks. Because these prices cannot adjust in response to a changing economic environment, the adjustment process is drawn out, and the allocation of resources may be less efficient in an economic sense due to changes in the relative prices of these goods or services.

Nominal Wage Rigidities in the Labor Market[4]

Another prominent contributor to the sluggishness of price adjustment, and one that has gained more attention following the Great Recession, is the downward nominal wage rigidity in the labor market. That is, it is difficult for employers to reduce nominal wages following a negative shock to aggregate demand. The unwillingness of firms to reduce, or of employees to accept, lower wages can lead to increased unemployment, as firms lay off workers instead of reducing wages or hours for all employees. Downward wage rigidities, therefore, slow the price adjustment process during business cycles. In a recovery period, it takes time for the economy to work through the "pent-up wage deflation" before hiring and wage gains can materialize. The concept of downward nominal wage rigidities and their implications will be discussed in more detail in a later chapter.

Prices as Incentive

Imperfect price adjustment can also be an incentive for participants in a marketplace. The lag in price adjustment often introduces opportunity for the clever arbitrageur in many markets, who may take advantage of the discrepancy in price. The simplest example, not surprisingly, is an application to financial markets. That said, the ideas in this section could easily be extended to account for many types of markets.

In financial markets, for example, there is evidence that suggests that price discovery occurs in futures markets rather than cash markets for some assets, and that the futures markets lead the spot market in responding to news.[5] The lag in response between prices in futures

---

[4] G. Mankiw, *Macroeconomics* (New York: Worth Publishers, 2009).

[5] Joel Hasbrouck, "Intraday Price Formation in U.S. Equity Index Markets," *Journal of Finance* 58, no. 62375-99 (December 2003).

and the cash market can create an arbitrage opportunity. The presence of this opportunity to buy in the lower-priced market and instantaneously sell to the higher-priced market should attract arbitrageurs who would do just this. Buying at the lower price and selling at the higher price would lead to the convergence of the two markets, eliminating the arbitrage opportunity. This introduces an interesting paradox in financial markets, which, stated loosely, suggests that efficient markets require a little bit of inefficiency to reward arbitrageurs, who then make the market more efficient.[6]

Extending this idea to the real economy, we see that there must be some reward for expending the effort and resources necessary to gather information regarding prices and their adjustment in order to better price one's own goods rather than simply taking prices as given. That is, if prices adjust perfectly and instantaneously, a firm would not expend resources to obtain information about the supply-and-demand schedules of a product and rather simply monitor the prevailing price in the marketplace, taking it as given.

IMPLICATIONS

Thus far, we have argued that the price adjustment process is imperfect because of a number of structural factors. In addition, we extended an argument in financial economics—that a little inefficiency is required to incentivize the arbitrageur who promotes inefficiency—to the real economy, arguing that an imperfect adjustment process may be necessary to incentivize firms to expend the effort and resources to obtain information relevant to the prices of goods they sell. We will now discuss a number of implications this imperfect adjustment process for economists.

Business Cycles

Likely the largest implication of sticky prices is the introduction of business cycles. If the economy instantaneously moved to a new equilibrium following an economic shock, the short-run aggregate supply curve would be a vertical line, the same as the long-run supply curve.

---

[6] Sanford J. Grossman and Joseph E. Stiglitz, "On the Impossibility of Informationally Efficient Markets," *American Economic Review* 70, no. 3 (June 1980), 393–408.

That is, a positive shift in aggregate demand would simply raise the price level and not impact output because prices instantly adjust. Dynamic adjustment, however, leads to a positive sloping short-run aggregate supply curve and allows actual output to persistently deviate from the long-run potential.

It is difficult to discuss economic fluctuations without mentioning the monetarism school of thought. Monetarist theory suggests that money is not neutral in the short run and the money supply is "the chief determinant of current dollar gross domestic product (GDP) in the short run and the price level over longer periods."[7] This can be seen through the quantity theory of money, which states that nominal output equals the money supply times the velocity of money.

$$MV = PQ$$

Where M is the money supply, V is the velocity of money, P is the price level and Q is output. This equation always holds true and is an accounting identity because the velocity of money is defined to make the equation hold. That said, monetarists argue that changes in the money supply can impact real output because prices on the right side of the equation are slow to adjust to a new equilibrium. This imperfect adjustment, therefore, is the foundation of many policy actions and is one of the justifications for the generally accepted belief that monetary policy can have real impacts in the short run.

Buildup of Imbalances

Prices that are mandated or set by governments are an example of frictions that lead to imperfect price adjustment. While there are a number of examples of mandated prices, one of the more straightforward examples with easily accessible data is in the case of currency pegs. When a country pegs its currency to another, it typically stands ready to transact (either buy or sell) at the peg or in some channel around the peg.

Take, for example, the experience of the Swiss franc (CHF) at the beginning of 2015, when the Swiss National Bank shocked markets

---

[7] Sarwat Jahan and Chris Papageorgiou, "What Is Monetarism?" *International Monetary Fund*, 2014.

by allowing the CHF to appreciate against the euro. The central bank had initially introduced the floor on the currency (thereby limiting the appreciation of the CHF) in an effort to maintain the competitiveness of its exports. The CHF, like the dollar, is often seen as a safe-haven currency. With the turmoil in the Eurozone, many traders preferred to hold assets denominated in Swiss francs. To prevent the currency from appreciating beyond the floor set by the Swiss National Bank, the central bank had to commit to buying an unlimited amount of euros, which would be financed by the sale of CHF. In order to defend the floor amidst a rapid depreciation of the euro relative to many currencies, including the dollar, the Swiss National Bank cut short-term interest rates into negative territory to make holding the CHF less attractive and rapidly expanded the monetary base—a by-product of buying euros with newly created CHF. The rapid expansion of the monetary base stoked fears of runaway inflation, which likely contributed to the central bank's decision to remove the peg. As illustrated below in Figure 4.4, the reaction to the move was abrupt, as the CHF rapidly appreciated versus the euro.

Similarly, we can look at the experiences of many Asian economies in the late 1990s, whose currencies came under downward

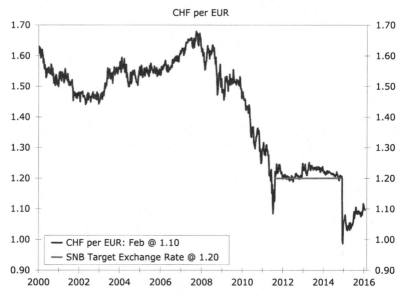

Figure 4.4 Swiss Exchange Rate
Source: Bloomberg LP

pressure rather than upward pressure like the CHF. In defending their currencies against depreciation, the Asian central banks were forced to sell foreign currency reserves and buy the local currency. This, naturally, cannot go on indefinitely as each country holds a finite amount of foreign currency reserves. If traders view the peg as unsustainable, the country is susceptible to a speculative attack. That is, if "the market" does not believe the country is willing and able to defend its currency peg through selling reserves or raising interest rates, which can exacerbate the problem by weakening the domestic economy and increasing borrowing costs, traders may aggressively sell the currency in question, leading to the peg breaking.

As you can see in Figure 4.5, Thailand consistently built up foreign reserves as their economy experienced rapid growth, leading the country to be viewed as a "model economy." This caused capital to flow into the country, which would normally put upward pressure on Thai baht. By accumulating foreign exchange reserves, Thailand was able to maintain the currency peg. Once some of the issues in the economy became more pronounced and the baht came under rapid selling pressure, foreign exchange reserves fell rapidly. Once the available reserves were all but exhausted, the central bank capitulated and devalued the baht.

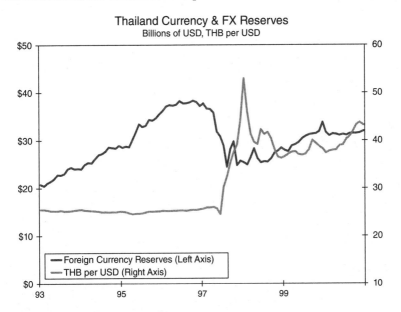

Figure 4.5 Thailand Currency and FX Reserves
Source: Bloomberg LP

Short Run to Long Run

Another impact of the lag in price adjustment is that short-run impacts and adjustments can spill over to the long run. In the post–Great Recession era, as we have emphasized, many things have changed in the economy. This has resulted in estimates for potential growth seeing significant downward revisions. While the excesses before the crisis masked some of the changes to economic fundamentals, the recession itself likely also contributed to reduced potential in many economies around the globe. The fact that short-term business cycle fluctuations can spill over and impact the long-term growth trajectory of an economy is not conventional wisdom in classical economics. In fact, a recent study found a relationship between the magnitudes of the decline in output relative to potential (output gap) and the subsequent downward revision in potential GDP since the downturn.[8] They conclude that the hysteresis effects—negative impact on potential growth from economy operating below potential—account for a large portion of this phenomenon.

FINDING DYNAMIC ADJUSTMENT IN THE DATA

We have discussed a number of causes of imperfect price adjustment in an economy as well as implications and examples of the imperfect adjustment process on the broader economy. We now will outline a few econometric techniques for identifying the imperfect price adjustment process and apply them to some of the data we mentioned earlier in the chapter.

Don't Assume Reversion to the Mean

Often, we hear economic data discussed in relation to the long-run average value. Many commentators cite a long-run average as a "normal" value for economic data series without justifying this assertion. As we have mentioned, many economic series are not mean reverting; that is, they do not tend toward a stable mean over time. Therefore, we must be careful when utilizing the long-run average as a guide in

---

[8] Laurence Ball, "Long-Term Damage from the Great Recession in OECD Countries," International Monetary Fund, 2014.

Table 4.1 Identifying a Structural Break Using the State-Space Approach

Real GDP-YoY (Not Mean Reverting)		
Break Date	Type of Break	Coefficient
Oct-08	Level Shift	–1.81
10-Year Treasury (Not Mean Reverting)		
Break Date	Type of Break	Coefficient
Apr-87	Level Shift	1.05
Existing Home Sales-YoY (Not Mean Reverting)		
Break Date	Type of Break	Coefficient
Apr-10	Additive Outlier	21.89
Oct-92	Additive Outlier	14.58
Home Prices-YoY (Not Mean Reverting)		
Break Date	Type of Break	Coefficient
Apr-12	Level Shift	5.15
Apr-86	Additive Outlier	3.25
Home Inventories-YoY (Not Mean Reverting)		
Break Date	Type of Break	Coefficient
Jan-90	Level Shift	17.29
Exchange Rate-USD/THB (Not Mean Reverting)		
Break Date	Type of Break	Coefficient
Jan-98	Additive Outlier	5.94
Apr-01	Level Shift	2.41

decision making by validating that the series is in fact mean reverting before proceeding to do so.

In Table 4.1 we display the results for a series of statistical tests to determine if many of the economic series we discussed in this chapter are in fact mean reverting. First, we utilize the Augmented Dickey-Fuller (ADF) test to test for mean reversion, and we then test for structural breaks using the State-Space approach. As you can see, all of the series we studied contained a unit root, meaning the series is not mean reverting. In addition, all of the series contain structural breaks, meaning their mean and/or variance changed between periods. Therefore, we must be careful when assuming the long-run average as a guide for future behavior with these series.

Time-Varying Equilibrium Rate Resetting Expectations

Similarly, we can investigate the time-varying equilibrium real interest rate (Figure 4.6). Statistical analysis confirms the structural break in the natural rate of interest during the Great Recession. This suggests that the myriad of comments indicating that interest rates should "normalize" or increase back to a "normal" level are statistically unfounded. While there are economic arguments for rates rising, we must be careful of arguments assuming they will rise back to historical levels.

Impulse Response Functions

Now that we have identified that the series we are interested in are not mean reverting, we must apply a few transformations (percent change is a convenient transformation) that would convert the series into one that is in fact mean reverting. Once we have done this, we

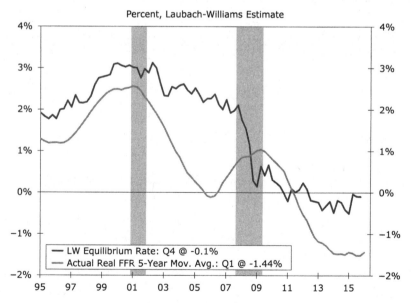

Figure 4.6 Natural Real Rate of Interest Estimate
Sources: Federal Reserve Board and Laubach & Williams

construct a simple model of the housing market, including home sales, home prices, inventories, and interest rates to illustrate the dynamic adjustment process. We acknowledge that this model fails to capture many of the dynamics in the housing market, but utilize this model for simplicity. We shock the model with a 1 percentage point increase in the 10-year Treasury yield and investigate the dynamics of the model through the impulse response functions plotted in Figures 4.7 through 4.9.

Following a 1 percentage point increase in the 10-year Treasury, home sales steadily decline and continue to decline for a year into the future. Similarly, home prices fall and inventories rise; these changes are also persistent. This simple model clearly illustrates the imperfect price adjustment process. A year after the initial shock to interest rates, the housing market is still in the adjustment process to the new equilibrium. Of course, this model contains significant uncertainty, and the confidence intervals of impulse response functions include zero. Nonetheless, it is informative that the mean response to a shock does display imperfect price adjustment.

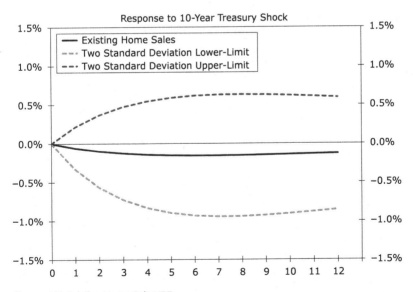

Figure 4.7 Existing Home Sales IRF

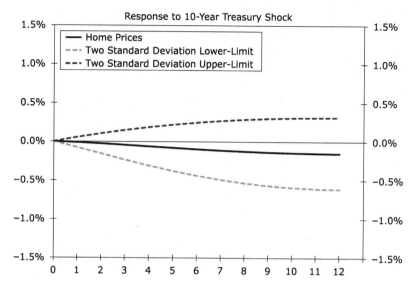

Figure 4.8 Home Prices IRF

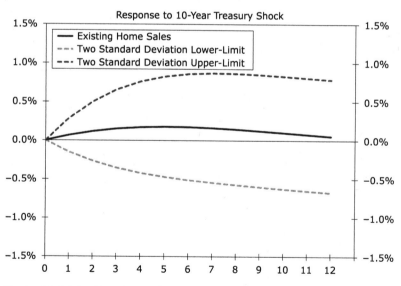

Figure 4.9 Existing Home Inventory IRF

CONCLUSION

In this chapter, we explored price adjustment to shocks and policy changes in an economy. We began by highlighting the numerous rigidities that cause imperfect price adjustment before discussing the important economic implications of the dynamic price adjustment process, including real business cycles, the potential for imbalances to build up and lead to sharp adjustments, and the risk that short-run deviations can affect long-run potential growth. Finally, we investigated a number of techniques for finding imperfect adjustment in the data and took a look at the dynamic adjustment process of the U.S. housing market.

CHAPTER 5

Business Investment

This Time Is Different

C apital investment is a critical component of long-run economic growth. The growth rate of the capital stock has implications for the pace of gains in labor productivity and long-run potential growth, which is fundamental to improving standards of living in an economy. In addition, although business investment comprises a smaller share of gross domestic product (GDP) than consumption, it is highly cyclical and can be a leading indicator for turns in the business cycle (Figure 5.1). In this chapter, we highlight the drivers of business investment spending and how the behavior of capital investment has changed following the Great Recession.[1] It is clear that business investment has disappointed for much of this cycle. Despite a rapid rebound initially following the large declines seen in the recession, equipment has been frustratingly slow during this expansionary period.

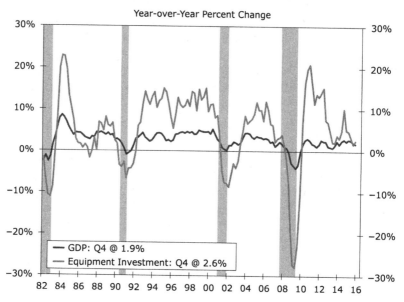

Figure 5.1 Real GDP and Equipment Investment
Source: U.S. Department of Commerce

---

[1] For our purposes, we define investment spending as business fixed investment in equipment. We will use business investment and capital investment interchangeably.

DRIVERS OF BUSINESS SPENDING

Investment spending directly impacts the capital stock; therefore, businesses' investment decisions are related to their desired capital levels. Recall that the change in the capital stock (ΔK) from one period to another is equal to net investment, or gross investment (I) less depreciation (δK).[2]

$$\Delta K = I - \delta K$$

Notice from the equation above that an economy requires positive investment to simply hold the capital stock constant, and to increase the capital stock in any given period investment must outpace depreciation.

A firm's desired capital stock should reflect the trade-off between the profit generated from additional capital and the cost of the capital. As is often the case in economics, the firm should continue to invest until the marginal benefit of holding an additional unit of capital equals the marginal cost of the additional unit, that is:

$$MP_{K^*} = MC_{K^*}$$

where MP_{K^*} is the marginal product of capital and MC_{K^*} is the marginal cost of capital at the desired capital level (K^*). We will now discuss various economic indicators that we can look at that impact each side of the above equation and, therefore, the desired capital stock and business fixed investment.

Expected Sales

A large driver of the marginal product of capital is expected future sales. Potential growth can be a proxy for future sales, and the Congressional Budget Office (CBO) publishes forecasts for potential output for years into the future. The potential growth rate of the U.S. economy has downshifted markedly following the Great Recession as a result of trends in place prior to the recession that were masked by

---

[2] Gregory Mankiw, *Macroeconomics*, 7th edition (New York: Worth Publishers, 2010), 196.

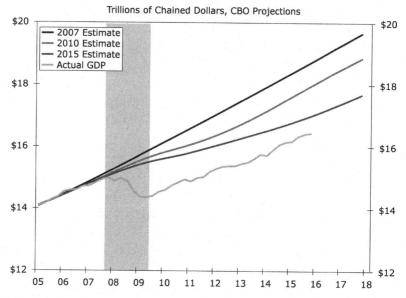

Figure 5.2 Potential GDP Revisions
Source: CBO

the rapid growth leading up to the recession and structural shifts that occurred during the recession (Figure 5.2).

A downshift to expected growth as we have experienced likely weighs on the marginal product of capital. That is, lower expected sales in the future require less capital and the marginal benefit of additional capital in the future is decreased. This is one plausible explanation for the slow pace of business investment during this cycle. When the rate of business investment is compared to GDP growth, investment in the current cycle looks more typical (Figure 5.3).

Capacity Utilization

Capacity is another indicator that can be indicative of business investment plans. Capacity utilization represents the share of resources for production that are being utilized in the mining, utilities, and manufacturing sectors of the economy.[3] It is fairly intuitive to state that

---

[3] Unfortunately, we do not have data on capacity utilization for the large services side of the economy.

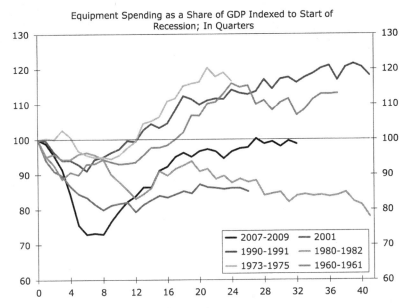

Figure 5.3 Equipment Spending Share Cycles
Source: U.S. Department of Commerce

capacity utilization impacts the marginal benefit of additional business investment. If there is significant excess capacity—as has been the case for much of this cycle (Figure 5.4)—the marginal product of additional capital is likely low as there is already excess capacity that is going unused. Therefore, additional investment is unlikely to be utilized right away making the marginal benefit of the additional capital lower, ceteris paribus. Of course, expectations for the future also are important as capital investment decisions and implementation are not immediate. As discussed earlier, however, lower sales expectations reflected in the downward revisions to potential growth estimates are not supportive of strong capital spending.

It seems clear that the growth rate of the desired capital stock following the Great Recession declined compared to the pace of growth before the recession. This has likely reduced the marginal benefit of additional investment for firms in the economy and been a reason for the sluggish pace of capital investment during this cycle.

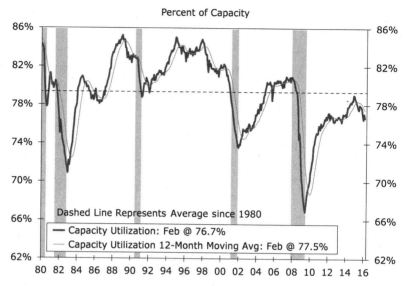

Percent of Capacity

Figure 5.4 Total Capacity Utilization
Source: Federal Reserve Board

Expected Useful Life

Expectations regarding depreciation and the useful life of an asset also impact the expected benefit that asset will provide. A more durable and flexible capital stock suggests that depreciation will be lower and the capital will maintain its productive capacity for longer. Trivially, an asset that is expected to produce for a longer period of time will lead to higher expected profits from that activity, increasing the expected marginal benefit of the asset. In addition, a more durable capital stock is associated with a lower rate of depreciation. Therefore, the required investment to maintain the capital stock declines. This means that an increase in the expected useful life of the capital stock has an ambiguous impact on investment, depending on the increased expected benefit of additional capital investment and the reduced replacement costs to maintain the current stock.

Presently, the capital stock is "old" relative to history (Figure 5.5). While this could be indicative of more durable economic capital, it also may reflect a lack of willingness to invest in new capital because of the uncertainty about the economy. The composition of the capital stock

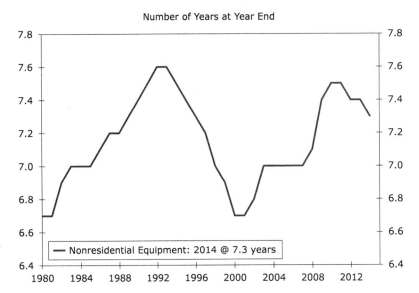

Figure 5.5 Current-Cost Average Age of Private Fixed Assets
Source: U.S. Department of Commerce

also clearly can impact the average age, as new technologies may have longer or shorter expected useful lives.

In addition, some have indicated that the older age of the capital stock may be a reason for the slower growth in labor productivity during this cycle as older capital, all else being equal, is likely less productive than new capital.

Interest Rates

We now turn to the right side of the marginal benefit marginal cost equation, the marginal cost of capital. This can be a tricky concept to pin down; what exactly is the cost to a firm for their economic capital? Because many firms own their capital outright, we cannot look at rental costs. Therefore, we agree with the notion that the cost of capital can be thought of as the cost of financing the purchases. While the theory surrounding the cost of capital could form a text of its own, we will highlight a few of the important drivers.

Interest rates are an important driver of the cost of capital. Historically low interest rates—both nominal and real yields—should, in

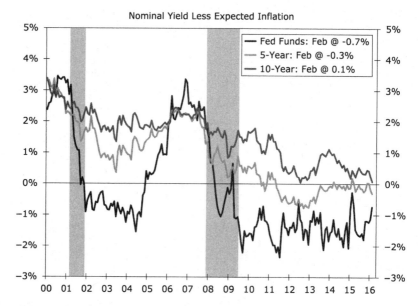

Figure 5.6 Real Interest Rates
Source: Federal Reserve Board

theory, lower the cost of capital and supported capital investment, all else being equal (Figure 5.6). As is always the case in economics, it is impossible to measure the counterfactual, and it is likely that capital investment would have been even weaker had interest rates not been lowered like they were following the financial crisis.

In addition, as we have mentioned before, it is rare for the ceteris paribus assumption to hold and a firm's access to capital markets can vary with market conditions and over the business cycle. Firms trying to raise funds to finance the purchase of economic capital would have likely found it more challenging during the turmoil of late 2011 and early 2012 stemming from the European debt crisis. In addition, lending standards tightened markedly following the recession (Figure 5.7). Thus, despite the low level of rates, firms might not necessarily have been able to borrow to finance their capital investments.

Although interest rates impact business investment decisions, they are clearly not the only factor. The violation of the ceteris paribus assumption can clearly be seen when investigating business investment in Fed tightening cycles (Figure 5.8). As you can see, business investment

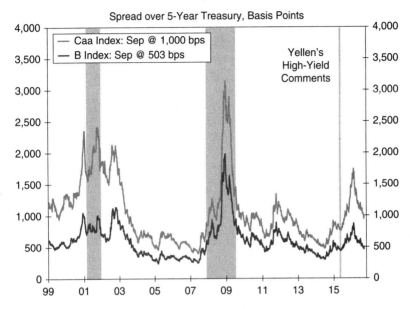

Figure 5.7 High-Yield Spreads
Source: Bloomberg LP

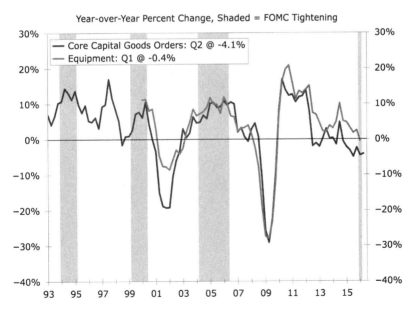

Figure 5.8 Core Capital Goods Orders vs. Equipment Spending
Source: U.S. Department of Commerce

typically accelerates at the beginning of a tightening cycle. This may seem counterintuitive at first, but taking a broader context, we know that the Fed is generally raising interest rates in a strong economy where the other drivers of business investment compensate for higher interest rates, at least initially.

Corporate Profits

In addition to interest rates, corporate profits are an important source of funding for many businesses. In a frictionless economy, capital investment decisions are independent of the amount of funds available from corporate profits because there are no borrowing constraints. However, there are frictions in the economy, including borrowing constraints and costs associated with borrowing. As such, internally generated funds are often used to finance capital investment. As seen in Figure 5.9, the financing gap—the difference between internally generated cash flow and capital expenditures—was positive for much of the recovery period. As we mentioned earlier, firms were hesitant to

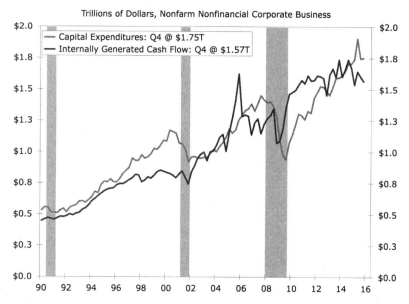

Figure 5.9 Capital Expenditures vs. Internally Generated Funds
Source: Federal Reserve Board

invest following the crisis because of uncertainty about the economic outlook and many firms chose instead to pay down debt, buy back stock, or expand through acquisitions rather than capital investment. Capital expenditures have recently picked up, however, leading to the financing gap turning positive. This means that outside funding, or drawdown in cash balances, must finance the difference in internal funds and capital expenditures.

Policy—Tax and Policy Uncertainty Index

Tax policy can also impact the cost of capital for firms. We will not explore the nuances of corporate tax policy in this text, although special tax treatment of interest payments and depreciation of the capital stock can alter the incentives of corporations and the marginal cost of capital. In addition, uncertainty about future policy and the uncertain regulatory environment can weigh on business investment decisions. As you can see in Figure 5.10, policy uncertainty was at extraordinarily high levels following the recession, which likely weighed on capital investment.

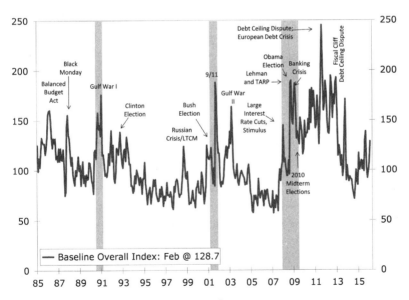

Figure 5.10 Index of Economic Polity Uncertainty
Source: Baker, Bloom, and Davis

Discrete Jumps

Finally, business investment is not continuous. That is, a firm can only add capital in discrete amounts. In an overly simplified example, consider a firm that makes clothing using a combination of labor and capital, which consists of sewing machines. Business is booming for our clothing manufacturer and they would like to expand. Clearly, they cannot add half a sewing machine and can only increase their capital stock by a discrete amount. While this is an unrealistic example for modern firms, it is instructive that a certain threshold must be met for the marginal benefit of capital to be worth the additional costs, and adjustments are not necessarily smooth.

PUTTING IT ALL TOGETHER: EXPLAINING SLOW RECOVERY IN CAPITAL INVESTMENT

Analyzing the different drivers of the desired capital stock and, therefore, capital investment, we can now analyze why business investment has disappointed during this cycle. Many economic commentators are puzzled as to why business investment has not grown more rapidly given the low-interest-rate environment and above-potential economic growth. When we investigate all the pieces together, not in isolation, we can see that there are numerous headwinds to business investment. Lower expected sales and low capacity utilization has weighed on the marginal benefit of additional capital. Firms are unlikely to ramp up spending in a meaningful way if they do not expect the additional equipment to be utilized. In addition, uncertainty about future policy—both monetary and fiscal—has likely weighed on business investment despite an attractive interest rate environment. Corporate profit growth has also moderated as of late, meaning a pickup in capital investment will likely increasingly have to be funded from external sources. As we have discussed, financial market conditions and investor sentiment can impact capital market funding, although lending standards from banks have eased considerably since the recession.

CHAPTER 6

Corporate Profits

Reward, Incentive, and That Standard of Living

*For the engine that drives enterprise is not
thrift, but profit.*

—John Maynard Keynes

INTRODUCTION: PROFITS AS ESSENTIAL PARTNER

By autumn, something appeared amiss. While the equity markets soared, there was talk of rising interest rates and questions about the viability, as well as the momentum, of corporate profits going forward. There was an increased willingness to overlook traditional metrics and certainly the existence of a credit/profit cycle. But, of course, that was 1999 and investors had learned their lesson. Or had they?[1]

Our perspective is that there is a critical role of profits in economic growth in any economy and there is also a clear cycle in corporate profits within each economic recovery and over the long run. When those principles of cyclical variation are ignored, trouble usually follows. Now under way is our review of the historical patterns of profits over the business cycle.[2] In this chapter, we examine the role of profits in our society and the many links profits have throughout our economy, including providing future income for retirees or other investors. To anticipate, there is a clear pattern of profits over the business cycle, and, contrary to many critics, profits are an essential partner in the success of the overall economy.

Profits are frequently disparaged in our society. However, profits, in many forms, drive a large part of economic activity. We often find that a political candidate "profits" from another candidate's mistakes. Each year, many college football athletes will profit from hard work and a bit of luck with an opportunity to play in the NFL. A writer profits from her efforts and imagination by writing a best seller. Hollywood writers, producers, and actors profit from their efforts and imagination.

Yet when profits accrue to a "corporation" through the efforts of its employees and the insight of its leaders, those profits are often

---

[1] For more on the stock market in the late 1990s, read Roger Lowenstein, *Origins of the Crash* (New York: Penguin Press, 2004).
[2] John Silvia, Michael Brown, and Zachary Griffiths, "Corporate Profits and the Business Cycle: A Preliminary Review of the Data Part I," May 12, 2014.

disparaged. Moreover, the profits of the corporation do not accrue to the "corporation," but instead benefit its employees and investors—often in the form of pension plans for households and charitable contributions to their communities.

Profitable companies find many ways to contribute to their communities. Bankrupt firms do not. Profitable firms pay taxes. Bankrupt firms do not. The failure to appreciate the role of profits as a reward, incentive, and a fundamental building block for the standard of living for savers and investors and their many goals—including retirement—is a sad commentary in today's public rhetoric.

THE ROLE OF PROFITS IN THE ECONOMIC CYCLE: FIVE DRIVERS

When viewed from the context of the business cycle, profits are a residual, or a buffer to fluctuations in the economy. Relative to real factors such as economic growth and employment, as well as inflation and wages, profits are more variable, as illustrated in Figure 6.1.

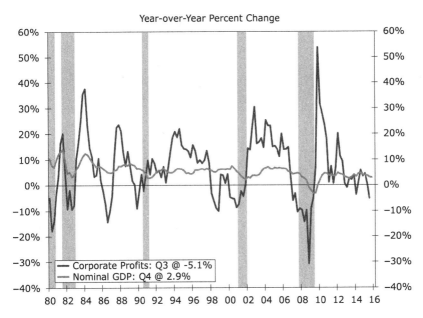

Figure 6.1 Corporate Profits before Taxes and Nominal GDP
Source: U.S. Department of Commerce

What accounts for this variability? Profits reflect the effects of cyclical and exogenous forces. Since the timing of these forces is random, profit volatility is a natural outcome. Five factors dominate the pattern of profits. First, profits tend to follow the gap between actual output and potential output in the economy. The key issue here is fixed costs and idle capacity. When the economy is strong, actual output is close to capacity and firms are using their replete complement of capital and fixed resources, so the fixed cost per unit of output is low and thereby the firm is making efficient application of its land, equipment, and labor (Figure 6.2). However, when the economy is weak, per-unit fixed costs are higher due to more under- or unutilized physical capital; this is simply the concept of operating leverage for a company on a macro scale. In addition, there will be less work for an existing workforce, and this is associated with lower productivity and/or lower employment.

Second, there is the cyclical pattern between output prices and input costs for many firms, which is shown in the comparison between output prices (as measured by the gross domestic product

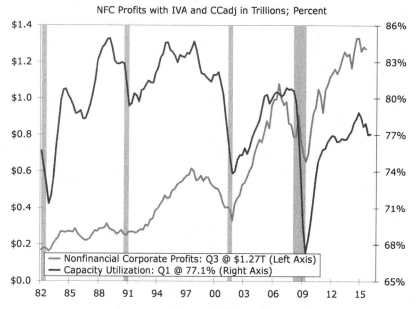

Figure 6.2 Nonfinancial Corporate Profits vs. Capacity Utilization
Sources: U.S. Department of Commerce and Federal Reserve Board

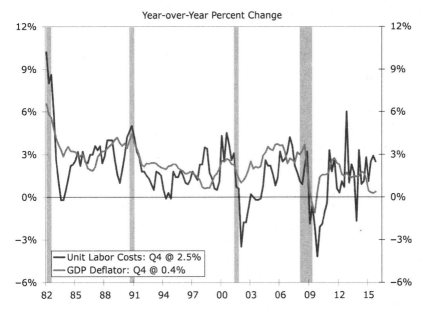

Figure 6.3 GDP Deflator vs. Unit Labor Costs
Sources: U.S. Departments of Commerce and Labor

[GDP] deflator) and input prices, proxied by unit labor costs (Figure 6.3).[3] Both series tend to move with the business cycle. A weak economy is associated with weak aggregate demand and weaker output prices relative to trend; thereby profit growth is weaker when compared to a stronger economy. In Figure 6.3, the rise in output prices tends to be faster than the increase in unit labor costs in the early years of the economic recovery (1983–1984, 1992–1995, 2002–2006, and 2009–2010) and thereby tends to boost profits in the early recovery period. However, as the economic expansion ages, unit labor costs catch up (1986–1988, 1997–1998, 2007, and 2012–2014) such that profit growth tends to slow.

Third, interest rates tend to fluctuate over the business cycle such that interest expense tends to be low in the early phase of an economic recovery as the Federal Reserve keeps rates low to boost economic growth, while during boom periods the Fed will tend to

---

[3] See Mark Bils, "The Cyclical Behavior of Marginal Cost and Price," *American Economic Review* 77, no. 5 (December 1987): 838–855.

raise rates. In addition, during boom periods, the financial markets will reinforce the upward trend on interest rates to compensate for higher inflation and rising credit demand in a search for financing that usually accompanies the latter phases of the economic cycle. Furthermore, credit spreads often widen late cycle, exacerbating this phenomenon.

To complicate the cyclical factors, two exogenous factors are also at work. Energy price shocks have had a significant impact on aggregate demand and input costs. Changes in fiscal policy can alter the after-tax profits independent of the current stage of the economy.

THE ROLE OF PROFITS: INCENTIVES AND REWARDS

Profits are the returns on investment and are a prime motivating factor in the economy. Past profits and anticipated future profits directly affect business actions such as capital expenditures and hiring workers. Profits have three interesting roles in economic activity. First, profits act as a reward for entrepreneurship and innovation, as evidenced in the fortunes that accrued to innovators such as Thomas Edison, Henry Ford, Andrew Carnegie, John D. Rockefeller, Steve Jobs, Larry Page, Sergey Brin, Jeff Bezos, Bill Gates, and Paul Allen.

Second, profits act as an incentive to invest and speculate on the possibility of above-market returns. Higher anticipated future returns prompted individuals to invest in the auto and radio industries in the first half of the twentieth century and in consumer services such as department stores and fast food after WWII. In recent years, consumers have invested in technology, specifically technology focused on processing and communicating information—such as the exercise of apps on mobile phones. Profits also served as an incentive for the establishment of the Virginia colony in American history.[4]

Finally, profits often serve as a key contributor to the rising values in savings and investment accounts that are employed by households to meet many financial goals, including home purchases, college

---

[4] Charles O, Paullin, *Atlas of the Historical Geography of the United States,* ed. John K. Wright (New York and Washington, D.C.: Carnegie Institution of Washington and American Geographical Society, 1932).

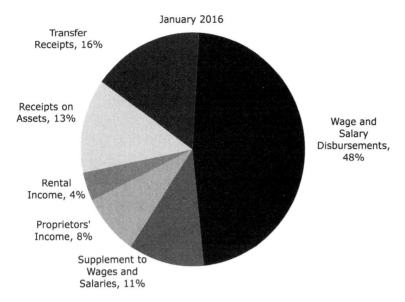

Figure 6.4 Personal Income Sources
Source: U.S. Department of Commerce

education, and retirement funding. Although overlooked or simply not understood by many, profits are the key to the growing nest eggs that finance much of economic activity. Innovations such as mutual funds, individual retirement accounts (IRAs), pensions, and, more recently, exchange-traded funds (ETFs) gain value over time as profits grow. As illustrated in Figure 6.4, profits contribute to personal income through the receipts on assets, proprietors' income (self-employed profits), and as a supplement to wages and salaries (via contributions to employee pensions and government social insurance).

Defining Terms: Economic Profits—
A Return to People, Not Corporations

Profits are a form of income and accrue to someone—not a corporation. Although referred to as "corporate" profits, the actual flow of funds accrues to investors. Investors are often individuals invested in pensions and mutual funds, direct shareholders of a specific company stock, and the company's workers, who receive additional compensation today or in the future (profit sharing). In addition, corporate profits are taxed and are therefore a source of government funding. Pretax profits less corporate tax payments equals after-tax profits, which are either retained or paid out as dividends—again a return on investment and risk taking to someone.

Providing Character to Profits over Time: Over the Cycle and Relative to Trend

How can we characterize profits to better analyze the economy and gather insights into future patterns of employment, investment, and personal income growth? Profits have a pervasive influence on economic activity so our development of a better understanding of the patterns of profit growth will aid in our decision making about the economy.

Economists often face complex time series, such as corporate profits, and yet are asked to provide understanding and forecasts of its behavior to noneconomists, especially investors. We raise three fundamental questions about U.S. corporate profit growth, which are also common and critical questions faced by economists in characterizing the behavior of any macroeconomic series. First, can we identify a long-run trend component for profit growth and thereby separate the cyclical component from the trend? That is, at any given phase of the business cycle, are we positioned for above-trend growth (boom) or below-trend growth (slowdown)? Second, how volatile is profit growth, and does this volatility obscure the message of average profit growth? Third, does profit growth over time exhibit a mean-reverting behavior? That is, do profits exhibit a tendency to return to some average growth rate?

U.S. corporate profit growth can serve as a case study to identify the properties of any time series. First, we look at the data, plotted earlier in Figure 6.1. This reveals the historical pattern of the series and helps to visually identify whether the series has a deterministic trend over time, any unusual outliers, or a volatile pattern that might obscure a trend. In the next step, we compare profit growth between subsamples. This would help to analyze profit behavior in different time periods.

Separating the Trend from the Cycle: Benchmarking Profit Growth over the Economic Cycle

How can we tell when profit growth is faster or slower than its under-lying trend? This is a key question since the answer forms the basis for our understanding of an acceleration or deceleration in profits, and thereby the contribution of profits to income growth and invest-ment spending. Periods of accelerating profit gains are associated with a pickup in personal income growth, financial asset prices, business investment, and hiring. Decelerating profit growth indicates a slower, possibly even contractionary, economic environment.

Our approach here utilizes the Hodrick-Prescott (H-P) filter tech-nique that identifies the trend in an economic time series outside of the business cycle.[5] Our results are presented in Figures 6.5 and 6.6. In Figure 6.5, nonfinancial profits as a share of nonfinancial output (NFC

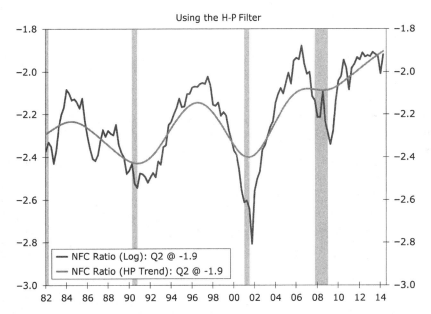

Figure 6.5 Decomposing NFC Ratio
Source: U.S. Department of Commerce

---

[5] This technique is covered in John Silvia, Azhar Iqbal, Kaylyn Swankoski, Sarah Watt, and Sam Bullard, *Economic and Business Forecasting* (Hoboken, NJ: John Wiley & Sons, 2014).

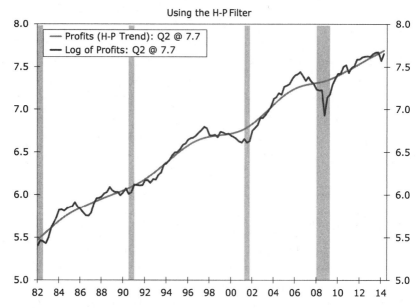

Figure 6.6 Decomposing Corporate Profits
Source: U.S. Department of Commerce

ratio) takes on a clear cyclical pattern as the share rises in the early phase of an economic recovery (1991–1996, 2003–2006) but declines when growth slows down or the economy is in a recession (1997–2001). In the expansion that began in late 2009, we again can see the pickup in the profit share. Meanwhile, the trend of the NFC ratio series has drifted upward since 2002 in contrast to a more cyclical pattern from 1982 to 2002.

In Figure 6.6, we illustrate the log form of profits and show that there is a clear uptrend in the level of profits as well as the cyclical property of profits around its long-term trend.[6] This cyclical pattern around the trend sets up investment opportunities for investors, who may look for markets that represent value relative to trend. That is, below-trend profits during 1994–1995 set up an opportunity for investment returns when profits returned to trend.

---

[6] We utilize the log form of the profits series here since percent changes in profits would yield negative values and would not be amenable to the H-P cycle/trend breakdown.

Linear, Nonlinear: Characterizing the Trend

Figures 6.5 and 6.6 provide the initial evidence of the trend and cyclical patterns of corporate profits for the complete sample period of 1982–2014:Q2. We also divide profit growth and profit margins into period subsamples so that we can apply statistical tools on the series and characterize its behavior in each sample.

First, we test whether profit growth and profit margins contain a time trend. There are two types of trends—linear and nonlinear. A linear trend indicates a constant growth rate, while a nonlinear growth rate is variable (see Silvia et al., 2014, for more detail). One of the tripwires in financial thinking is that all relationships are linear, and linearity is at play in many spreadsheets when strategists and economists operate their models.

In Table 6.1, we examine the sample period of 1982–2014 and provide the results from an identification process, which results in the finding of no trend in the growth rate of profits, while there is evidence of a nonlinear trend in the NFC ratio. This was foreseen given that we saw a clear cyclical pattern around a trend that itself moves up and down and is more characteristic of a nonlinear, rather than linear, trend in Figure 6.5.

Stability Ratio over Different Economic Cycles

In addition, Table 6.1 provides the results of calculations of the mean and standard deviation for each subsample since 1982 as well as for

Table 6.1 Results from Identification Process (1982–2014)

	Profits (Year-over-Year)				NFC Ratio			
	Mean	Standard Deviation	Stability Ratio	Trend	Mean	Standard Deviation	Stability Ratio	Trend
1982-1989	7.46	13.52	181.2	No Trend	0.10	0.01	10.9	Nonlinear Trend
1990-2014	7.47	11.96	160.1	No Trend	0.11	0.02	20.4	Linear Trend
2007-2014	5.54	16.60	299.8	N/A-Short History	0.13	0.02	13.0	N/A-Short History
1982-2014	7.47	12.31	164.8	No Trend	0.11	0.02	19.3	Nonlinear Trend

Source: U.S. Department of Commerce

the complete sample period of 1982–2014. We do this to identify whether all subsamples have the same mean and standard deviation. Moreover, we calculate a stability ratio—standard deviation as percent of the mean—for each subsample and for the complete period. The stability ratio helps us to identify how profit growth varies by sample. A higher stability ratio indicates a more volatile series.

We find that U.S. corporate profit growth is mean reverting. A high degree of volatility in profits is evident, however, with a higher standard deviation (12.31 percent) than the mean (7.47 percent). Finally, among the subsamples, the 1990–2014 period is more stable in terms of profit growth (lowest stability ratio) and the subsample since the Great Recession (2007–2014) contains the most volatile profit growth rates. The H-P filter reveals that profit growth was higher than its long-run trend growth during the 2003–2006 period, indicating an above-trend (and unsustainable?) pace of profit growth.

Results in Table 6.1 indicate that the average growth in profits since 1982 is remarkably stable at around 7.47 percent, with a standard deviation of 12.31 and a stability ratio of 164.8. However, once we isolate the 2007–2014 period, there is a clear break in the mean growth rate of profits which would be anticipated given the Great Recession in that period. In this case, the standard deviation is also larger than the mean, and as a result the stability ratio is also high. Contrary to popular commentary, profit growth has not picked up in recent years; rather, it has slowed in the most recent period.

For the NFC ratio, there is also remarkable stability in the mean value as well as in its standard deviation. For this ratio, there does not appear to be a significant break with the past for the 2007–2014 period.

Mean Reversion: Key Benchmark for Pursuing Accurate Analysis

Does the rate of growth in profits tend to revert to a mean value over time? This is a critical issue. First, effective statistical analysis requires that an economic series does not exhibit any trend (nonstationary). Second, if profit growth tends to rise continuously (or fall continuously), there are significant consequences for the overall economy. In a similar way, do profits as a percent of nonfinancial sector output also rise or fall over time?

After applying simple statistical tools, we move to the more sophisticated econometric technique of unit root testing. We apply an Augmented Dickey-Fuller (ADF) unit root test on profit growth. The ADF unit root test was introduced by Dickey and Fuller (1979, 1981) and has the null hypothesis of a unit root, with the alternative that the series is stationary.[7] If a series contains a unit root, we call it nonstationary; if not, it is stationary. A stationary series fluctuates around a constant long-run mean that implies that the series, profit growth in this case, has a finite variance that does not depend on time; hence, it is mean reverting.

In Table 6.2, the results for a test of mean reversion (stationarity) are presented. For the rate of growth of profits, the series is stationary (mean reverting) over the 1982–2014 period, and therefore can be utilized in statistical analysis. Unfortunately, the series for nonfinancial profits as a percent of nonfinancial output is nonstationary, and therefore must be transformed into a series that would be applicable in further statistical analysis.

Table 6.2 1982-2014 Profits and NFC Ratio Results

Profits (Year-over-Year)			NFC-Ratio		
Testing for Stationary					
Stationary (Mean Reverting)			Nonstationary		
Identifying a Structural Break Using the State-Space Approach					
Break Date	Type of Break	Coefficient	Break Date	Type of Break	Coefficient
Q4-09	Additive	34.5867*	Q2-08	Additive	0.015*
Q4-08	Additive	–21.606*	Q1-11	Additive	–0.014*
Q1-83	Shift	9.32*	Q4-01	Additive	–0.014*
			Q1-14	Additive	–0.012*
			Q2-05	Additive	–0.011*

*Significant at 1 percent

[7] D. Dickey and W. Fuller, "Distribution of the Estimators for Autoregressive Time Series with a Unit Root," *Journal of American Statistical Association* 74 (1979): 427–431; D. Dickey and W. Fuller, "Likelihood Ratio Tests for Autoregressive Time Series with a Unit Root," *Econometrica* 49 (1981): 1057–1072.

A common practice is to utilize the mean of a series for decision making, which is naïve, in our view, as average values may not be constant over time. We provide a more accurate framework to analyze a variable of interest for decision making, that is, whether we should utilize the mean for decision making. In addition, the proposed framework is easy to apply, as an analyst can perform statistical tests using Excel and any standard statistical software. First, plot the series to learn about overall behavior. Then the mean, standard deviation, and stability ratio can be calculated for different business cycles to examine variation in these statistics between business cycles. The H-P filter helps to determine current behavior of the series relative to the long-run trend. The ADF test is a more appropriate method to determine whether the long-run average is practical in decision making. For instance, profit growth is mean reverting in our sample period, implying that any deviations from the 7.5 percent average are temporary in nature, statistically speaking.

Structural Break: History Discontinued

Naturally, there is an interest in knowing whether profit growth or the NFC ratio contained a structural break during the 1982–2014 period. The results in Table 6.2 indicate that there were no structural breaks in either series.[8]

We employ the State-Space approach to identify structural changes in the profits series. The approach identifies the change based on the chi-square test. In the present case, the chi-square test determined the five largest breaks in the profits series using the 0.01 level of significance. The null hypothesis is that the underlying variable does not contain a change and the alternative hypothesis is that there is a change in the behavior of the variable during the specified time period. After we are aware of the existence of a break, the State-Space approach would then determine the break date and the nature of the change (e.g., level shift, additive outlier, or temporary change).

Although we are only interested in level shifts (structural breaks), the other forms of breaks in a series are additive outliers and

---

[8] Although the Q1-83 "shift" observed in profits in Table 6.2 would typically be judged a structural break, we have disregarded it since it occurred at the very beginning of the 1982–2014 time period and is not indicative of a break in the entire sample.

temporary changes. Identifying a level shift demonstrates that a variable has two or more "structures." Thus, the data set can be divided into multiple subsamples depending on the number of breaks, and each subsample will have statistically significant differences in the descriptive statistics (e.g., mean and standard deviations). An additive outlier indicates that an observation is just that, an outlier in the data set. A temporary change, however, identifies a fixed duration of change in a variable before the variable returns to the previous level. For example, the GDP growth rate will turn negative during a recession, but then returns to positive territory once the recession ends. Where a temporary change is often the result of the business cycle, a structural shift is often due to a change in policy or a more fundamental economic change.

Summing up, profits, as a return to entrepreneurship and real capital investment, play a crucial role as both incentives and rewards in our economic system. While profits are frequently disparaged by many commentators, profits take many forms and are essential for economic growth. Profitable companies find ways to hire, to contribute to their communities, and to pay taxes. When viewed in the context of the business cycle, profits act as a buffer to fluctuations in economic growth. As a buffer, profits fluctuate significantly over the cycle. Over time, however, profit growth tends to remain stable, indicating that the pace of profit growth corresponds with the pace of economic growth and the offsetting effects of changes in input costs and sales revenues. We also note that pricing margins and productivity tend to vary over the economic cycle. This provides a challenge to business leaders and financial investors in determining the profitability of an enterprise at any stage of the economic cycle.

In the first half of this chapter, we have provided an approach to separating trend from cycle so as to help decision makers in these areas. Volatility in corporate profits can be measured by calculating the mean, standard deviation, and stability ratio of data. All three measures should be calculated over several economic cycles to pin down the volatility of profits and provide perspective on equity market volatility and a sense of risk for equity investors. Profit data is also available for different sectors. Calculating measures of volatility will also provide perspective to investors and business leaders to better characterize the behavior of each sector. Later in this chapter, we will focus on modeling economic profits over the business cycle and the drivers in that model.

Profits: Behavior over the Economic Cycle

As a residual between two moving objects—revenues and costs—corporate profits can be quite volatile in the short run. Yet corporate profits are one of the clearest examples of the principles of dynamic adjustment and the role of information over the economic cycle.

On the revenue side, both output growth and output price fluctuations contribute to the change in revenues. Revenues will rise in response to an increase in economic output driven by higher aggregate demand in the economy. However, aggregate demand in the economy fluctuates over the business cycle. In the early phase of the economic recovery, a more rapid increase in demand will lead to an increase in output and thereby revenues. Prices are slower to respond to an increase in aggregate demand, making them lagging indicators of the economy. These observations reflect the dynamic and partial adjustment process in the economy. As a result, the actual day-to-day operations of output markets are not consistent with a frictionless, perfectly competitive view—particularly manufacturing. Therefore, our modeling of the profits process should reflect that imperfection.

Meanwhile, on the cost side, the short-run supply curve of any product is upward sloping owing to some factors of production (land, business structures) being fixed in the short run while other factors (labor) are variable, but subject to diminishing returns. That is, an increase in the application of the marginal factor, labor, applied to the other factors of production (land, business structures) generates a diminishing return in terms of output per unit of labor and a positive second derivative to the short-run supply curve.

$$\pi = R - C$$

The Internal Dynamics of Prices, Labor Costs, and Profit Margins

Dynamic partial adjustment under conditions of imperfect information is also a characteristic of profit margins. As we have witnessed with the current cycle, firms tend to be extremely cautious to hire workers early in the economic recovery, and, as a result, employment gains have been modest. Yet labor costs are often the largest component of the marginal costs of any adjustment by a firm while increasing production. As a result, output increases are accompanied by modest price increases but even more modest marginal cost increases. Therefore, the spread between price and marginal cost widens in the early phase of an economic recovery. As the cycle progresses, unit labor costs tend to rise faster as labor productivity slows and compensation rises. The rise in unit labor costs tends to outpace the rise in output prices and thereby profit margins shrink (Figure 6.7). Interestingly, the consumer price index (CPI) outpaces unit labor costs in the early phase of recoveries (1982–1985, 1992–1997, 2001–2004, and 2010–2011) but then lags in the latter phase of the expansion.

Increases in demand in the short run are not fully met by an increase in output as upward price movements along a supply curve come into play. In the short run, the output supply curve is upward sloping. Meanwhile, while short-run marginal costs do increase with increases in output, the price of outputs will rise relative to input prices.

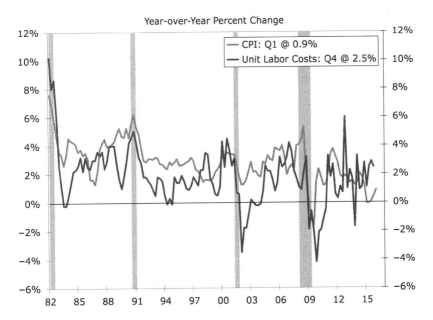

Figure 6.7 CPI vs. Unit Labor Costs
Source: U.S. Department of Labor

In contrast to the perfectly competitive economic model, input prices do not respond quickly to variations in demand—labor compensation flexibility is limited. As we have witnessed in the current recovery, employment is not perfectly flexible. We are in an economic world characterized by frictions rather than perfect competition. Firms require specific skills, preventing perfect labor mobility, so firms prefer steady employment levels since decreases in employment engender trained workers to leave or have their skills depreciate. Moreover, varying employment is costly to firms' reputations as workers prefer stable employment.

Productivity improves in the early phase of an economic recovery while compensation picks up in the latter phase of an economic expansion (Figure 6.8). Although productivity gains are certainly tied to real wages over a longer time frame, within a business cycle the slack in the labor market is a more important driver of wages. As a result, the marginal costs for labor are extremely pro-cyclical. Therefore, profit margins decline as the economic expansion continues. Imperfections in the labor and goods markets play a central role in the cyclical pattern of corporate profits.

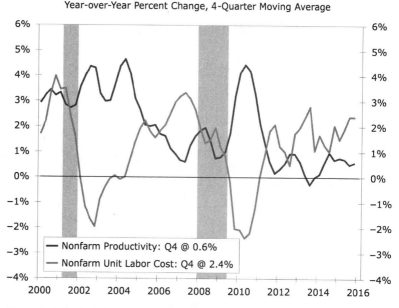

Figure 6.8 Productivity, Compensation Unit Labor Costs: Nonfarm
Source: U.S. Department of Labor

Corporate Profits and the Midpoint of the Business Cycle

One of the most basic metrics for business decision makers is corporate profitability. With such an emphasis placed on this one metric, it is important to understand how profits evolve over the business cycle in order to anticipate the future needs of the business. For example, as we reach further into the current business cycle, it is time to contemplate cost-cutting strategies in order to mitigate potential losses as profitability growth begins to slow. Conversely, if profitability growth is anticipated to increase, it would be in a firm's best interest to take advantage of expansion opportunities sooner in order to build or maintain a competitive advantage over time. In addition to the importance of understanding the economic operating environment, we find that, through analyzing corporate profits and their economic determinates, we can apply these metrics to more precisely identify the midpoints of business cycles. In addition, we explore one of the most commonly employed metrics to gauge business optimism, the debt-to-equity (D-E) ratio, which we find may not be the most applicable metric in determining fluctuations in corporate profits or business cycles.

Key Macroeconomic Drivers of Corporate Profit Growth

We began our analysis by decomposing the corporate profits cycle and describe its relationship to the business cycle to help decision makers determine where they are in the business cycle. We now turn to some key macroeconomic variables that economists focus on throughout the business cycle to help anticipate future trends in corporate profits during economic contractions and economic expansions. Finally, we analyze the aggregate corporate profits and their links to several business optimism metrics to also help determine how firms are responding to expectations about the future path of economic growth.

Productivity and Unit Labor Costs

Now that we have a sense of how corporate profits evolve throughout the business cycle, we turn to metrics that can provide some framework for determining future growth in corporate profits. There are two key metrics that economists exploit as inputs to determine the trend behind corporate profit cycles: labor productivity and unit labor costs. Although capital is also an important component of the business input-output equation, in a large, service-driven economy like the United States, labor productivity and unit labor costs explain most of the variance in corporate profits since 1947.[9]

Labor productivity is a measure of output per hour worked. Unit labor costs refer to the rise in labor compensation per hour relative to the labor's real output per hour. Monitoring the trends behind these two metrics can provide some predictive power in understanding future trends in corporate profits (Figure 6.9 and Figure 6.10). Productivity tends to decline rapidly as output slows heading into a recession (2006–2007). More telling is the trend in unit labor costs, which tends to accelerate before an economic downturn as the labor market

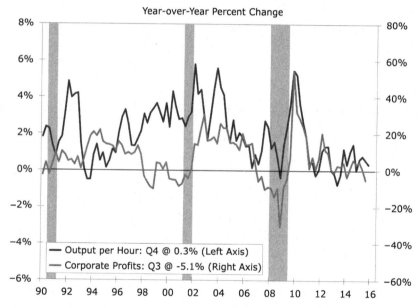

Figure 6.9 Nonfarm Productivity vs. Corporate Profits
Sources: U.S. Department of Commerce and U.S. Department of Labor

---

[9] A simple regression analysis of productivity and unit labor costs on corporate profits show that combined productivity and unit labor costs explain 89 percent of the variance in corporate profits from 1947 through 2013.

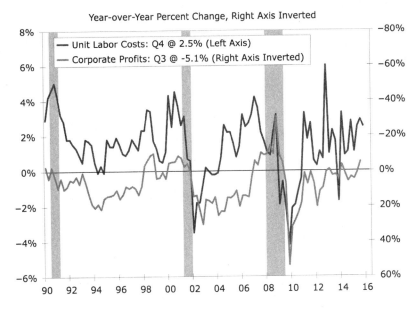

Year-over-Year Percent Change, Right Axis Inverted

— Unit Labor Costs: Q4 @ 2.5% (Left Axis)
— Corporate Profits: Q3 @ -5.1% (Right Axis Inverted)

Figure 6.10 Unit Labor Costs vs. Corporate Profits
Sources: U.S. Department of Commerce and U.S. Department of Labor

tightens and wages rise (1990, 2000, and 2006). Thus, the higher labor costs in light of falling output places downward pressure on corporate profits. Conversely, during the early recovery phase of an economic expansion, growth in output and profitability outpaces labor compensation and unit labor cost decline. The net result is higher corporate profit growth (1992–1994, 2002, and 2010).

The relationship between corporate profits and productivity and unit labor costs can be utilized to define turning points in the business cycle. As can be borne out during the past three expansions, the point at which productivity growth begins to exceed corporate profit growth has typically signaled the midpoint of a business cycle (1985–1986, 1996–1997) and a danger signal toward the end of the cycle (1989, 2000, 2007). Looking at unit labor costs compared to corporate profits, the midpoint of business cycles since the 1980s has been marked by unit labor costs growing more rapidly while at the same time corporate profits begin to contract (1985–1986, 1998, 2006–2007).

Saving vs. Spending Decisions

Profits are the major source of corporate cash flow and dividend payments, which serve as a return to savers and investors over time. Corporate cash flow roughly equals profits less dividend payments and inventory adjustment (often negative) plus deductions for capital consumption allowances (depreciation). Profits and retained earnings are the driving sources for dividend payments that, in turn, provide the returns to savers and investors via their 401(k)s, pensions, and individual retirement accounts (IRAs). As illustrated in Figure 6.11, there is a clear, positive link between profits and dividends. Two points are worth mentioning. Profits tend to lead dividends, as illustrated in the periods 1988–1991, 1994–2000, 2002–2007, and, most recently, from 2009 to 2012. This leading relationship exists on both the up- and downside of the economic cycle. This link establishes the importance of profits to the returns on financial investments and is a key to middle-income households in achieving a certain standard of living in retirement. Dividends, in turn, are a major, and increasingly sizeable, component of personal

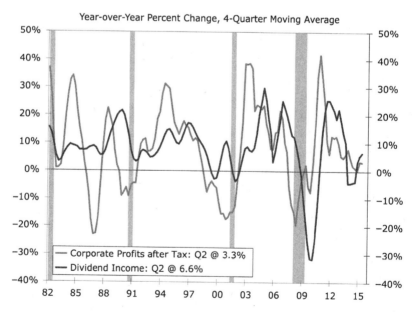

Figure 6.11 After-Tax Corporate Profits vs. Dividend Income
Source: U.S. Department of Commerce

Percent

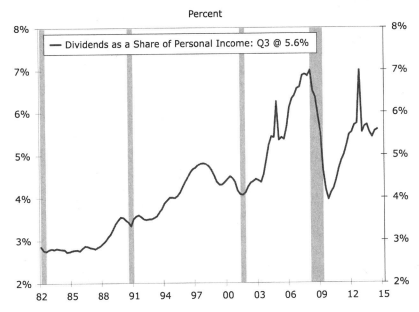

Figure 6.12 Dividends as a Share of Personal Income
Source: U.S. Department of Commerce

income, as illustrated in Figure 6.12, as pensions and other investment vehicles become more widely held among all households.

Profits and Risk

In economics, profits are a signal of financial success and credit quality. As a result, there is a sense that profits are negatively related to risk. As profits improve, there is less risk associated with the provision of credit in any given economic activity. For equity investors, an increase in profits is associated over time with a rise in dividends and, thereby, a reduction in the cost of equity finance. This tends to make profits and equity issuance pro-cyclical. For example, profits have a tendency to lead gains in equity prices, benchmarked here by the Standard & Poor's (S&P) 500 index (Figure 6.13). In turn, gains in initial public offering (IPO) issuance and merger-and-acquisition activity tend to follow the S&P 500 (Figure 6.14). The cost of equity finance reflects the anticipated dividend yield plus expected nominal growth of dividends. Gains in profit growth provide the basis for dividend growth and lower the cost of equity finance.

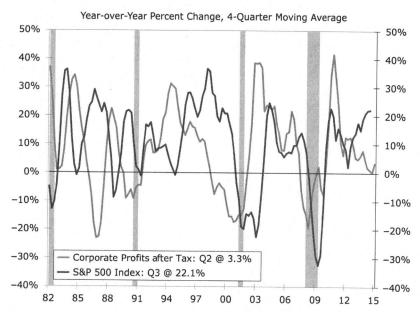

Figure 6.13 After-Tax Corporate Profits vs. S&P 500 Index
Sources: U.S. Department of Commerce and S&P

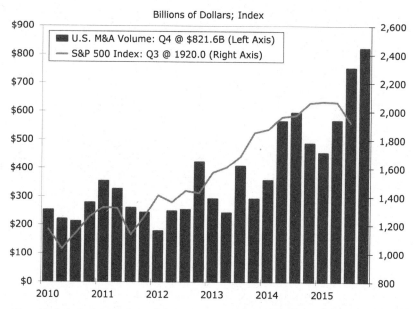

Figure 6.14 U.S. Merger-and-Acquisition Volume and S&P 500 Index
Sources: Bloomberg LP and S&P

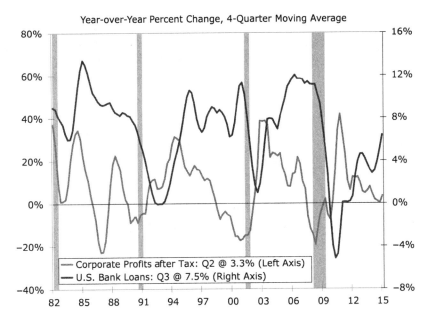

Figure 6.15 After-Tax Corp. Profits vs. Bank Loans
Sources: U.S. Department of Commerce and Federal Reserve Board

Profit growth also tends to lead credit finance activity. Profit growth is again a signaling device for greater opportunity and a reduction in the credit risk associated with bank lending. Gains in profit growth in 1993–1994, 2002–2004, and again in 2012 are associated with growth in bank loans (Figure 6.15). On the bond side, improvement in profit growth tends to be associated with declines in credit spreads (Figure 6.16). Strong profit growth in 1988, 1994–1996, 2004–2006, and 2009–2011 is associated with a decline in the Baa over the 10-year Treasury spread. As a result, profits provide a signal about the viability of repayment from the lender's point of view. Improvement in profit growth signals an improving view of credit quality and likelihood of repayment down the road by borrowers to lenders.

Profits as Return for Innovation, Entrepreneurship: Signals of Success, Opportunity

Profit growth alters the nonfinancial corporate ratio of capital spending minus internally generated funds (Figure 6.17). The rise in profits

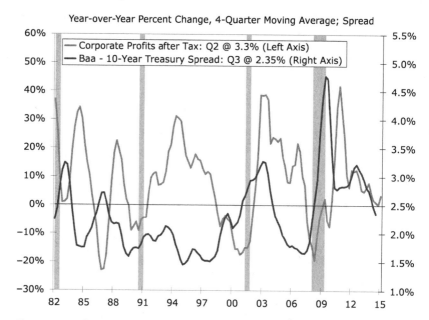

Figure 6.16 After-Tax Corporate Profits vs. Baa Corporate Bond Spread
Sources: U.S. Department of Commerce and Federal Reserve Board

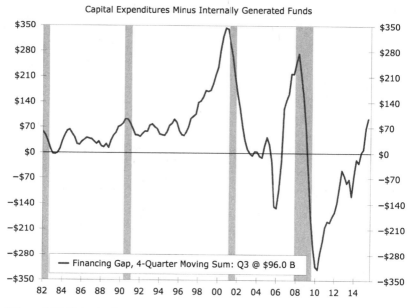

Figure 6.17 Financing Gap
Source: Federal Reserve Board

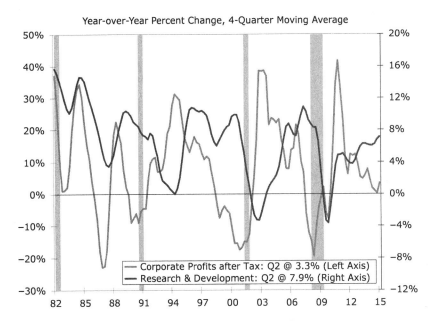

Figure 6.18 After-Tax Corporate Profits vs. Research & Development
Source: U.S. Department of Commerce

leads to gains in internally generated funds that, in turn, can provide greater financial support for investment and encouragement to entrepreneurial spirits—as proxied by improving profit expectations and equity valuations (Figure 6.18).

Finally, profit growth tends to be associated with gains in business investment in plants and equipment (Figure 6.19). Profit growth that is directed to capital spending will tend to maintain the capital-output ratio and, along with that, the hiring of workers. Moreover, the investment undertaken would be anticipated to increase corporate share values and thereby feed back into earnings and dividends and the improvement of household incomes over time.

One Final Note: Cyclical Profits and Stationary Benchmarks

Many investment decisions reflect a judgment on profits as a return on equity, and yet we see that this measure of investment performance has a distinct cyclical character. Given this cyclical character, establishing an absolute level of value attached to any return on equity is likely to be

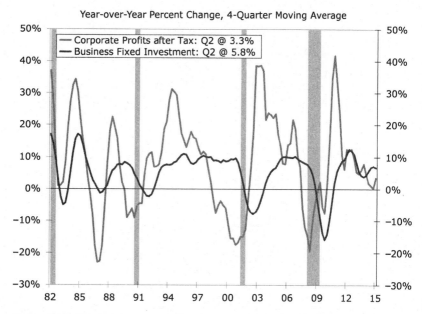

Figure 6.19 After-Tax Corporate Profits vs. Business Fixed Investment
Source: U.S. Department of Commerce

a misleading guide to investing, since both profit growth and profits as a percentage of GDP vary significantly over the economic cycle. Establishing a single value for the return on equity would run counter to the cyclical character of the series. Therefore, an investor would view values above average as too expensive when, in fact, those values would reflect an improving economy. In turn, a slower pace of profit growth, especially when equity valuations look attractive, may reflect a weakening economy and might represent a challenge to current market valuations.

Moreover, the cyclical behavior of profit growth will also vary between economic sectors over the business cycle. Two sectors of the economy could exhibit different returns on equity patterns over the same economic cycle. At the sector level, some economic sectors, such as manufacturing, may be more sensitive to the economic cycle than other sectors, such as health care. This reinforces the view that any absolute benchmark for value in investing might be misleading when dealing with a cyclical series such as the return on equity, that itself varies by the sector under study. There is not a uniform standard for all sectors or for a uniform standard for the stage of the economic cycle.

Modeling the Profit Process

We model the pattern of profit growth as a function of the behavior of revenues and costs over the business cycle. On the revenue side, we examine the patterns of economic growth and prices. On the cost side, we examine unit labor costs, the unemployment rate, and interest rates as a proxy for capital (nonlabor) costs.

Some Fundamental Rules of Building a Forecasting Model

We present a model-based forecasting approach to generate reliable forecasts of an economic/financial variable, such as corporate profits.[10] Here are some fundamental rules. First, a preferred model should perform better (produces a smaller forecast error, on average) than a benchmark or competing models in a simulated out-of-sample forecasting experiment. Second, it is necessary to establish a benchmark forecasting approach for comparison, so we adopt an autoregressive of order one, AR(1), method as a standard benchmark. All competing models should perform better than the AR(1) model's forecasts.

Third, different forecasting approaches should be employed in a modeling process. That is, one possible approach would be a pure statistical method, which does not include any additional variables. One such technique is called an Autoregressive Integrated Moving Averages (ARIMA) model. In the forecasting process, it is always preferable to include as much information (in terms of predictors) as possible, along with a better econometric method to lead to a better forecast. In the Bayesian Vector Autoregressions (BVAR) modeling procedure, we can incorporate more information than a traditional econometric framework. The AR, ARIMA, and BVAR techniques are explained in great detail in Silvia et al. (2014).

The final rule to building a reliable forecasting model is that the model selection criterion should correspond with the forecast objective. For instance, our objective is to forecast the near-term (up to one year ahead) outlook of corporate profits. That implies we are interested in a four-quarter-ahead out-of-sample forecast of corporate profits growth. Therefore, we set a four-quarter-ahead simulated

---

[10] For a comprehensive forecasting modeling, see Chapter 9 of Silvia et al. (2014).

out-of-sample root mean square error (RMSE) as the forecast evaluation criterion for the competing models. The model that produces the smallest four-quarter-out RMSE (i.e., smallest average forecast error) would be the preferred model.

A Recursive Method of Model Selection

To calculate the out-of-sample RMSE, we assume that data is available between $t = 1$ and $t = T$ for modeling purposes, where T represents the most recent data point—in this case, 2014:Q2. In addition, we are interested in h-step-ahead forecasts, where $h = 1, 2, 3, 4$, up to four quarters ahead. Assume an integer variable q that varies from 1 to q using one quarter as a unit. For each q, we choose data between $t = 1$ and $t = T - q$ to build a model and apply it to generate h-step-ahead forecasts. We then calculate the out-of-sample RMSE for each step (from one quarter ahead to four quarters ahead). The magnitude of the RMSE statistic is utilized to compare the out-of-sample performance of each model, and the model with the smallest RMSE is the best model among its competitors.

We estimate all three models using data from the sample period 1982:Q1—2002:Q4 and generate four-quarter-out forecasts. Then, we move one quarter ahead, using data from 1982:Q1 to 2003:Q1, and again produce forecasts for the next four quarters. We employ this recursive method until we reach the final data point that is 1982:Q1–2013:Q2. We then calculate the out-of-sample RMSE for each quarter. In total, we have 42 forecast errors for each quarter ahead forecast. Table 6.3 shows the out-of-sample RMSE for each quarter ahead, up to four quarters, as well as the average RMSE for corporate profit growth rates.

The one-quarter-ahead RMSE for the BVAR model is 4.59 and four-quarter RMSE is 7.44. On average, as well as for each quarter,

Table 6.3 Simulated Out-of-Sample RMSE for Corporate Profits

Model	Forecast Horizon, Quarters Ahead				
	1	2	3	4	Average
AR	6.21	10.66	12.77	12.85	10.62
ARIMA	5.78	8.96	11.07	12.41	9.55
BVAR	4.59	5.06	5.89	7.44	5.74

the BVAR model produces the smallest RMSE compared to the benchmark AR(1) model and the competing ARIMA model. Therefore, the BVAR model is our preferred model to generate forecasts for corporate profits.

As suspected, the RMSE values increase with the forecast horizon for all three models, which indicates forecast uncertainty increases with the forecast horizon. A model selection criterion should be consistent with the forecast objective, since values of the four-quarter-out RMSE are much larger than those of one-quarter-out RMSE. In fact, for the AR and ARIMA models, four-quarter RMSE values are more than twice the values of one-quarter-ahead RMSE. That corresponds with the notion that further-out forecasting contains higher uncertainty. In addition, the out-of-sample RMSE is a practical statistic to build a forecast band (upper and lower limit). If we build a forecast band based on the one-quarter-out RMSE value, then that band will be narrower (and, ideally, more precise) than the one based on the four-quarter-ahead RMSE.

Table 6.4 shows the out-of-sample RMSE for the ratio of nonfinancial corporate profits to output of nonfinancial corporate business (NFC ratio). The BVAR model produces the smallest RMSE for each quarter as well as the average RMSE.

The forecasting performance of the BVAR approach is the best among all three models as it produces the smallest out-of-sample RMSE, on average, or the smallest average forecast error. Therefore, we employ the BVAR approach to forecast corporate profits growth rates (Figure 6.20) and the NFC ratio (Figure 6.21). In addition, in Figures 6.20 and 6.21, we plot the out-of-sample forecast with actual data and in-sample fitted values from all three approaches for corporate profits and NFC ratio.

Table 6.4 Simulated Out-of-Sample RMSE for NFC Ratio

Model	Forecast Horizon, Quarters Ahead				
	1	2	3	4	Average
AR	0.008	0.014	0.016	0.021	0.014
ARIMA	0.007	0.012	0.015	0.020	0.013
BVAR	0.005	0.009	0.011	0.012	0.009

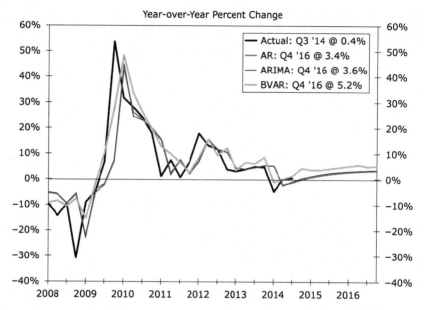

Figure 6.20 Corporate Profits Growth Forecasts
Source: U.S. Department of Commerce

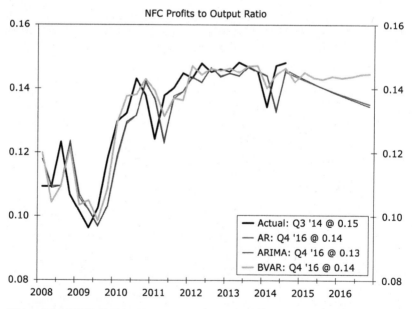

Figure 6.21 NFC Ratio Forecasts
Source: U.S. Department of Commerce

One observation from the out-of-sample forecast from these three models is that the AR and ARIMA models produce similar forecasts and connote a continuously upward trend in corporate profits. That is one potential issue with both AR and ARIMA approaches, especially during multiperiod-out forecasting. Typically, and in the present case, both AR and ARIMA models linearly extend the series for the out-of-sample period. However, many economic and financial series experience nonlinear growth rates. For instance, profit growth rates are volatile over time, that is, profit growth was 4.7 percent for 2013:Q4 and –4.8 percent for 2014:Q1. The BVAR model, however, shows a bounceback for 2014:Q4 and then slower growth for the next couple of quarters, which is more realistic than the linear upward trend indicated by the AR and ARIMA models. The same observation can be observed in the case of the NFC ratio as the AR/ARIMA models both produce a linear downward trend.

CONCLUDING REMARKS: MODELING PROFITS

Profits exhibit a complex set of behaviors over the business cycle since there are a number of influences on both the cost and revenue side of the equation. The common approach to modeling profits fails to deal with this variable, cyclical character. When we apply the BVAR technique on profit growth and profits as a share of nonfinancial corporate output, our results are superior to standard linear models and allow us an added advantage, which can prove serviceable to investors and decision makers.

CHAPTER 7

Labor Market Evolution

Implications for Private-Sector and Public-Policy Decision Makers

One of the distinguishing characteristics of monetary policy in the United States as opposed to other central banks is the Federal Reserve's dual mandate of maximum employment and price stability. While many other major central banks are commissioned solely with the goal of price stability, that is, a healthy rate of inflation, the Federal Reserve seeks to control inflation along with what can often be a conflicting goal of seeking full employment. Why, then, focus on full employment?

Employment as a policy priority first came to light during the Great Depression when widespread unemployment exacerbated the decline in demand, production, and the general standard of living. Public works programs under the New Deal offered some relief, but periods of uncomfortably high unemployment continued to occur in subsequent business cycles. The Humphrey-Hawkins Full Employment Act in 1978 formalized employment as a federal government policy priority and required the Federal Reserve to pursue full employment alongside price stability when formulating monetary policy.

The idea of full, or maximum, employment is an important gauge of output and price pressures. A labor market that is far from full employment, characterized by high unemployment, suggests an underutilization of resources in the economy. Not only does high unemployment lead to workers struggling to earn a living, but also indicates the economy is growing below its potential, which means a slower improvement in the standard of living. On the flip side, extremely low unemployment would indicate the demand for labor outstrips the supply of labor, leading to wage pressures that could in turn ignite inflation beyond desired levels. Full employment is therefore judged as the delicate balance between the demand for labor and the supply of labor, with neither underutilized resources nor upward pressure on wages. Estimates vary as to what constitutes full employment, but economists often center their assessments on the unemployment rate as a benchmark, offering a narrow, but still uncertain, range of values around the jobless rate.

Basic models of the economy assume full employment as a benchmark, but the reality is that most of the time the economy is far from full employment (Figure 7.1). In other words, the labor market is typically in disequilibrium. The unemployment rate is above what would

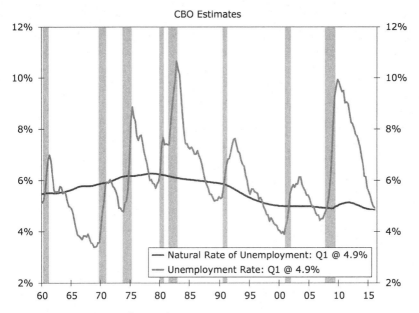

Figure 7.1 Natural Rate of Unemployment
Sources: Congressional Budget Office and U.S. Department of Labor

be considered full employment in the recession, recovery, and, quite often, early expansion phases of the business cycle. Further on in the expansion and late phase of a business cycle, the unemployment rate can fall below what would be considered full employment as the economy heats up and the demand for labor intensifies, causing employers to bid up wages more quickly.

PART I: LABOR MARKET IMPERFECTIONS

The result of the frequent overshooting and undershooting of full employment is due to the fact that, in the real economy, there are many imperfections of the labor market. Workers are far from uniform, with differing skills, education, experience, and willingness to work. Employers are equally heterogeneous in their needs for labor. These differences lead to frictions in the labor market that prevent the market from maintaining equilibrium over time. Moreover, determining full employment can be obfuscated by structural trends in the labor market. Long-term trends may complicate assessments of the current cyclical state of the labor market, as these structural trends may also impact determinants of labor market tightness or slack, such as the labor force participation rate.

In this chapter, we discuss the frictions that can keep the labor market from balancing at full employment. These frictions include search frictions, heterogeneity among workers, and the inability of workers to change their skills in the short run. We then discuss how structural trends can change what constitutes full employment as well as complicate the determination of this state that plays such an important role in U.S. monetary policy.

Labor Market Frictions and the Persistence of Disequilibrium

When assessing the state of the labor market, policy makers, analysts, and the media typically focus on the unemployment rate and the number of jobs being created or eliminated over a given period of time. Yet job growth and the unemployment rate fluctuate widely over time. As illustrated in Table 7.1, job growth in the previous cycle averaged just 0.2 percent per year, compared to 1.8 percent in the business cycle before that and more than 2 percent in the 1982–1991 business cycle. The unemployment rate has also varied widely throughout different business cycles, indicating that the labor market has not behaved in a consistent manner over the past three cycles.

The boom-and-bust dynamic of the business cycle leads to jobs being cut as economic activity contracts. Businesses are quick to cut employment, leading to payrolls falling and an excess supply of labor

Table 7.1 Unemployment Rate

Variable	1982:11-1991:3			1991:3-2001:11			2001:11-2009:6			2009:6-2015:4*		
	Mean	S.D.	Stability Ratio	Mean	S.D.	Stability Ratio	Mean	S.D.	Stability Ratio	Mean	S.D.	Stability Ratio
UR	6.81	1.47	21.59	5.50	1.17	21.17	5.58	1.05	18.84	8.05	1.40	17.41
(T-statistic)	(2.97)			(-6.16)			(-5.37)			(9.44)		
Employment (YoY)	2.35	1.62	69.03	1.78	1.29	72.21	0.20	1.64	806.50	0.67	2.05	308.56
(T-statistic)	(5.19)			(2-73)			(-6.08)			(-2.77)		

*Not a complete business cycle

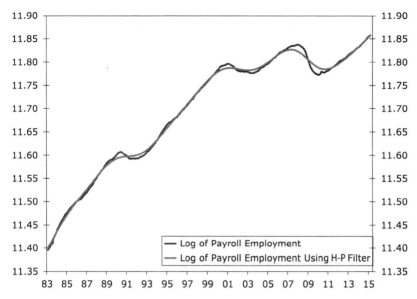

Figure 7.2 Nonfarm Payrolls Trend
Source: U.S. Department of Labor

that drives the unemployment rate above equilibrium levels. Even accounting for trends in the business cycle using a Hodrick-Prescott (H-P) filter, payroll levels and the unemployment rate are often out of sync with their underlying trend and what could be considered full employment (Figures 7.2 and 7.3).[1]

Through the cyclical variation in joblessness, the unemployment rate tends to revert back to its mean over time. Since 1982, the unemployment rate has averaged 6.4 percent, and an Augmented Dickey-Fuller (ADF) test confirms econometrically a single mean of the series.[2] It is worth noting that the mean is also above what is typically considered full employment by Federal Reserve officials, which is currently just below 5.0 percent.

---

[1] R. Hodrick and E. P. Prescott, "Post-War Business Cycles: An Empirical Investigation." *Journal of Money Credit and Banking* 29 (1997) Issue 1, pages 1-16.

[2] D. Dickey and W. Fuller, "Distribution of the Estimators for Autoregressive Time Series with a Unit Root," *Journal of the American Statistical Association* 74 (1979): 427–431; D. Dickey and W. Fuller, "Likelihood Ratio Tests for Autoregressive Time Series with a Unit Root," *Econometrica* 49 (1981): 1057–1072; and J. Silvia, I. Iqbal, and K. Swankoski, "How Stationary Is My Economic North Star? The Study of Drift in Benchmarks," *Wells Fargo Economics*, March 20, 2013.

Figure 7.3 Unemployment Rate Trend
Source: U.S. Department of Labor

In contrast, the U-6 rate of unemployment, the broadest measure, which includes workers employed part time but who would like full-time work and those marginally attached to the labor force, is not mean reverting. This is consistent with the view that in some ways, the labor market of the twenty-first century is behaving differently than in prior periods. Although the data only begin in 1994, an ADF test, along with the plot shown in Figure 7.4, suggests that the mean of this series has actually moved up over time. Therefore, policy makers and analysts should be cautioned against using past levels of U-6 unemployment as a benchmark for what may be considered "normal" levels.

Unemployment rates and topline payroll figures also mask the churn going on underneath the surface of the labor market. While the net number of jobs being created in an expansion or cut during a downturn is in the low hundreds of thousands each month, millions of workers actually leave a job and/or start a new one each month. For example, when 201,000 jobs were created in January 2015, five million jobs had a new employee in the position, either the product of a

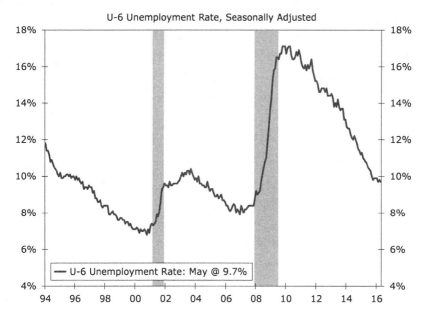

U-6 Unemployment Rate, Seasonally Adjusted

— U-6 Unemployment Rate: May @ 9.7%

Figure 7.4 Broad Unemployment
Source: U.S. Department of Labor

new employee filling an existing position or an employee being hired for a new position in a growing business (Figure 7.5).[3]

Similarly, millions of workers separate from their job in a given month. This can be due to voluntary separations, that is, workers quitting their position to go to another job, retire, or temporarily leave the workforce (Figure 7.6). A high rate of workers quitting their jobs is viewed as a positive trend for the economy. Quitting is a sign of improved job prospects, either realized if a job is already lined up or confidence that one won't be hard to find. Therefore, quits exhibit a cyclical pattern over the business cycle. Quits can also be positive for underlying productivity, as workers are likely to switch to jobs that better suit their skills and interests.

Of course, turnover can also be due to involuntary separations, such as a worker being fired or laid off as demand for a company's product falls during a downturn or the company's production becomes out of date in the current economy. Total hiring will outstrip

---

[3] U.S. Bureau of Labor Statistics Job Openings and Labor Turnover Survey, published monthly.

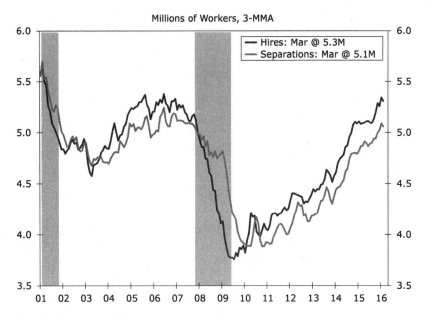

Figure 7.5 Hirings and Separations
Source: U.S. Department of Labor

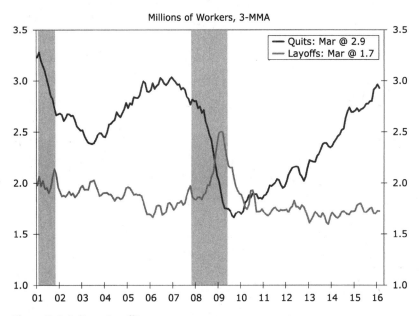

Figure 7.6 Quits vs. Layoffs
Source: U.S. Department of Labor

separations during the expansion phase of the business cycle, leading to an increase in the total number of jobs in the economy (Figure 7.5). In downturns, separations rise ahead of hiring and indicate an overall decline in the number of jobs in the economy.

Many workers quitting a job may do so because they found a better job elsewhere and start the new position within a matter of days or only a few short weeks. For others voluntarily leaving their job, they may find themselves unemployed for a spell as they hold out for a well-fitting job or look for a job in a new location following a job relocation of their partner. Similarly, finding a new job for a worker laid off that suits their skills may take some time as their industry may be in decline or demand conditions in general may be weak.

Search Costs: The Value of Imperfect Information

Finding a new job can take time for a number of reasons. First, information about what jobs are available, and at what wage, are neither instantly available nor widely distributed. It takes workers time to search out this information, whether through job postings online or through talking to people in their networks.[4] Even when workers learn of new job opportunities, the available jobs may require skills that the unemployed worker does not have, leading the worker to continue looking for jobs that match his skills. Furthermore, location may be an issue. The United States is a fairly homogenous society, making it easy in a cultural sense to move from one location to another if a job that matches the right skills and offers an acceptable wage is available. However, in practice, moving is costly, whether in terms of the financial costs of selling a home, breaking a lease, and the physical transportation of household items, or through the less measurable emotional costs of cutting community ties.

Unemployment during the time needed for workers to find a new job that suits their skills, in a location they are already in or willing to move to and at an acceptable wage, is known as frictional unemployment. Frictional unemployment is not necessarily a bad thing. It indicates that workers are taking some time to find a job that best matches

---

[4] Dale T. Mortensen, "Job Search, the Duration of Unemployment, and the Phillips Curve," *American Economic Review* 60, no. 5 (December 1970): 847–862.

their skills, rather than the first job available, which should be good for the workers' productivity and the economy's productivity more broadly. Although a benign type of unemployment, estimating this component of the unemployment rate is important for policy makers when assessing the amount of slack in the labor market or whether the labor market is tightening to the point where it would begin to put upward pressure on wages.

Making policy makers' jobs difficult in this arena is that the rate of frictional unemployment can change over time. Financial costs to moving were particularly steep in the wake of the Great Recession, when home prices collapsed and pushed many households into negative home equity positions. This likely raised the rate of frictional unemployment for at least a time. Evolving trends in the economy can also change the rate of frictional unemployment, as different sectors take on more or less importance. These sector shifts can raise frictional unemployment as the jobs demanding certain skills may be shrinking, making it more difficult for unemployed workers to find a job matching their skills. This may also be considered a form of structural unemployment, where the unemployed workers do not have the right skills for the jobs that are available.

Structural unemployment should dissipate over time as unemployed workers update their skills and retrain. However, in reality, not all workers will retrain. The cost-benefit trade-off of going back to school or undergoing a retraining program looks very different for older workers versus younger workers, the latter of which have longer time horizons to recoup their investment of updating their skills. The trade-off also would vary by location, depending on whether the new-skilled jobs are even available in a particular area. Therefore, structural unemployment may lead some workers to drop out of the labor force altogether.

We see evidence of frictional unemployment by looking at the unemployment rate and length of unemployment over time. Even during strong periods of economic growth and labor demand, the unemployment rate does not fall to zero. In fact, the lowest it has ever been was 2.5 percent in 1953, during a very different economy and labor market. Similarly, the median duration of unemployment fluctuates over the business cycle, but in recent decades has only fallen as low as five weeks, indicating the time it typically takes for an unemployed worker to find new suitable employment (Figure 7.7). The median duration of unemployment has drifted upward over time, or, in other words, is nonstationary. This comes as the series experienced two structural breaks following the financial crisis and Great Recession. The first was a shift upward in mid-2009, while the other was a shift lower in mid-2012, when the median duration began to fall more rapidly (both significant at the 1 percent level). The upward shift, however, was to a greater magnitude, implying the trend in the duration of unemployment has gravitated up since earlier business cycles.

The more severe structural type of frictional unemployment can be illustrated by the rate of long-term unemployment, or unemployment lasting longer than six months (Figure 7.8). The long-term rate of unemployment spiked to 4.0 percent in mid-2011, nearly four times its average since 1960 of 1.1 percent. Yet even the short-term unemployment rate, which better accounts for workers whose skills are up to date, never falls below 3 percent. The higher rate of long-term unemployment has persisted to where the series experienced multiple

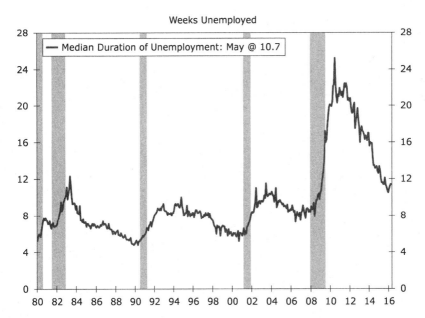

Figure 7.7 Median Duration of Unemployment
Source: U.S. Department of Labor

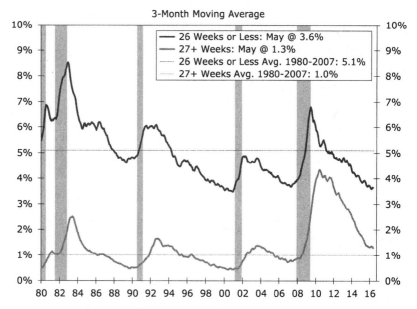

Figure 7.8 Unemployment Rate by Duration
Source: U.S. Department of Labor

structural breaks upward in 2009.[5] While long-term unemployment is nonstationary and has multiple means, the short-term unemployment rate is stationary.

The persistence of unemployment can also be seen by looking at the unemployment rate against the rate of job openings. Even in recessions, labor market turnover or secular growth in certain industries leads to companies needing to hire. However, when the economy weakens, fewer companies are looking to expand, and therefore the job openings rate tends to fall as the unemployment rate rises. This negative relationship is illustrated by the downward slope of the Beveridge curve, which plots the unemployment rate against the rate of job vacancies (Figure 7.9).[6] Frictional unemployment is evident in that no matter what the rate of unemployment, there are always some job openings that remain unfilled.

---

[5] A State-Space approach to determine whether the long-term unemployment rate experienced a structural break found a level shift in the series in April and September of 2009.

[6] Christopher R. Dow and Leslie A. Dicks-Mireaux, "The Excess Demand for Labour: A Study of Conditions in Great Britain, 1946–1956," *Oxford Economic Papers* 10, no. 1 (1958): 1–33.

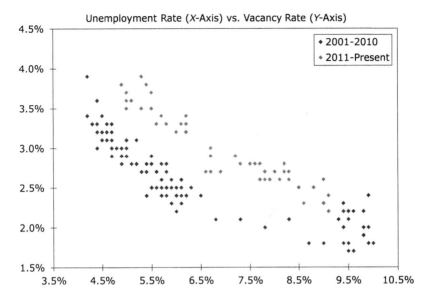

Figure 7.9 The Beveridge Curve
Source: U.S. Department of Labor

Insights into structural unemployment are also offered by the Beveridge curve. A higher rate of unemployment for a given level of job openings would suggest that workers do not have the right skills or are not in the right location for jobs that are currently available. A higher rate of structural unemployment would therefore be indicated by an outward shift in the Beveridge curve. It is typical for the Beveridge curve to move outward in the recovery phase of the labor market, when job openings begin to rise but employers take their time filling them.[7] However, a persistent shift outward, lasting through the expansionary phase of the labor market, would indicate that the needs of employers are changing more quickly than the skills of workers. This appears to be the case in the most recent labor market expansion. Even as the unemployment rate has fallen rapidly, the rate of job openings remains relatively high when compared to the labor market expansion of the 2000s, indicating less efficiency in matching available job opportunities to workers.

[7] Olivier Jean Blanchard and Peter Diamond, "The Beveridge Curve," *Brookings Papers on Economic Activity* 1 (1989).

PART II: HETEROGENEITY IN THE LABOR MARKET

Determining full employment and then steering macroeconomic policy can be made difficult by the fact that workers are far from homogenous, as often assumed by simplified theoretical models and public-policy projections. Instead, workers vary vastly in terms of their experience, skills, and desire or availability to work outside of the home. These differences are illustrated by the wide and often persistent ranges of labor market outcomes across demographic and educational characteristics. As the variations in the data show, workers are not always perfect substitutes for each other. As the composition of the working-age population and labor force changes, these differences can impact the aggregated measures of the labor market that policy makers rely on so heavily. Therefore, understanding these differences and how the labor force changes over time is important when determining the state of the labor market.

Experience Matters: The Different Labor Market Outcomes and Work Patterns across the Age Spectrum

Workers' experience level is one of three major factors that drive labor market outcomes. Measuring workers' effective experience across the economy would be difficult, to say the least, but age offers a good initial proxy, where older workers are presumed to be more experienced. Unemployment varies widely among different age groups (Figure 7.10). While the unemployment rate for 25- to 34-year-olds closely tracks that of the overall unemployment rate, there are significant differences among other age groups (Table 7.2).

Not surprisingly, more experienced workers—in other words, older workers—have stronger chances of employment. Older workers' years of experience in a specific field or company and longer track record of their ability to perform are clearly valued when looking at the unemployment rates for different age groups. Among the working-age population not of retirement age (ages 16 to 65), the unemployment rate tends to be lowest for workers aged 55 to 64, and only slightly higher for workers aged 45 to 54.

In contrast, unemployment among teenagers is significantly higher than the broad population. Over the past 50 years, the overall

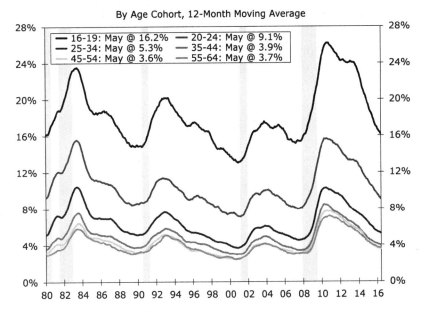

Figure 7.10 Unemployment Rate
Source: U.S. Department of Labor

unemployment rate has averaged 6.1 percent, while the rate for 16- to 19-year-olds has averaged 17.6. Similarly, although not as pronounced, this pattern holds true when looking at the unemployment rate for 20- to 24-year-olds, which has averaged 10 percent over the past five decades. The unemployment rates for both 16- to 19- and 20- to 24-year-olds have experienced a number of positive structural breaks, which suggests the unemployment rate has shifted upward over time. While unemployment is much less prevalent among 25- to 34-year-olds compared to teenagers and workers in their early 20s,

Table 7.2 Unemployment Rate by Age Group

1980-2015	16–19	20–24	25–34	35–44	45–54	55+	55–64	Unemployment Rate
Mean	18.3*	10.5*	6.4	4.9*	4.3*	4.0*	4.1*	6.4
St. Dev.	3.2	2.3	1.7	1.3	1.3	1.1	1.2	1.6
t Stat	67.6	30.2	(0.1)	(15.3)	(21.1)	(25.1)	(24.1)	

* Significant difference from total population at 1 percent level
Source: U.S. Department of Labor

it is notably higher than other prime-age workers (defined as workers aged 25 to 54) as these workers may possess some general work experience but less experience relevant to their career field.[8]

For young workers, the higher rate of unemployment comes as they tend to have higher rates of job separation. This may be due to the fact that when firms are under pressure, they first lay off workers with the least experience and tenure with the firm. However, it is also likely influenced by the voluntary separations of young workers as they seek out jobs in different industries or only work during certain times of the year.

Higher separation rates for younger workers are evident in the average length of employee tenure. While in 2014 the average length a worker had been with their current employer was 4.6 years, workers in their early 20s had been at the same employer for only 1.3 years and workers aged 25 to 34 an average of only 3.0 years.[9] In contrast, workers aged 55 to 64 had been at their current employer for an average of 10.6 years. The longer tenure and lower separation rates come as older workers have gained more specialized skills and knowledge in a particular field and are less likely to switch occupations or industries. Longer tenure is also associated with the institutional knowledge a worker who has been with the firm for a long time possesses, which can make the worker more productive and valuable to the firm.

In addition to facing higher unemployment, younger workers are also more likely to work part time. The high rate of part-time employment among 16- to 24-year-olds is to be expected, given the greater likelihood that these workers are also in school. However, underemployment is also highest among young career-age workers (Figure 7.11). The share of 25- to 34-year-olds who are working part time but would like to be working full time is about 10 percentage points higher than for workers older than age 35, as their more limited experience makes employers more reluctant to hire them full time.

---

[8] For a review of the issues surrounding dual labor markets, see William T. Dickens and Kevin Lang, "A Test of Dual Labor Market Theory," *American Economic Review* 75, no. 4 (September 1985): 792–805.

[9] Bureau of Labor Statistics, "Employee Tenure in 2014," September 18, 2014.

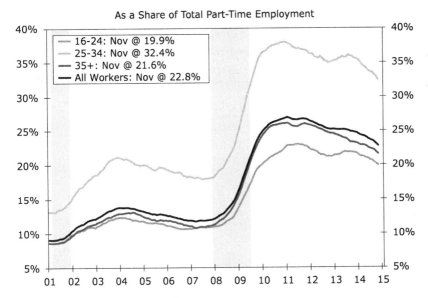

Figure 7.11 Part-Time for Economic Reasons
Source: U.S. Department of Labor

In addition to employment outcomes, age also plays an important role in the decision to participate in the labor market. The Bureau of Labor Statistics defines the working-age population as the population aged 16 and older, but participation rates vary widely across the age spectrum (Figure 7.12). The vast majority of teenagers are in some type of schooling, and therefore only around 30 percent participate in the labor market each year, most of whom engage only in the summer months. With the better income prospects afforded by a college degree, the participation rate among 20- to 24-year-olds is also lower than the general population since many members of this cohort are also in school. Between ages 25 and 54, however, participation rises dramatically to where about 80 percent of this group is involved in the labor market.

By age 55, however, the participation rate begins to fall noticeably. Even before workers hit the standard retirement age of 65, some have the income and wealth needed to retire. Others may not have the means, but either find themselves too old to retrain if unemployed or with disabilities that make it difficult to work. As workers hit 65, the traditional standard age of retirement, and are able to collect their full Social Security benefits, labor force participation falls even more, to around just 30 percent.

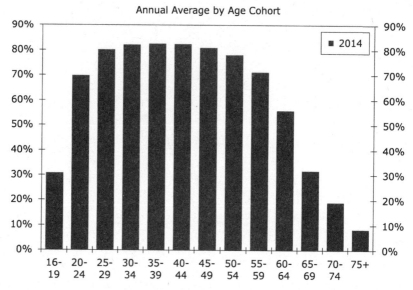

Figure 7.12 U.S. Labor Force Participation Rate
Source: U.S. Department of Labor

Education Pays: Labor Market Outcomes across the Skill Spectrum

Education is the second clear link between labor market outcomes and worker characteristics. Education levels provide a good approximation of workers' skill levels. Not surprisingly, more skilled workers have an easier time of finding employment and obtaining higher wages for their work. More broadly, a more skilled workforce is one of the factors that improves productivity in the economy. Stronger productivity growth is a key ingredient in boosting real economic growth and in turn raising the living standards of a society. This helps to explain policy makers' focus on improving the quality and access to education among the population.

Perhaps the most obvious way in which education impacts workers' experience in the labor market is through earnings. Workers with more skills can command higher compensation as the supply of labor in which to fulfill those jobs is smaller. Presumably, all college graduates could work a cash register, but few retail clerks have the training needed to work as an engineer. This leads incomes to rise alongside education. In 2013, a household headed by someone with a college degree earned $80,100, 72 percent more than the median household income and 120 percent more than the median household headed by someone with only a high school diploma. Furthermore, the premium of a college degree has held steady in recent years despite rising costs of attendance as income for non–college graduates has followed a similar trend over the past decade.[10]

Not only do workers with more education receive higher wages, but they have an easier time finding employment. As workers' education levels go up, unemployment rates go down (Figure 7.13). The differences in unemployment rates by education are statistically significant compared to the overall unemployment rate across all education levels (Table 7.3). Over the past two decades, the unemployment rate for college graduates has run three percentage points lower than the unemployment rate for workers with only a high school diploma, on average. The differences in unemployment rates become even more

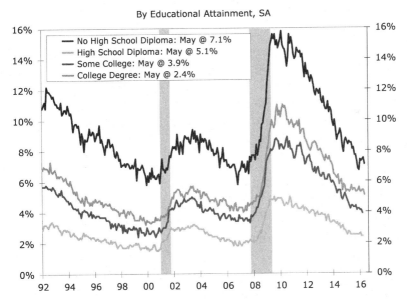

Figure 7.13 Unemployment Rate
Source: U.S. Department of Labor

---

[10] Jaison R. Abel and Richard Dietz, "Do the Benefits of College Still Outweigh the Costs?" *Current Issues in Economics and Finance* 20, no. 3 (2014), Federal Reserve Bank of New York.

Table 7.3 Unemployment Rate across Education Levels

	No High School Diploma	High School Diploma	Some College	College Degree	Unemployement Rate
Mean	9.4***	5.8**	4.8***	2.8***	6.1
St. Dev.	2.5	2.0	1.7	0.9	1.6
t Stat	18.6	(2.1)	(9.4)	(29.7)	

*** Significant difference from total population at 1 percent level
** Significant difference from total population at 5 percent level

Source: U.S. Department of Labor

pronounced during downturns in the labor market, which suggests that the impact of recession hits workers of different education levels in disproportionate ways. For example, in 2009, when the overall U.S. unemployment rate peaked at 10 percent, the unemployment rate for college-educated workers climbed only as high as 5 percent.

As employers had to make tough decisions about firing and hiring during the past recession, their preference for more educated workers was made clear. Bachelor's degree holders now account for 38 percent of employed workers compared to 34 percent at the start of the recession. As employers continue to seek workers who are able to add value in a more knowledge-based economy, relatively fewer opportunities have become available for low-skilled/semiskilled workers—often associated with those without a high school diploma. Younger generations have a higher share of college graduates, but with only 36 percent of 25- to 34-year-olds having college degrees, there is still great variation in educational attainment.

With higher wages and an easier time finding employment, participation in the labor force is positively associated with education. Labor force attachment rises with education as the opportunity cost of not working, that is, forgone wages, increases. The labor force participation rate for college-educated workers stood at 75 percent in 2014 compared to 58 percent among those with only a high school diploma. This participation gap has also widened in recent years, having stood at less than 15 percent in the mid-2000s. Not only do workers with less education earn less income, but a significantly higher share is not engaged in the labor market. The growing differences in participation rates, combined with higher unemployment and lower earnings prospects, have led to a wider divergence in income among educational groups.

Gender's Role in Labor Market Outcomes: Persistent Differences between Men and Women

Gender is a third important way in which workers' labor market experiences can vary drastically. Cultural norms that have dominated for centuries are still apparent in the modern labor market. Since in many households the role of primary breadwinner falls to the man, men have higher rates of labor force participation than women, who still bear the bulk of household and child-rearing responsibilities. In 2014, the participation rate among prime-age working males was 88 percent, 15 percentage points above the participation rate of women. For women who do work outside the home, they are much more likely to work part time. For most women, the decision to work part time is a choice, as they balance the same household responsibilities that keep some women out of the labor force altogether. Only around 20 percent of prime-age women working part time are underemployed in terms of hours worked, compared to about two-thirds of prime age men working part time (Figure 7.14).

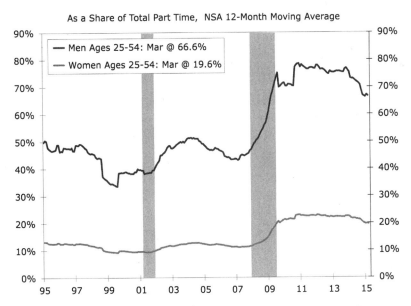

Figure 7.14 Involuntary Part-Time Workers
Source: U.S. Department of Labor

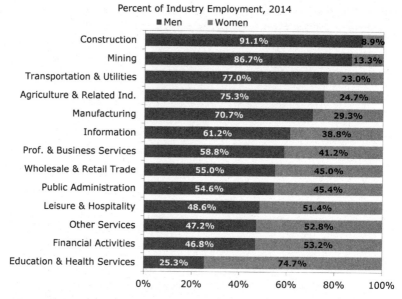

Figure 7.15 Employment by Gender
Source: U.S. Department of Labor

Different labor market patterns between men and women are also evident when looking at the types of jobs held. Men still tend to dominate employment in a number of industries, most notably the construction and mining sectors (Figure 7.15). On the flip side, women tend to comprise a relatively high share of employment in education and health services. While unemployment rates between men and women have tracked fairly closely since 1980, these industry differences can lead to shorter-term variations. For example, the unemployment rate for men rose to a high of 11.1 percent following the Great Recession versus 9 percent for women. This came as male-dominated industries were hit particularly hard by the downturn. Employment in the construction industry fell 30 percent from peak to trough and 14 percent in the manufacturing sector. Meanwhile, government employment, which is composed of a relatively high share of women, fell only 4 percent, and education and health services employment continued to grow throughout the recession and recovery.

However, even as unemployment outcomes are similar between men and women over the course of the business cycle and more women are now receiving college degrees than men, income among men remains higher. Some of this can be explained by the industry distribution of female workers, where women hold a relatively higher share of jobs in lower-paying industries. Yet even within individual industries and occupations, women almost always earn less than men. Part of this is due to different levels of experience, where women are more likely to take time off in their careers for child rearing or work part time. Another factor is that even among "full-time" workers, women still tend to work fewer hours than males. In 2014, women in their prime working years classified as full time (working 35 hours or more) worked an average of 41.0 hours per week compared to 43.9 hours for men working full time. Yet even when controlling for industry, education, experience, and hours worked, evidence suggests an unexplained earnings gap persists.[11]

Why Does Worker Heterogeneity Matter? Cyclical vs. Secular Trends in the Labor Market

Imperfect information and heterogeneity among workers make it difficult for the labor market to achieve and maintain the theoretical steady state. Fluctuations in the business cycle make it even more difficult as labor needs for employers change and wages adjust. Beyond the business cycle, the supply and demand for labor is constantly evolving as the economy grows. This creates structural trends that can outlast the business cycle and make the current position of the economy in the business cycle more difficult to determine. Many of these trends stem from the changing composition of the workforce. Given the different labor market outcomes and work patterns among different workers, shifts in the composition of the labor force can have meaningful effects on aggregate measures of the labor market. As a result, the movement of some indicators must be interpreted more carefully, accounting for the longer-term secular trends in the economy.

Labor market differences among age groups and the changing age distribution of the workforce are two ways in which secular trends can

---

[11] Francine Blau and Lawrence Kahn, "The Gender Pay Gap: Have Women Gone as Far as They Can?" *Academy of Management Perspectives*, February 2007: 7–23; Stephanie Boraas and William M. Rodgers, III, "How Does Gender Play a Role in the Earnings Gap? An Update," U.S. Bureau of Labor Statistics *Monthly Labor Review* (March 2003): 9–15.

obfuscate the current state of the labor market. Some analysts believe that the low rate of job turnover in recent years not only stems from the weak labor market but is also being held down by the relatively large share of the workforce in the later stages of their careers. As noted previously, older workers switch jobs at lower frequencies, and therefore the low rate of job turnover may not be as far from normal levels as it first appears. Similarly, the rising share of workers at the younger end of the wage spectrum, which tend to work in lower-paying industries and obtain lower wages in general, may be keeping average hourly earnings growth muted.[12]

Perhaps nowhere has the impact of the changing age composition of the adult population been more apparent and in need of more scrutinized interpretation than the labor force participation rate in recent years. In 2008, the labor force participation rate began to fall sharply as the Great Recession took hold and job opportunities for the most part disappeared (Figure 7.16). Since then, the labor force participation rate

Figure 7.16 Labor Force Participation Rate
Source: U.S. Department of Labor

---

[12] Sarah House, Erik Nelson, and Alex Moehring, "Millennials in the Economy IV: Who's Hiring Young Workers?" *Wells Fargo Economics*, January 26, 2015.

has fallen more than 3 percentage points. However, the drop in labor force participation also coincided with a major demographic milestone: the first of the Baby Boomers turned age 65 in 2011. Moreover, the link between education and employment/earnings outcomes has led to more young adults obtaining a college education. While some students work part time, many do not, which has led to labor force participation rates for the population under age 25 continuously sliding since the early 1990s as young adults join the workforce later in life.

Therefore, analysts and policy makers have sought to determine how much of the decline since the Great Recession is due to cyclical factors and how much is due to secular trends. In addition to cyclical factors weighing on the participation rate as workers of all ages were more discouraged over their job prospects, a historically large share of the working-age population was reaching the age in which participation declines dramatically even in a strong labor market. Understanding the cyclical component is an important facet in determining how much slack is in the labor market and in turn the most prudent stance of monetary policy.

Secular trends such as the aging of the population and young workers staying out of the labor force longer to obtain more education have made it difficult to determine precisely how much of the decline in the labor force participation rate since the Great Recession has been due to cyclical weakness. Therefore, it has been difficult to determine how much the labor force participation rate may bounce back once the labor market strengthens. To assess the degree to which demographics have weighed on the labor force participation rate since 2007, we can examine how the distribution of the working-age population has shifted in recent years. As the Baby Boomers have aged, the share of the population aged 55 and older has grown (Figure 7.17). Holding constant the participation rate for each detailed cohort since the recession began, demographics alone would have lowered the participation rate to 64.6 percent between 2007 and 2013, or by 1.5 percentage points.[13] Therefore, demographics appear to have accounted for a little over half of the 2.8 percentage point drop in participation between 2007 and 2013.

---

[13] John E. Silvia and Sarah Watt House, "Labor Force Participation: Where to Now?" *Wells Fargo Economics*, April 9, 2014.

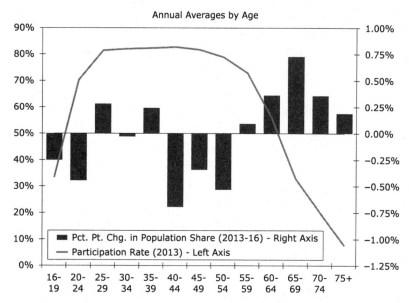

Figure 7.17 Labor Force Participation and Demographic Shifts
Source: U.S. Department of Labor

At face value, the decline in the labor force participation rate, without taking account of the different work patterns of older workers, would lead to an overestimation of the amount of slack in the labor force.

Even as the participation rate has been influenced by population trends, additional secular trends have weighed on the participation rate in recent years. The participation rate for prime-age workers—ages 25 to 54—had started to fall well ahead of the 2007–2009 recession. Between 2000 and 2007, the prime labor force participation rate declined 1 percentage point. The drop in the prime-age participation rate ahead of the Great Recession suggests a structural decline in the total participation rate beyond the widely discussed demographics and educational trends.

The labor force participation rate in the second half of the twentieth century was dominated by secular trends. Female labor participation rate for prime-age women steadily increased beginning in the early 1960s through the mid-1990s (Figure 7.18). Between 1950 and its peak in 1999, the labor force participation rate among women nearly doubled. The steady secular trend of women increasingly working outside of the

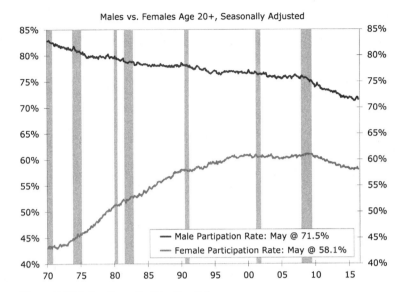

Males vs. Females Age 20+, Seasonally Adjusted

Male Partipation Rate: May @ 71.5%
Female Participation Rate: May @ 58.1%

Figure 7.18 Labor Force Participation Rate
Source: U.S. Department of Labor

home often masked the cyclical variations in labor force participation. By looking at the aggregate data, there would be little reason to believe that labor force participation varied with the business cycle, increasing when demand for employment and wage growth was strong, and declining when unemployment rose and job opportunities became relatively scare.

By the early 2000s, the trend in female labor force began to level out and could no longer mask the trends in male participation rates. The rate for prime-age men has been declining since the mid-1950s. There is no widely agreed-upon reason for the ongoing decline in prime-age male labor force participation. However, one possible reason is increased social insurance—particularly disability insurance.[14] Another possible explanation for the long-term decline in prime-age male participation is declining real wages for lower-skilled jobs.[15] In other words, the opportunity cost of leisure has declined for

---

[14] David H. Autor and Mark Dugan, "The Rise in Disability Rolls and the Decline in Unemployment," *Quarterly Journal of Economics* 118, no. 1 (2003): 157–206.

[15] Chinhui Juhn, "Decline of Male Labor Force Participation: The Role of Declining Market Opportunities," *Quarterly Journal of Economics* 107, no. 1 (1992): 79–121; Robert A. Moffit, "The Reversal of the Employment-Population Ratio in the 2000s: Facts and Explanations," *Brookings Papers on Economic Activity*, Fall 2012.

lower-skilled workers. This may also account for the plateau in female participation rates, as the income earned from working outside the home for many women is not enough to offset its costs, such as child care or higher marginal tax rates.

The rise in female labor force participation in the second half of the twentieth century was an important factor in raising the supply of labor available in the economy. As labor is an input into production, the increased labor supply helped to spur stronger growth in the economy, as well as raise the real income of households, as many now included a second breadwinner. However, now it seems that female labor force participation has hit a ceiling, which will limit the future rate at which the labor supply, and therefore the economy, can grow. In other words, the leveling off of the participation rate among women, combined with the continued decline in the labor force participation rate for prime-age men, has limited the potential gross domestic product (GDP) growth of the economy.

PART III: HOW DO SECULAR LABOR MARKET TRENDS IMPACT ECONOMIC POLICY?

In combination with other long-term trends in the economy, the decline in the labor force participation rate will impact the rate of job creation in the economy. Job growth is a function of both the supply of and demand for labor. With the labor force participation rate having fallen sharply since the Great Recession and growth in the working-age population slowing, growth in the supply of labor, measured by labor force growth, looks to have downshifted in recent years. As a result, the number of new jobs needed each month to keep the unemployment rate steady has also declined.[16]

How many jobs does the economy need to add each month to be associated with a decline in the unemployment rate? A good benchmark is the trend rate of job growth. The trend rate of job growth is effectively the number of jobs needed to absorb new entrants to the labor force without affecting the unemployment rate. Above-trend job gains would

---

[16] Daniel Aaronson and Scott Brave, "Estimating the Trend in Employment Growth," *Chicago Fed Letter* 312 (July 2013), Federal Reserve Bank of Chicago.

reduce the unemployment rate, whereas below-trend job growth would drive the unemployment rate higher. Determining this trend is useful for U.S. monetary policy in the context of current and projected rates of job growth, as it will affect the timing for when full employment is reached.

Job growth is ultimately a function of the supply of and demand for labor. Although fluctuations in demand are the driving factor of job growth in the short run, the supply side plays a key role in the overall trend in job growth. Labor supply is driven by growth in the working-age population as well as this group's rate of participation in the labor market. Admittedly, the participation rate can be affected by demand conditions in the short run. Over time, however, the labor force participation rate has been dominated by secular trends independent of the business cycle, as previously discussed.

Historical estimates for the trend in job growth have centered around 150,000 new jobs per month.[17] This is close to the average number of jobs created per month from 1960 to 1999 (145,000). Of course, during this period, labor force growth was bolstered by the demographic effect of the Baby Boomers joining the workforce beginning in the late 1960s and a cultural shift of rising labor force participation among women beginning in the early 1960s.

To better understand how many new jobs are needed each month in order to lower the unemployment rate, we estimate a model of the trend in payroll growth. Job gains above the trend, likely to be seen in the expansionary phase of the business cycle, would lead to a lower unemployment rate. Conversely, job gains below trend, likely to be seen when the economy is in a recession, would lead to an increase in the unemployment rate.

Included in our model are four variables that capture demand and supply drivers of labor. The growth rate of the economy, in other words aggregate demand, will influence business's needs for labor. Therefore, we include the Congressional Budget Office's (CBO) estimates of potential GDP.[18] The potential rate of growth for the U.S.

[17] Todd Clark and Taisuke Nakata, "The Trend Growth Rate of Employment: Past, Present and Future," *Federal Reserve Bank of Kansas City Economic Review* (2006 Q1): 43–85.

[18] "Key Assumptions in Projecting Potential GDP—February 2014 Baseline," Congressional Budget Office, February 4, 2014, www.cbo.gov/publication/45070.

economy is estimated to have fallen from an average of 3.1 percent per year in the 10 years prior to the Great Recession to an average of 2.1 percent in 2015–2020.

We also include estimates for the natural rate of unemployment, or the unemployment rate at which inflation remains steady. Over the business cycle, the demand for labor will fluctuate, leading to variations in the unemployment rate and the pace of hiring. The natural rate of unemployment is included to account for the general demand for labor over the forecast horizon outside of cyclical factors. We use the historic and projected estimates of the natural rate of unemployment published by the CBO (Figure 7.19).[19] The CBO estimates that the natural rate of unemployment has drifted higher following the Great Recession and will average 5.5 percent over the next six years compared to 5.0 percent from 1998 to 2007.

For the United States, the supply of labor is partially dependent on the size of the working-age population. The working-age population is derived mainly through domestic population growth but also through

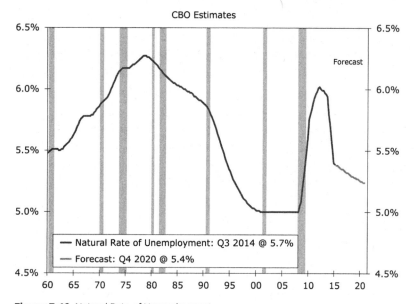

Figure 7.19 Natural Rate of Unemployment
Sources: Congressional Budget Office and U.S. Department of Labor

---

[19] Ibid.

immigration. The Bureau of Labor Statistics (BLS) publishes estimates for the growth in the working-age population, including assumptions about immigration, which we use for the population component in our model (Figure 7.20).[20] The BLS estimates that the civilian working-age population is set to grow even more slowly over the next six years, increasing around 0.9 percent per year.

We also include the labor force participation rate for the working-age population in our model. Currently, the future path of the labor force participation rate is a source of great uncertainty. The precipitous decline since early 2008 has undoubtedly been due in part to the weak-demand environment, signaling a cyclical component to the drop. However, as the recovery has turned into expansion, it has become more difficult to separate the initial cyclical forces from structural changes in labor force participation. For example, older job losers who would have temporarily left the labor force in a short downturn may instead retire as the labor market is slow to recover. Therefore, the extent to which the labor force participation rate bounces back over the next few years—if it does at all—is perhaps the biggest wild card when it comes to determining a benchmark for the number of jobs needed to keep the unemployment rate steady.

To account for this uncertainty and to get a sense of how sensitive our estimates are to the labor force participation rate, we run the model using three scenarios for the labor force participation rate. The scenarios take into account the structural trends in the participation rate among age cohorts ahead of the Great Recession (Figure 7.17). In the most optimistic scenario, we assume that the downward trends in younger cohorts' (ages 16 to 49) participation rates stabilize, and older cohorts' (ages 50+) participation rates continue to trend higher. In the moderate scenario, we assume that pre-recession trends remain in place; that is, younger cohorts' participation rates continue to trend lower, while older cohorts' participation rates continue to trend higher. Under the third and most pessimistic scenario, we

---

[20] "Employment Projections," Bureau of Labor Statistics, December 19, 2013. We use historical data through 2014 and base our projections on the percentage increase from 2015 onward rather than published projected levels. www.bls.gov/emp/ep_data_labor_force.htm.

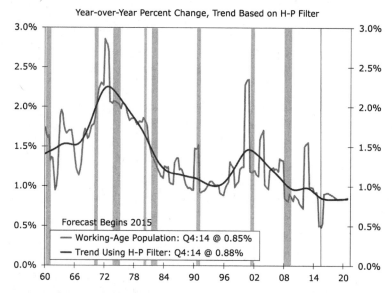

Figure 7.20 Working-Age Population Growth
Sources: Congressional Budget Office and U.S. Department of Labor

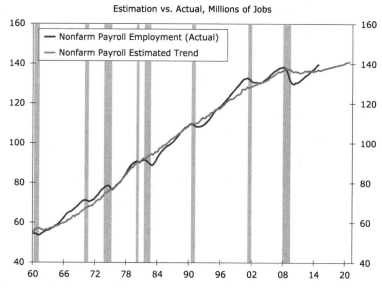

Figure 7.21 Trend Employment Level
Source: U.S. Department of Labor

assume the participation rate of younger cohorts continues to trend lower, while older workers' participation rates level off (which began to occur around 2012).

Our measures of trend employment suggest that nonfarm payrolls would need to grow by an average of only 65,000 jobs per month from 2015 to 2020 to keep the unemployment rate unchanged (Figure 7.22). Even under our optimistic scenario for labor force participation rate trends, job gains would need to average only 94,000 per month to be neutral on the unemployment rate (Figure 7.22). This compares to an average monthly change of 108,000 in the previous labor market recovery and expansion of 2001–2007.

Implications for Private-Sector Hiring and Policy Makers

Although job gains have picked up notably in 2014, the subpar pace of job growth compared to prior expansions should be taken within the context of a slower trend in payroll gains. Much has been made of the unemployment rate not fully capturing remaining slack in the labor

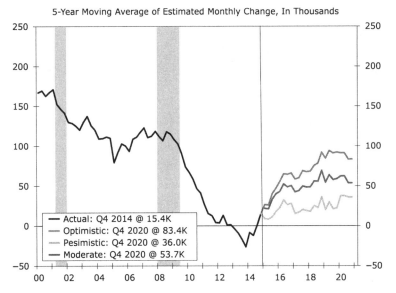

Figure 7.22 Trend Employment Monthly Change
Source: U.S. Department of Labor

market, but if the trend in payroll growth has downshifted as appears to be the case, it should be less surprising to analysts and policy makers that the unemployment rate has fallen so swiftly.

Accurately assessing the trend in job growth will have important implications for businesses and policy makers. First, with labor force growth set to slow in the coming years, it may not be a "buyers' market" for labor as long as some employers currently expect. Instead, employers may find themselves facing talent shortages, particularly for specialized professions, and may have a tougher time filling jobs at prevailing wage rates. If hiring continued to proceed well above its trend level, workers should finally see the long-awaited pickup in wages and salaries, which could also lure some nonparticipants back into the labor force.

Second, for governments that rely heavily on income taxes, a lower trend in job growth would suggest slower growth in tax revenues, particularly as it implies weaker economic growth more broadly. The weaker rate of growth in tax revenues would make it more difficult to meet entitlement expenditures promised under more optimistic scenarios. A persistently lower rate of labor force participation would also challenge tax revenues, as a smaller share of the population is engaged in the economy and earning income that would generate tax revenues. In turn, it would lead to a higher dependency ratio, not just for the population of typical working age, and suggest a greater share of working-age adults are dependent on the earnings of family, charity, or government support programs. This in turn could lead to higher taxes for businesses and individuals to fund entitlement programs and other government spending.[21]

Third, establishing appropriate monetary policy would also hinge on understanding how trends in job growth can change over time. If Federal Reserve policy makers overestimate the trend in payroll growth, they risk ignoring signs that the labor market may be

---

[21] For example, current Social Security tax revenues fall short of current expenditures. The Congressional Budget Office estimates the gap, which was 0.4 percent of GDP in 2013, to grow to 1.7 percent in 2038 and 2.2 percent in 2088, which, unless benefits are reduced, would lead to additional taxes or borrowing by the government to fulfil future outlays. "CBO's 2014 Long-Term Projections for Social Security: Additional Information," Congressional Budget Office, December 18, 2014.

overheating. In contrast, underestimating the trend in payroll growth may lead to the Fed's tightening too early in a business cycle. With the labor market constantly fluctuating and made up of a heterogeneous workforce, finding this balance remains no easy task. Fluctuations around the unemployment rate and the dynamic estimates of what constitutes full employment make it difficult for policy makers to determine when the labor market is in equilibrium.

CHAPTER 8

Inflation

When What You Get
Isn't What You Expect

INTRODUCTION

One of the most persistent deviations between actual and expected outcomes since the financial crisis has been the behavior of inflation. A lack of inflation has been a ubiquitous problem among advanced economies since the global financial crisis, even as monetary policy has been pushed to what can only be considered as ultra-accommodative. With price stability one of the Federal Reserve's goals mandated by Congress and the primary benchmark of success for other central banks, the dearth of inflation has presented a clear challenge for policy makers seeking to normalize interest rates and employ the traditional tools of monetary policy.

Prior to the financial crisis, central banks had established command over inflation. After stagflation in the 1970s, in which inflation flourished and the real economy languished, monetary policy makers established credibility in fighting inflation by adjusting interest rates. In recent years, however, with interest rates at record lows, inflation continues to run well below what models have predicted. Federal Reserve officials have been steadily nudging down medium-term inflation forecasts while standing pat that inflation will return to 2.0 percent over the longer run.

Policies aimed at stoking inflation back up to more palatable levels have fallen short all across the developed world. Record low interest rates, unprecedented expansion of the monetary base, and even a foray into negative interest rates have all failed to generate inflation in the way models predicted. Is this a case of the dynamic nature of price adjustments not being properly captured in models, or is the post–Great Recession inflation environment different from the past?

The deviation between the actual and expected path of inflation has consequences for consumers, businesses, investors, and policy makers. Any variance between the path of realized versus expected inflation alters the real rate of interest. The recent shortfall in inflation therefore has provided a relative benefit to savers (lenders), while adversely affecting borrowers who thought the real value of debt would be lower. For the Federal Reserve, the discrepancy between realized and expected inflation has led to an adjustment in the expected path of interest rates. In early 2012, Federal Reserve officials expected the fed funds target rate would be raised twice by the end of 2014, but the fed funds target rate was instead held at its record low until the end of 2015.

In this chapter, we review the importance of inflation for consumers, investors, and policy makers. If consistent with expectations, inflation should be neutral for economic actors. However, economic reality often varies from what is expected, and inflation is no different. To understand how inflation may deviate from expectations, we look at the historical drivers of inflation and how the post–Great Recession environment in many ways marks a departure from the past. We then turn to statistical methods that help us better understand how inflation may evolve in the future across the United States and other advanced economies.

WHAT IS INFLATION?

Inflation is the aggregate change in prices for goods and services within the economy. Over any period, prices for individual products are changing to reflect individual supply-and-demand dynamics. For example, a bumper crop of tomatoes one season may send prices for them lower, as the rise in supply exceeds the initial level of demand at the previous price. At the same time, drought may ravage cattle herds, sending prices for beef higher as supply falls. What matters for inflation, however, are not these individual price movements, but the *overall* fluctuation in prices when looking across the economy.

As consumers and businesses go about their purchases, the level cost of goods is what stands out. For example, between June 2014 and June 2015, the average price of a gallon of gas fell $0.89. Inflation, however, is viewed as the rate of change in the price level, that is, the percent change in prices over a given period. Therefore, whether prices stabilize at historically high or low levels does not have a bearing on inflation, so long as prices stabilize, since the rate of change would be zero.

The term *inflation* is broadly applied to describe how prices change in the economy. More specifically, however, inflation refers to a *rise* in prices over time. Deflation, on the other hand, refers to a *decline* in prices over time. Between the spectrum of inflation and deflation is

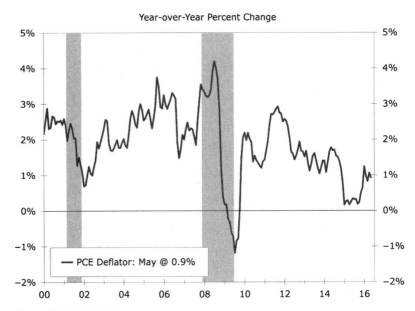

Figure 8.1 PCE Deflator
Source: U.S. Department of Commerce

disinflation, which denotes an increase in overall price levels, but at a slower rate. For example, when the annual rate of inflation slowed from 1.8 percent to 0.2 percent from 2014 to 2015 following the collapse in oil prices, the economy experienced a bout of disinflation, but not deflation, as the aggregate price level did not decline (Figure 8.1). Hyperinflation is an extreme inflationary scenario, where prices rise extraordinarily fast, even exponentially.

WHY DOES INFLATION MATTER?

For anyone trying to save money for a future purchase, inflation may seem undesirable. With the cost of goods and services generally rising over time, the purchase is likely to cost more in the future than it does today. In other words, inflation erodes the value of money over time. Therefore, it may seem odd that central bankers actually *want* inflation, rather than try to keep prices stable over time.

While for savers the positive rate of inflation may be unwelcome, the alternative of deflation is significantly more dangerous for the economy. If consumers see prices falling on a sustained basis, they will begin to hold back their spending. As they hold back their spending, aggregate demand falls further, leading to even lower prices in order for the market to clear. At the same time, businesses postpone investment, as investment will be cheaper in the future. The combined effects lead to a collapse in growth, as was seen during the Great Depression.

In addition to holding back spending and investment, deflation makes deleveraging more difficult for debtors. As aggregate prices decline, workers will receive less income, businesses will receive less revenue, and governments will receive less tax revenue, all else being equal. As a result, the fixed amount of debt owed becomes more burdensome to repay as the real value of their debt rises. The result can be defaults, which negatively impact both borrower and lender but also lead to a greater share of income being devoted to debt rather than current consumption, which can help support overall demand.

Why, then, do central bankers not simply aim for a zero rate of inflation? Monetary policy is a blunt instrument. Inflation can fluctuate significantly around policy makers' objectives. Developments outside their control can lead to significant price changes in some items and overall inflation levels. The 2014–2016 collapse in oil prices offers an example, as the political decision among Organization of the Petroleum Exporting Countries (OPEC) members not to cut production was a major factor in driving prices lower. Floods and droughts are other examples of how prices can also be affected by factors outside monetary policy makers' control and keep inflation from running at its target for a period of time. Yet even among specific episodes that clearly impact inflation, inflation is difficult to fine-tune. The post–Great Recession environment offers a good illustration, where despite historically accommodative monetary policy, inflation fell short of the Federal Reserve's goal for the better part of seven years (Figure 8.2).

Therefore, policy makers prefer to have some cushion between the target rate inflation and deflation, as the negative effects of modest inflation are significantly smaller than the costs of slipping into a deflationary spiral. For example, the Federal Reserve, Bank of England, and Bank of Japan all have inflation targets of 2.0 percent, while the European Central Bank and Swiss National Bank target inflation at

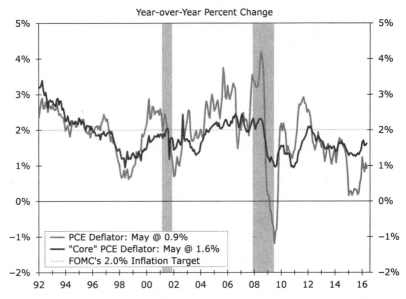

Figure 8.2 PCE Deflator vs. Core PCE Deflator
Source: U.S. Department of Commerce

less than 2 percent. Other major central banks may aim for slightly higher inflation (Norges Bank of Norway at 2.5 percent, Bank of Mexico at 3 percent) or a target range, as seen in Canada (2.0 percent +/− 1.0 percent) and Australia (2.0 to 3.0 percent).

Ultimately, the impact of inflation depends on the realized rate of inflation versus what was expected. If households and businesses expect 2 percent inflation and incorporate that into their wage demands, selling prices, and decisions to take out debt and investment plans, then an actual inflation rate of 2 percent would be neutral on their real finances.

In other words, realized inflation, and inflation expectations and forecasts in particular, play a central role at every level of decision making for economic agents. Households, businesses, and governments and policy makers all must factor in assumptions about future inflation into their spending and investment decisions. Households must consider future inflation when negotiating wages, taking on debt at a given nominal interest rate, and choosing how to direct savings into investments. The expected rate of inflation is a critical input to many key business decisions, including planning for wage and salary increases, adjusting rents and budgeting for facilities maintenance and upkeep. Governments must take into account future inflation when estimating revenues and outlays, particularly when those outlays may extend well into the future.

Inflation forecasts influence investment and budget planning both directly and indirectly. A higher inflation forecast suggests more monetary (nominal) funds will be needed to purchase resources or complete tasks. Since nearly all organizations, public, private, and nonprofit, operate with limited funds, an accurate inflation forecast is critical in order to properly allocate resources. For instance, a higher inflation forecast suggests that a larger sum of monetary resources is required to complete a task compared to the past, all else being equal. If actual inflation comes in at a lower level than the forecast had predicted, decision makers will have overestimated costs, meaning they may have missed the opportunity to acquire certain materials or assets and/or complete certain tasks. Inflation forecasts also indirectly influence investment and budgetary decisions via interest rates. Investment and budget planning relies on careful consideration of borrowing costs, as higher (or lower) expected borrowing costs would greatly influence many business decisions. Therefore, inflation rates (particularly inflation forecasts) are essential elements of decision making for economic agents.

The expected rate of inflation is also important for monetary policy makers who aim to keep inflation running at a moderate rate in order to help facilitate an appropriate rate of growth for the economy. The Federal Open Market Committee (FOMC) takes into account the forecast for inflation when forming monetary policy decisions. Monetary policy works with a lag, and therefore policy makers must be particularly mindful not only of the current rate of inflation but how inflation is likely to evolve over the medium term, which is typically considered about two to three years.

Furthermore, private-sector forecasters, including many members of the Blue Chip Economic Indicators group, believe that the FOMC will change the stance of monetary policy if the economy/inflation moves in a different direction than the Fed's forecast. Some observers believe that the Fed has more information or more accurate forecasts than private forecasters, and therefore the forecasts of policy makers provide signals about the future path of policy. In addition, private forecasters may modify their forecasts according to the signals provided by the Fed's forecasts. Put differently, inflation forecasts from the FOMC, to some extent, set inflation expectations as well as expectations for the overall economy.

WHAT DETERMINES INFLATION?

While economists are in agreement as to why inflation matters, there is somewhat less consensus around the drivers of inflation. There are several theories of inflation, and each theory suggests somewhat different drivers of inflation. The different theories exist since, over time, the magnitude of the association between different variables has fluctuated as the economy has evolved. In addition, some inflation drivers may be more influential in the short run and other drivers more impactful on long-run inflation, with different theories focusing on different time horizons for inflation. Over the years, however, different theories of inflation have fallen in and out of favor depending on how adequately they fit with the current inflationary environment.

Quantity Theory of Money

The money supply is one of the key drivers of inflation rates, as suggested by the quantity theory of money. That is, the quantity theory of money postulates that the money supply has a positive (direct), proportional relationship with the inflation rate. Put differently, ceteris paribus, a 1 percent increase in growth of money supply would increase inflation rate by 1 percent. The magnitude of the relationship between the money supply and inflation may vary (depending on phases of the business cycle along with other factors), but the relationship between the two variables is well established in the literature.

Interest rates also play a role in driving inflation. Imbedded within the nominal interest rates is an inflation component. As described in the Fisher equation, the nominal interest rate is equal to the real inflation rate plus inflation.

$$i = r + \pi$$

Since interest rates are the cost of holding money, interest rates (nominal interest rates in particular) influence the demand for money. From the quantity theory of money we know that the money supply also influences prices and therefore inflation may have a two-way causal relationship with interest rates. Higher inflation expectations may therefore boost nominal interest rates because the FOMC would be expected to raise the fed funds rate to control inflation. Therefore, in theory, there is a link between money supply/demand, interest rates, and the inflation rate.

A Phillips Curve Framework

The money supply and interest rates alone, however, do not determine inflation. Other factors, such as aggregate demand, can affect the strength of the relationship between the monetary base, interest rates, and inflation. A practical example is the U.S. economy following the Great Recession. The FOMC increased the money supply significantly. Between late 2008 and mid-2014, the monetary base expanded by more than $2.5 trillion as the Federal Reserve embarked on three rounds of asset purchases, or *quantitative easing*. Over the same period, the fed funds target rate was left at 0 to 0.25 percent from December 2008 to December 2015. The inflation rate, however, continued to register significantly below the FOMC's target of 2 percent. The average rate of inflation from 2009 to 2014 was just 1.4 percent, as measured by the PCE deflator.

The post–Great Recession environment runs contrary to the quantity theory of money as well as Milton Friedman's statement that inflation is a monetary phenomenon. A possible justification of the broken link between the inflation and monetary variables is lack of aggregate demand. That is, following the 2007–2009 recession, the economy's recovery was painfully slow. While the economy began to grow again in mid-2009, the pace was well below its historic average. In addition, slack in the labor market persisted, with full employment not being reached for another seven years. Demand remained weak as credit growth slowed and households and businesses deleveraged, leading to a slower velocity of money.

The impact of aggregate demand on inflation is typically explained through the Phillips curve framework. The Phillips curve suggests a relationship between the unemployment rate—a proxy for demand in the economy—and wages and inflation. The unemployment rate is inversely correlated with inflation. Greater demand drives lower unemployment, and as excess resources in the economy, in this case labor, are absorbed, prices move higher. This relationship between stronger demand and higher prices is referred to as demand-pull inflation. With more workers earning higher wages, aggregate spending increases, pulling up prices as "too much spending follows too few goods." Therefore, at least in the short run, the effectiveness of money supply and interest rates as inflation drivers may depend on the aggregate demand.

Throughout history, the strength in the link between inflation and the unemployment rate has varied. After Arthur Phillips first published work on the link between unemployment and wages in the United Kingdom in 1958, economists Paul Samuelson and Robert Solow found a similar relationship in the United States between unemployment and inflation.[1] However, the link seemed to break down in the 1970s, when both inflation and unemployment in the United States soared (Figure 8.3).

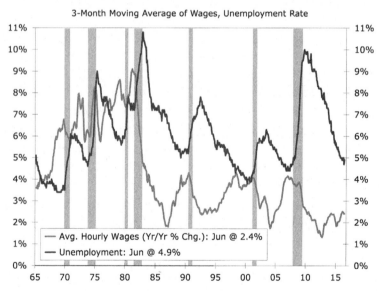

Figure 8.3 Unemployment and Wage Growth
Source: U.S. Department of Labor

---

[1] A. W. H. Phillips, "The Relation between Unemployment and the Rate of Change of Money Wage Rates in the United Kingdom, 1861–1957," *Economica* 25, no. 2 (1958): 283–299; Paul A. Samuelson and Robert M. Solow, "Analytical Aspects of Anti-inflation Policy," *American Economic Review* 50, no. 2 (1960): 177–194.

The breakdown highlighted how the trade-off between lower unemployment and inflation was only a short-run phenomenon and excluded supply shocks. Policy makers could boost aggregate demand in the short run, leading to temporarily higher inflation, but actual inflation also depends on expected inflation. If economic agents expect higher inflation, then for a given level of unemployment, inflation becomes higher. The inclusion of inflation expectations is known as the augmented Phillips curve and can be written as follows:

$$\pi = \pi_{-1} - \beta(u - u^n) + v$$

where π is inflation, $u - u^n$ is the difference between the actual and estimated natural rate of unemployment, and β measures how sensitive inflation is to unemployment. The term π_{-1} illustrates that current inflation depends in part on recent inflation, as recent inflation affects inflation expectations and therefore price setting, wage demands, spending, and so on. Shocks, such as the oil price collapse in 2014–2016, also influence inflation and are represented by the term v.

More recently, the unemployment rate in the United States has fallen from a peak of 10 percent following the recession to less than 5 percent. Yet inflation has been little changed, leading some to question the efficacy of the Phillips curve. Stable and relatively low inflation expectations in recent years in part explain why actual inflation has remained so low in the Phillips curve framework. However, even when accounting for inflation expectations, the relationship between unemployment and wages/inflation has diminished (i.e., the slope of the Phillips curve has declined), although the relationship is still found to be present.[2]

Moreover, the relationship between unemployment and wages/inflation depends on the economy being at full employment. If the economy is not yet at full employment, then excess labor reduces the need for employers to raise wages. This leads to the idea of the nonaccelerating inflation rate of unemployment (NAIRU), also known as the natural rate of unemployment. Stronger demand would not be

---

[2] For example, see International Monetary Fund, "The Dog That Didn't Bark: Has Inflation Been Muzzled or Was It Just Sleeping?" *World Economic Outlook,* 2013.

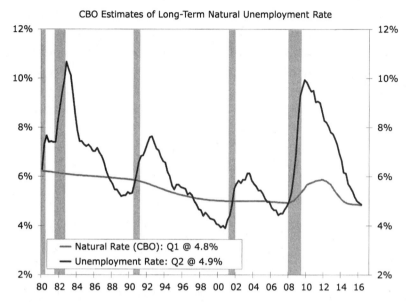

Figure 8.4 Unemployment Rate and NAIRU
Sources: U.S. Department of Labor and Congressional Budget Office

expected to drive inflation higher until unemployment has reached its natural rate. Estimates of the natural rate of unemployment vary over time as structural factors in the economy change (Figure 8.4). In recent years, Federal Reserve officials and the Congressional Budget Office estimate the natural rate of unemployment at around 4.8 percent. Through the first half of 2016, the unemployment rate averaged 4.9 percent, suggesting wage and broader inflationary pressure would only now begin to be building in the post-recession environment.

Cost-Push Inflation

In addition to demand, supply side shocks can also alter inflation, particularly in the short run. Sharp reductions in the supply common products can send price higher, raising overall inflation. This scenario is known as "cost-push" inflation. The most well-known example of this situation is the oil crisis of the 1970s. In retaliation for supporting Israel in the 1973 Arab-Israeli war, OPEC members placed an embargo on exports to the United States and other countries supporting Israel and also cut production. Between the middle of 1973 and the end of 1974, oil prices more than tripled. The rapid rise in energy costs sent overall inflation, as measured by the consumer price index (CPI), up from 3 percent in 1972 to 11 percent in 1974.

Cost-push inflation can also work the other way and lead to lower inflation. More recently, OPEC's decision not to cut production to prop up prices amid rising North American supply sent shockwaves through the oil market. Oil prices fell around 75 percent from the middle of 2014 to early 2016. The lower cost of oil and related products pushed overall inflation lower, with the CPI briefly falling below zero. In addition to prices for energy goods falling, prices for transportation services also declined, pushing core goods prices lower, as it was cheaper to ship products.

Sometimes, past events (either demand-pull or cost-push) or expectations lead to inflationary pressures in an economy, which is referred to as built-in inflation. For example, a persistent demand-pull or cost-push scenario may increase inflation expectations and workers may push for higher wages in anticipation of higher inflation. In addition, producers may raise prices expecting higher input prices as well as higher wages.

Inflation Expectations

Recent inflation experiences can play an important role in expectations of future inflation. The inflation effects of short-term fluctuations in demand or supply previously discussed can shape how businesses and consumers think about future inflation. Following the 2014–2016 drop in oil prices, both market and consumer expectations for inflation fell. Given the significant role of energy prices on overall inflation, the decline in short-term inflation expectations reflected recent price movements. However, long-term inflation expectations (both market-based measures of compensation and consumer expectations) also fell to record lows (Figure 8.5). The drop in long-term expectations came even though oil prices could not fall forever and prices only needed to stabilize, let alone rise, for inflation—which, again, is the rate of change in prices, not a level—to move higher.

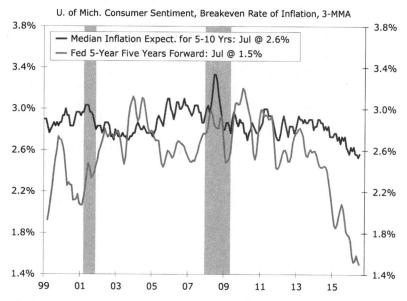

U. of Mich. Consumer Sentiment, Breakeven Rate of Inflation, 3-MMA

— Median Inflation Expect. for 5-10 Yrs: Jul @ 2.6%
— Fed 5-Year Five Years Forward: Jul @ 1.5%

Figure 8.5 Median Inflation Expectations 5 to 10 Years Ahead
Sources: University of Michigan and Federal Reserve Board

The drop in the public's inflation expectations may have in part been driven by the Federal Reserve's own forecasts. As mentioned earlier, the FOMC publishes its forecast for key economic variables, including inflation, regularly and market participants (financial markets in particular) pay close attention to those forecasts. Inflation forecast from the FOMC play a role in shaping the inflation expectations among economic agents. For more than two years, the FOMC repeatedly cut its inflation forecasts for the 2016 core PCE deflator (Figure 8.6). The persistent cuts to the Fed's own forecasts of future inflation, along with the recency bias of lower realized inflation, likely weighed on the public's perception of future inflation. A simple ordinary least squares (OLS) regression of core inflation based on the unemployment rate gap (measured by the unemployment rate minus its estimated natural rate) and long-term inflation expectations shows inflation expectations play a significantly larger role in determining core inflation.

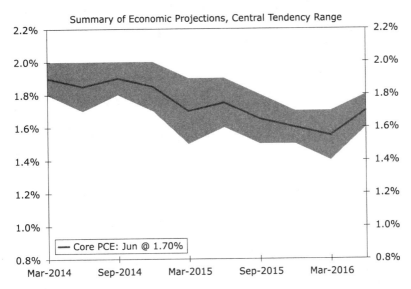

Figure 8.6 2016 Core PCE Projections
Source: Federal Reserve Board

INFLATION AFTER THE GREAT RECESSION

The leading theories of inflation appear to do little to explain the post–
Great Recession price environment. After more than seven years of
expansion and a labor market near full employment, core inflation in
the United States has remained stubbornly low. With the exception of
a few months in early 2012, the core PCE deflator has continuously
run below the Federal Reserve's 2 percent target. Inflation measured
by the core CPI has been somewhat stronger, as it often is due to its
different methodology, but it too has proved weaker than many expected this far from the financial crisis.

The lack of inflation has come as a surprise to many, particularly
those who follow the quantity theory of money. Central bankers
around the world have embarked on extensive asset purchase programs, that is, quantitative easing (QE), in recent years with the
aim of boosting inflation and lowering interest rates beyond main
policy rates. Modeled after efforts made by the Bank of Japan back in

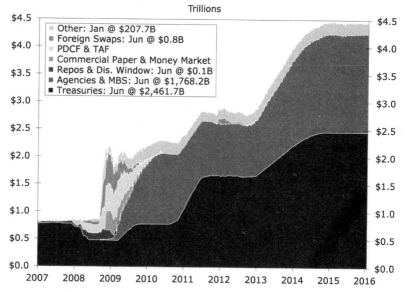

Figure 8.7 Federal Reserve Balance Sheet
Source: Federal Reserve Board

2001 to boost Japanese inflation, the Federal Reserve was the first major central bank to turn to QE following the global financial crisis (followed shortly by the Bank of England). Between three rounds of quantitative, nearly $4 trillion in assets were added to the Fed's balance sheet (Figure 8.7), sparking fears of runaway inflation. Yet where was the inflation?

What the monetarist adherents of inflation failed to take into account were the dynamics beyond the money supply. While ceteris paribus, a multitrillion-dollar increase in the money supply would spur inflation, all was not equal. Aggregate demand in the economy remained far weaker than in previous expansions and slower than even downgraded estimates of potential growth. The Congressional Budget Office estimated that the output gap, the difference between potential output and actual economic output, at one point reached more than $1 trillion and has yet to fully close (Figure 8.8). The lingering slack in the economy led to little inflationary pressure despite the massive increase in the Fed's balance sheet and money supply.

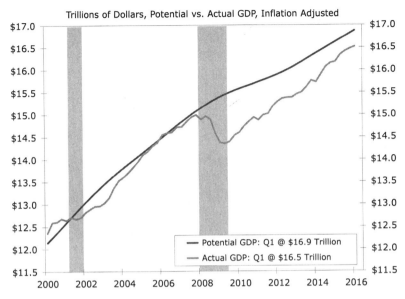

Figure 8.8 U.S. Output Gap
Sources: Congressional Budget Office and U.S. Department of Commerce

Also underappreciated was the potential for an altered transmission mechanism between the Fed's balance sheet and overall credit growth in the post-crisis environment. The weak growth backdrop limited both the demand and supply of new credit. Perhaps more important was the new regulatory environment. The emergence of new capital requirements contributed to banks' desire to be more cautious in credit expansion following the financial crisis. Additionally, new liquidity requirements led banks to increase their investment in safe, liquid assets, such as excess reserves held at central banks. The new rules, and even the anticipation of the changes, led to a different allocation of assets than would have been expected prior to the crisis, altering the course in which credit was expanded. Following QE, excess reserves at banks rose closely in line with the Fed's balance sheet (Figure 8.9). The weaker transmission mechanism between money, credit, and growth led to a sharp slowdown in the velocity of money (Figure 8.10).

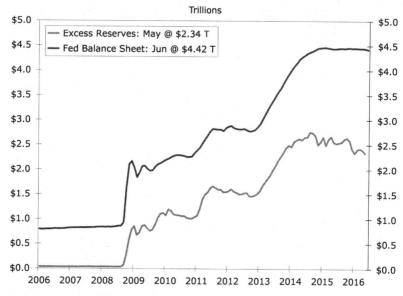

Figure 8.9 Excess Bank Reserves
Source: Federal Reserve Board

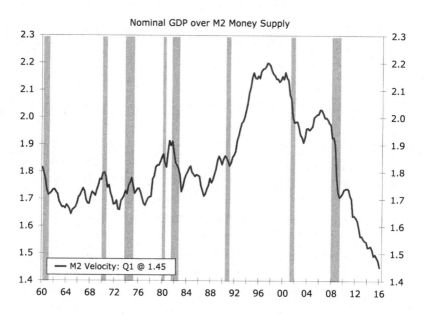

Figure 8.10 M2 Money Supply Velocity
Sources: Federal Reserve Board and U.S. Department of Commerce

Inflation Expectations and the Case of the Missing Deflation

Even as credit growth and broad demand have improved as the expansion has continued, inflation has remained stubbornly low. Yet this is not the first time in this cycle where inflation has been "stickier" than predicted by slack-based models. The rise in the unemployment rate to 10 percent and 4 percent decline in real gross domestic product (GDP) signaled a collapse in demand that should have also ushered in a collapse in prices, at least temporarily. However, core inflation slowed by only a little more than 1 percentage point and, despite the worst downturn since the Great Depression, remained around 1 percent. The mild weakening in inflation compared to what models predicted led economists on a search to explain the "missing deflation."

The search has highlighted the importance of inflation expectations in determining realized inflation. While the unemployment rate more than doubled and hit nearly a 30-year high, long-term inflation expectations, measured by the University of Michigan's Consumer Sentiment Survey, fell from an average of 3.1 percent in 2008 to 2.8 percent in 2010. Models including inflation expectations, and their relative stability in the downturn, better captured the behavior of inflation.[3]

Wages and Productivity in Inflation

As the expansion has proceeded and inflation has remained low, the modest rates of inflation now look to be altering consumer and business inflation expectations for the future. While the labor market has neared full employment and core inflation has improved, inflation expectations—both short and long term—began to slide from what were already low levels in late 2014.

The reduction in inflation expectations alters the path and intensity of future price and wage increases. Disappointing wage growth has been a common refrain since the recession. Explanations include the traditional slack arguments where, with the labor market only recently reaching levels that could be considered full employment, employers

---

[3] Marco Del Negro, Marc P. Giannoni, and Frank Schorfheide, "Inflation in the Great Recession and New Keynesian Models," NBER working paper No. 20055, April 2014.

had little need to boost wages in order to attract or maintain workers. Research has also pointed to the stickiness of wages, where employees are reluctant to accept wage cuts. Therefore, even as slack rises, wages do not fall. In order for employers to adjust real wages, they therefore reduce the rate of future wage increases in what is referred to as pent-up wage cuts.[4]

However, the path of productivity plays an important role in the wage debate as well as its impact on inflation. Productivity is the ultimate driver of real wage gains as workers earn the marginal product of their labor. After an initial bump in 2009–2010 when demand began to rise again, yet employers were hesitant to hire, labor productivity slowed to a crawl, averaging just 0.5 percent per year from 2011 to 2016 (Figure 8.11). The weak rate of productivity growth along with low inflation was consistent with slow nominal wage growth.

If productivity remains weak, then diminishing slack in the labor market can more quickly lead to inflation as employers need to increase nominal wages faster than labor's output. If workers are not

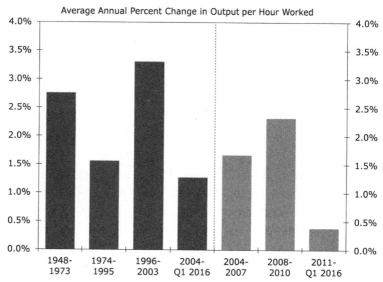

Figure 8.11 Nonfarm Labor Productivity
Source: U.S. Department of Labor

---

[4] Mary C. Daly and Bart Hobijn, "Downward Nominal Wage Rigidities Bend the Phillips Curve," FRB San Francisco working paper 2013-08, 2014.

producing more with each hour worked, raising topline revenues, employers cannot boost wages without cutting into margins or passing on higher labor costs through higher prices. The result is either a shift in income allocation from capital (profits) to labor, or inflation that offsets any nominal wage gains.

Recently, however, the link between labor costs and inflation has broken down more generally. The inability for employers to cut wages during the downturn (downward nominal wage rigidity) has been pointed to as one factor that kept inflation from falling as much as output-gap models would have suggested following the Great Recession. Yet the pass-through effects of higher wages and labor costs to inflation have weakened since the early 1980s, suggesting a diminished link between inflation and economic activity.[5] The breakdown follows a declining share of income derived from labor earnings over the past few decades, weighed down by an aging population and falling labor force participation among prime-age workers (Figure 8.12).

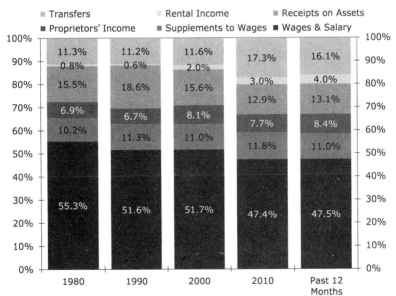

Figure 8.12 Personal Income Sources
Source: U.S. Department of Commerce

---

[5] Ekaterina V. Peneva and Jeremy B. Rudd, "The Passthrough of Labor Costs to Price Inflation," Finance and Economics Discussion Series 2015-042 (Washington, DC: Board of Governors of the Federal Reserve System, 2015), http://dx.doi.org/10.17016/FEDS.2015.042

Not Going It Alone: Low Inflation Globally

The United States is not alone in its low-inflation experience. Around the world, many other advanced economies have struggled to bring inflation back up to rates consistent with central banks targets. In the Eurozone, where the European Central Bank aims to keep inflation under 2 percent, core consumer price inflation has hovered around 1 percent in recent years, while headline inflation has been near zero (Figure 8.13). In Sweden, inflation has been below the Riksbank's target since 2012, while inflation in Switzerland has been well below 2 percent since the financial crisis (Figure 8.14).

Japan has struggled most of all with low inflation. Prices have bordered on the brink between inflation and deflation for the past two decades, averaging just 0.1 percent per year. The inflation history of Japan highlights the challenges of persistently weak demand, exacerbated by unfavorable demographic trends. While Japan's shrinking population makes the country's demographic challenges more severe than any other major economy, other advanced economies, including

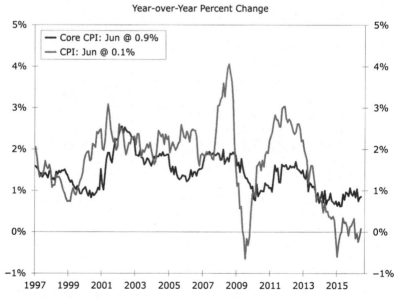

Figure 8.13 Eurozone Consumer Price Inflation
Source: Eurostat

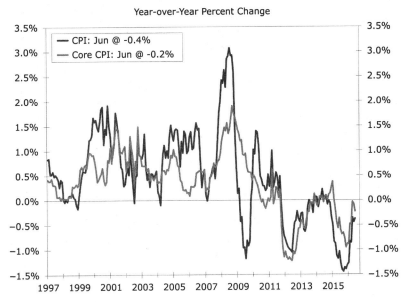

Year-over-Year Percent Change

Figure 8.14 Swiss Consumer Price Index
Source: Swiss Federal Statistics Office

the United States, face slower population growth and an aging population that portends slower growth and weaker inflation pressure.

The ubiquitous story of inflation running too low for the comfort of central banks follows the similarly common story of record monetary accommodation. Even as the Federal Reserve's quantitative easing generated little help for inflation, it did not stop the European Central Bank from embarking on QE in early 2015 and for the Bank of Japan to further expand its balance sheet. QE was also undertaken with the aim to lower interest rates beyond central banks' main policy rates. However, to further support inflation, a number of countries have lowered policy rates into negative territory, in the hopes of spurring credit growth and therefore demand in the economy. Less explicitly stated by central bankers is the currency effect of greater policy accommodation. As monetary policy eases, currencies depreciate amid capital outflows, all else being equal. The weaker currency can at least temporarily boost inflation via import prices. Yet, as evidenced with the inflation performance of the Eurozone, Sweden, and Japan, negative rates have done little to boost inflation.

The United States has been at the losing end of the currency/inflation dynamic. Even as the Federal Reserve has been slow to remove policy accommodation since the Great Recession, the relative strength of the U.S. economy has led to expectations that policy is more likely to tighten than ease, and is likely to tighten ahead of other major central banks. While the Fed has been talking about lifting rates, monetary policy in other advanced economies has become more accommodative or signaled that tighter policy would come at a later date than expected by the Fed. The divergence in policy and even the outlook for future policy caused the dollar to strengthen against a wide range of currencies. Between mid-2014 and the end of 2015, the broad trade-weighted dollar index strengthened more than 20 percent.

Lower import prices ensued. The strength in the dollar led to the effective cost of imported products falling as it took fewer dollars to purchase the same amount of foreign-denominated goods. Import prices for nonfuel items sank between autumn 2014 and the end of 2015 (Figure 8.15). Although the impact on overall consumer price inflation was limited since the majority of consumer spending is devoted to

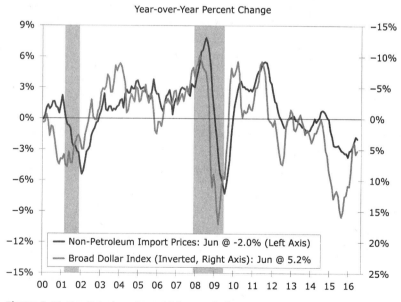

Figure 8.15 Non-Petroleum Import Prices vs. Dollar
Source: U.S. Department of Labor and Federal Reserve Board

Year-over-Year Percent Change

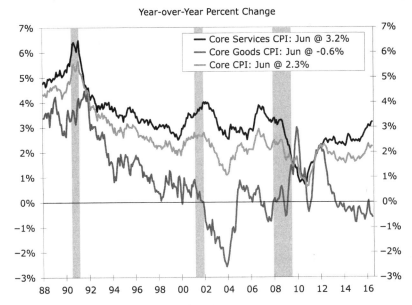

Figure 8.16 Core Goods vs. Core Services CPI
Source: U.S. Department of Labor

services, very few of which are imported, the stronger dollar contributed to weaker goods inflation. The CPI for goods excluding food and energy fell for the better part of 2013–2016, making it a drag on overall inflation (Figure 8.16).

The dollar is not the only factor, however, in weaker goods inflation. Globalization has opened up more markets, generating new sources of low-cost labor. Stronger productivity growth in manufacturing compared to services has also helped to reduce goods inflation in the United States and other economies.

Although inflation has not been as low as in advanced economies, developing countries have also experienced disinflation since the global financial crisis (Figure 8.17). At the forefront has been lower inflation in China. Consumer price inflation has slowed to around 2 percent after reaching 6 percent as recently as 2011. Overcapacity in the country's industrial sector has led to the producer price index falling since 2012. The ongoing deflation in the "world's factory" has contributed to lower goods inflation elsewhere in the world, via both cheaper prices for Chinese-made products, as well as tougher competition for foreign producers.

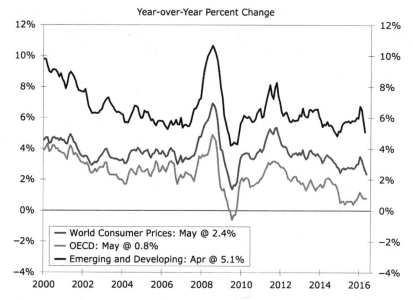

Figure 8.17 World Consumer Price Inflation
Sources: International Monetary Fund and the Organization for Economic Cooperation and Development

The disinflationary trends over the past few years have been more welcome in many emerging markets, as inflation remains far from deflation territory. However, the similar trends in both advanced and developing countries highlight the weakness in demand globally since the recession, evidenced by global growth remaining under its long-run trend since 2012. Amid the slowdown, lower commodity prices have been a common theme across the world, but have played a larger role in developing nations since food and energy make up a larger share of consumer purchases.

APPLICATION: PREDICTING IF CENTRAL BANKS CAN ACHIEVE PRICE STABILITY

As we have discussed, inflation forecasts are a key input in many financial decisions, including interest rates, investments, budgets, and wage rates. Yet the recent inflation environment looks very different from the past. Traditional explanations for inflation, such as the quantity theory of money and the Phillips curve, no longer appear to explain

price dynamics as successfully as they once did. As a result, the outlook for inflation has become more uncertain, with many wondering
whether central banks will ever achieve their inflation goals.

To examine the path of future inflation in advanced economies and
the global economy more broadly, we use an ordered probit approach
to quantify the probability of disinflationary pressure in the future. We
estimate the six-months-ahead probability of three distinct price scenarios: inflationary pressure, disinflationary/deflationary pressure, or
price stability. Inflationary pressure can be viewed as inflation running
above a central bank's target. The disinflationary/deflationary scenario
describes the likelihood that inflation would run well below target,
while the price stability scenario can be described as the probability
that inflation will be within or closely aligned with the target.

Although there is no single central bank for advanced economies,
most target inflation to be around 2 percent. We therefore consider
inflation of 1.5 to 2.5 percent to be consistent with price stability when
looking at advanced economies. The probability of achieving price stability, however, has fallen since 2012, as has the likelihood of an inflation overshoot. Instead, it looks like the most likely price scenario for
advanced economies is the continued undershoot of inflation, labeled
as the "deflationary" scenario (Figure 8.18).

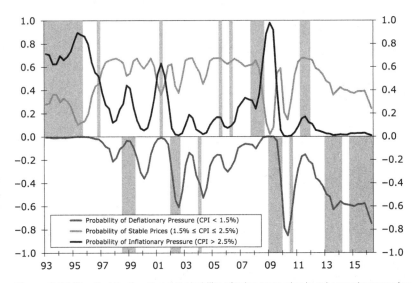

Figure 8.18 The Six-Months-Ahead Probability of Price Scenarios in Advanced Economies

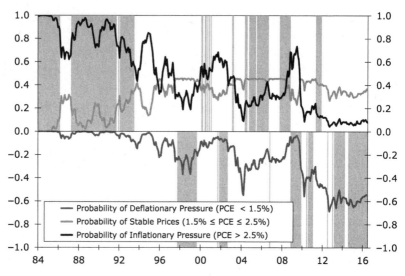

Figure 8.19 The Six-Months-Ahead Probability of Price Scenarios in the United States

Looking specifically at the advanced economies of the United States, Eurozone, and Japan paints a similarly bleak picture for central bankers aiming to revive inflation. The most likely outcome for U.S. economy is that inflation will remain stuck noticeably below the Fed's 2.0 percent target, although the outlook for price stability looks marginally better than in 2015 (Figure 8.19). A similar story holds for the Eurozone, despite the efforts of the European Central Bank to stimulate credit growth and inflation since the Eurozone sovereign debt crisis (Figure 8.20). Even with the Bank of Japan's herculean efforts to support inflation in recent years, returning inflation to around 2 percent remains a pipe dream (Figure 8.21).

With so many major economies struggling to bring inflation back up to targeted levels, it is not surprising to see that inflation globally is expected to remain low by historical standards. Inflation in developing countries tends to run higher than advanced economies. From 1996 to 2014, global inflation averaged 4.4 percent per year, which we use as a benchmark for global "price stability" since there is no institution targeting global inflation. Our probit analysis finds that returning global inflation within half a percent of its long-term average is unlikely in the next six months. In fact, the likelihood that global inflation falls

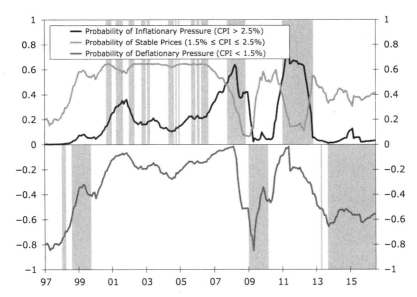

Figure 8.20 The Six-Months-Ahead Probability of Price Scenarios in the Eurozone

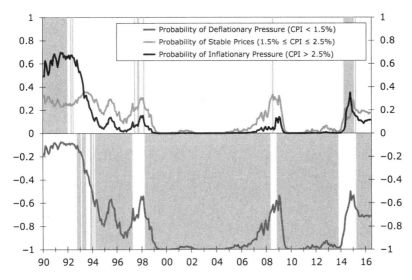

Figure 8.21 The Six-Months-Ahead Probability of Price Scenarios in Japan

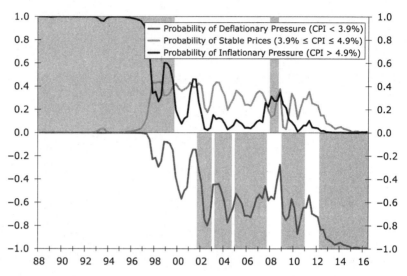

Figure 8.22 The Six-Months-Ahead Probability of Price Scenarios in the Global Economy

short of 3.9 percent is 100 percent (Figure 8.22). Such a high probability that global inflation will continue to run below its historic benchmark suggests a significant shift in the behavior of inflation over the past five years.

The likelihood that inflation will continue to fall short of policy makers' goals and its long-run averages highlights how the inflation environment has changed since the recession. Low inflation is a new challenge to central bankers, who over the years have grown comfortable in their tools to combat excessive inflation. The low inflation environment has paved the way for record policy accommodation from central banks, whether through expanding balance sheets or negative interest rates. Determining the sources of inflation—or in recent years, the source of disinflation—is vital for decision makers since different sources may require distinct policy actions.

CHAPTER 9

Interest Rates and Credit

Capital Markets in the Post–Great Recession World

As we have explored in previous chapters, the patterns of growth and inflation have changed relative to prior cycles. Many models of the economy that assumed perfect adjustment to a new equilibrium have failed, and this is also true in capital markets. Recent years have witnessed the rise of imperfection in the operation of capital markets. The assumptions of perfect information, costless adjustments, and price flexibility have fallen—the rise of imperfections is here. We will begin by highlighting a number of imperfections evident in capital markets.

IMPERFECT GUIDANCE IN AN UNCERTAIN WORLD

From both the Federal Open Market Committee's (FOMC) and the market's point of view, the role of the dot plot (Figure 9.1) remains unclear. For the FOMC, the plot appears to represent its anticipated path of the funds rate if economic conditions play out as expected. However, over the past three years the FOMC has overestimated inflation and underestimated the decline in the unemployment rate. So is the problem with the imperfect information put into the policy model,

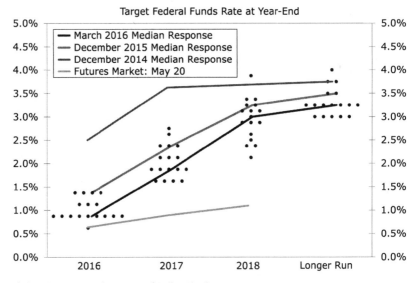

Figure 9.1 Appropriate Pace of Policy Firming
Sources: Federal Reserve Board and Bloomberg LP

236

or is the problem the economic model that estimates the path of the funds rate given the inflation/unemployment inputs?

For private markets, what is the dot plot telling us? The persistent downsizing of the fed funds projections since December 2014 hints that there is some bias in the projections—certainly an imperfect guide to the future.

Dynamic Adjustment: The Problem of Pro-Cyclical Behavior

As illustrated in Figure 9.2, banks adjust their lending standards over time, but, unfortunately, the dynamic adjustment of credit standards appears to impart a very pro-cyclical bias to the credit cycle. From the graph we can see that the percentage of banks that tighten credit drops dramatically in the early phase of an economic recovery (1992–1994, 2002–2004, 2010–2011) and stays easy for most of the economic expansion. Then the percentage of banks that tighten credit rises sharply just before a recession (1999–2000, 2007–2008). This credit

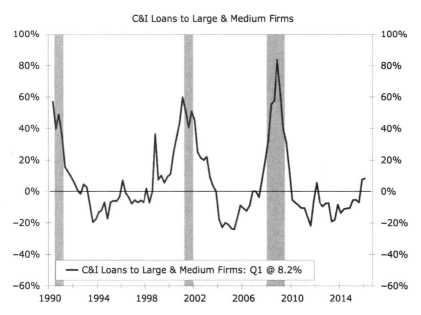

Figure 9.2 Net Percentage of Banks Tightening Standards
Source: Federal Reserve Board

cycle, while certainly rational from an individual bank's point of view, becomes quite pro-cyclical when viewed in the aggregate.

Price/Rate Adjustments: Sudden and Uneven

Interest rate movements, changes in the price of credit, are both sudden and uneven—a distinct break from the assumption of smooth movements to new information.

As illustrated in Figure 9.3, the variability of the real one-year Treasury yield is dramatic. This variability reflects the impact of several forces that are part of the interest rate framework. What is intriguing is that while the framework may be steady over time, the variability of the individual forces impacts the behavior of the one-year rate. In particular, this economic expansion has witnessed a significant change in the path of anticipated economic growth, expected inflation, and the context for monetary policy actions. Indeed, in recent years, we have witnessed the emergence of a new factor, global markets, into the FOMC's reaction function. In addition, long-term interest rates

Figure 9.3 Real 1-Year Treasury Yield
Sources: Federal Reserve Board and U.S. Department of Labor

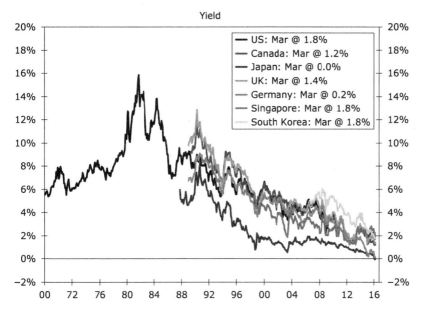

Figure 9.4 10-Year Government Interest Rates
Source: Bloomberg LP

are trending downward as several members of the Organization for Economic Cooperation and Development (OECD) have experienced downward trending 10-year Treasury yields since at least the mid-1990s (Figure 9.4). One potential reason for this downward trend may be the lower inflation and subpar gross domestic product (GDP) growth rates in some developed economies.

As these forces evolve, so does our model for interest rate behavior as evidenced by the movement in the short- and long-term yield curves, which we will examine later in this chapter. In economics, the framework constantly evolves, and nowhere is this more evident than in the realm of interest rates.

What Was Our Starting Point?

As illustrated in Figure 9.5, the starting framework posited that the pattern of the funds rate set by the FOMC would be based on the distance from a perceived equilibrium unemployment rate and a target inflation rate. For the period of 1990 to 2008, this appeared to work

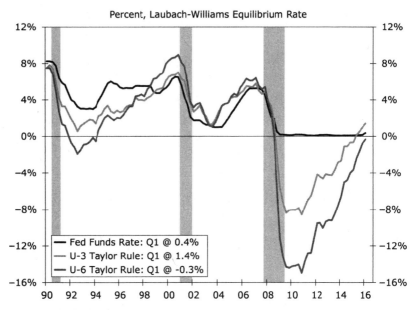

Figure 9.5 Taylor Rule Implied Funds Rate
Sources: Federal Reserve Board, U.S. Departments of Labor and Commerce

fairly well. Unfortunately, since 2008, this framework has begun to generate serious errors.

What changed? Our previous research has noted that there was a structural break in the behavior of several series subsequent to the credit crisis/recession of 2008–2009.[1] For the unemployment rate, the decline to the perceived measure of full employment was not associated with a strong labor market and a rapid rise in labor compensation. Meanwhile, the speed of the economy's approach to the 2 percent inflation target was far slower than anticipated. As a result, current FOMC policy is more cautious in raising the funds rate than implied by the Taylor rule using the traditional unemployment rate (Figure 9.5).

Enter a New Player: Global Developments

Global developments have always lurked off-stage and occasionally made a rude appearance in the interest rate environment, yet these

---

[1] John Silvia, Azhar Iqbal, and Alex Moehring, "Quantifying Frictions: Long-run Average a Useful Guide for Future?" *Wells Fargo Economics Group Special Report*, May 11, 2015.

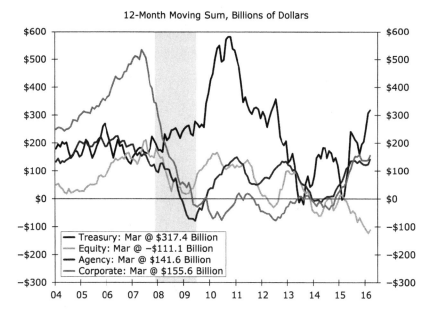

Figure 9.6 Foreign Private Purchases of U.S. Securities
Source: U.S. Department of the Treasury

developments have now added two elements of uncertainty. First, how do we measure this factor? Second, how does this factor fit our model? Since the FOMC introduced this factor into its policy statements, the importance has become evident. One measurement of the importance can be approximated by the safe-haven buying of financial assets as illustrated, in part perhaps, by private sector purchases of U.S. financial assets (Figure 9.6). In fact, when we include global developments in a forecasting model, we get a better forecast for the U.S. 10-year Treasury.

Moreover, the persistent decline in global yields in recent years has reinforced the message of a change in global growth expectations and the inability of key G7 central banks to reignite inflation toward a 2 percent target.

Choices: A New Framework and a Bullish Flatter Yield Curve

Ever since the taper tantrum discussion in 2013, there have been two distinct moves in the yield curve as illustrated in Figure 9.7. The long end of the yield curve has exhibited a bullish flattening trade with the

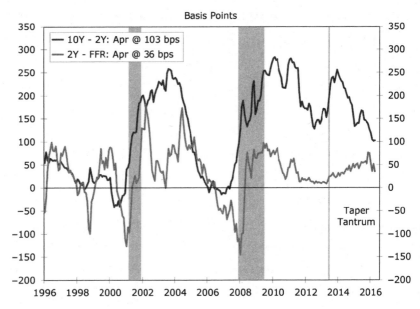

Figure 9.7 Yield Curve Spread
Source: Federal Reserve Board

decline in the 10-year 2-year spread. This reflects the yield pick-up for U.S. Treasury debt relative to what is available for investors in Europe and Japan while also reflecting the incentive of a stronger dollar to attract foreign inflows. Meanwhile, the short end of the yield curve reflects the anticipation of a FOMC increase in rates or at least some form of tighter policy going forward. The uncertainty in the market provides the motivation for a safe-haven move while limiting the extent of Fed tightening.

Previously, we dealt with the reality that the framework for interest rate behavior has evolved over recent years. But what happens if policy itself is inconsistent and what are the broader implications for the market?

The Price of Success

Since 1994, the PCE deflator has averaged less than 2 percent (Figure 9.8). Shall we, then, just declare victory and go on vacation? Alternatively, given this success, what happens if a policy maker

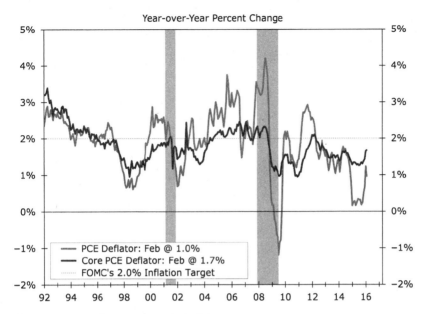

Figure 9.8 PCE Deflator vs. Core PCE Deflator
Source: U.S. Department of Commerce

wishes to push the envelope to achieve greater economic growth/ employment given the current below 2 percent inflation even as the unemployment rate has reached the full employment level? This is our trade-off today.

For the policy maker, the advantage is that, with current inflation so low and inflation expectations falling over the past six months, the marginal cost of additional inflation is low. Even if inflation were to run above 2 percent for a while, the perceived damage to inflation expectations appears limited to some.

Collateral Damage along the Road to Inflation

However, there are economic issues associated with continued easing in the pursuit of growth, and the risk of rising inflation through increased injections of liquidity. The flow of liquidity can, like water, move anywhere. As a result, the distortions in private markets may already be appearing, not through mispriced goods (inflation), but through financial/real assets.

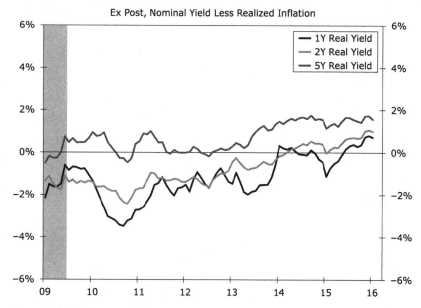

Figure 9.9 Real Treasury Yields
Sources: Federal Reserve Board and U.S. Department of Labor

Persistent zero rates made it easy to justify the purchase of new equipment in an industry (energy) perceived to have a growing output potential. The result was excess capacity in an industry now undergoing retrenchment. In the meantime, low rates allowed firms with visions of limited potential to substitute capital for labor.

As illustrated in Figure 9.9, the policy of administered low short-term rates has produced an era of financial repression where the real return to short-term investments, one- and two-year Treasury yields, was negative. The proper pricing of a risk-free short-term rate is not possible given that the rate is an administered rate by policy makers and not the marketplace. For savers to gain a real return, the imperative is to extend maturity out to five years.

Buy Existing, Not New

With persistent low interest rates, firms may find it easier to purchase existing equipment rather than buy new. This helps to explain the coincidence of high levels of merger and acquisition activity this cycle

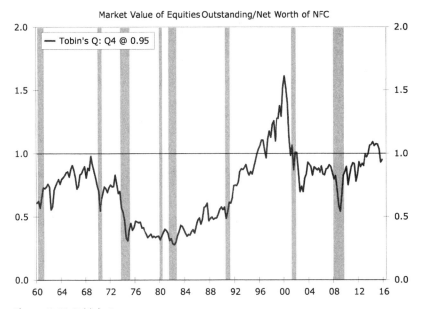

Figure 9.10 Tobin's Q
Source: Federal Reserve Board

along with subpar business investment. As illustrated by the Tobin Q ratio (Figure 9.10), when the Q ratio is below 1.0, then the market value is less than the recorded value of the assets of the company, intimating the market may be undervaluing the company. In this case, the incentive is to buy the company rather than buy new capital. Low interest rates are providing an incentive to invest—not in new equipment but rather in existing equipment given an environment with excess capacity.

On the Variability of Pricing Risk over the Cycle

Another means to judge the credit cycle is the pricing of high-yield debt. As illustrated in Figure 9.11, late-cycle pricing tends to show a steady rise in the risk premium even before the signs of recession are evident in the real economy. From 2000 to 2001 and again over the past year, there has been a rise in the risk premium for high yield credit. During 2007, the premium rose dramatically and spiked in 2008 with the onset of the recession. As the economic recovery takes hold,

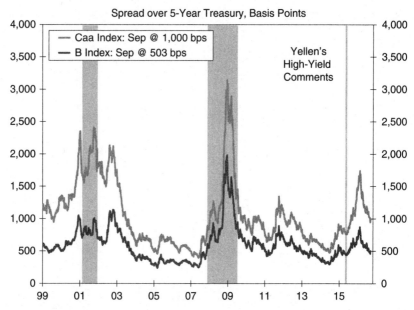

Figure 9.11 High-Yield Spreads
Source: Bloomberg LP

the risk premia tend to decline fairly steadily until just before the next recession starts the cycle again.

The outcome is that pricing of risk in the high-yield bond market is actually quite sensitive to changes in market perceptions. This pattern is reminiscent of the pattern of corporate profit growth we have written about before as another signal of potential economic difficulties. Both indicate that credit premia are rising with the aging of the credit cycle.

On the Variability of Credit Delinquencies over the Cycle

Household debt delinquencies (Figure 9.12) have their own interesting cyclical pattern. Delinquencies are fairly steady mid-expansion (2004–2006) but then gradually start to rise as the latter stages of the economic cycle appear (2006–2007) before they rapidly escalate into the recession. Delinquencies peak after the recession and then gradually decline as the recovery proceeds. One notable exception has been the secular rise of student loan delinquencies.

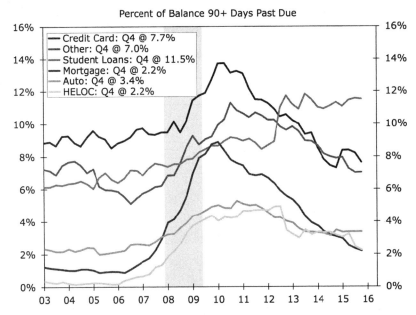

Percent of Balance 90+ Days Past Due

Credit Card: Q4 @ 7.7%
Other: Q4 @ 7.0%
Student Loans: Q4 @ 11.5%
Mortgage: Q4 @ 2.2%
Auto: Q4 @ 3.4%
HELOC: Q4 @ 2.2%

Figure 9.12 Household Debt Delinquencies
Source: Federal Reserve Bank of New York

So Why Are Downturns More Predictable?

Our three patterns of the credit cycle raise the question of why recessions are not more often easily predicted or recognized. From our work, the conditions for a recession may be present but the timing and source of the spark that lights the recession lamp is seldom obvious.[2] At present (based on 2016:Q1 data) the probability of recession remains below 50 percent for the next six months, but we are on watch given the elevated risk premia.

A LOOK AT ACTUAL HISTORY OVER THE LONG RUN

In broad terms, the equilibrium real interest rate is the real short-term rate consistent with an economy operating at full potential once cyclical shocks to the economy have dissipated. Empirical work indicates

---

[2] John Silvia, Azhar Iqbal, and Michael Pugliese, "Recession Talks in the Spotlight: Should We Worry?" *Wells Fargo Economics Group Special Report,* February 24, 2016.

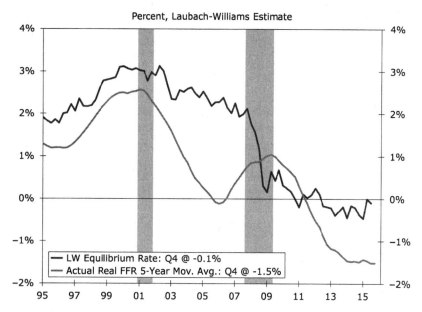

Percent, Laubach-Williams Estimate

Figure 9.13 Natural Real Rate of Interest Estimate
Sources: Laubach and Williams (2003) and Federal Reserve Board

that the natural rate of interest has actually declined over time as illustrated in Figure 9.13. In this graph, we plot the five-year moving average of the real fed funds rate and a more sophisticated estimate of the equilibrium interest rate. Both series have declined, and statistical analysis confirms that both series are not mean reverting and, moreover, exhibit structural breaks in the behavior of these series following the Great Recession.

A Look at Policy History in the Short Run

There also appears to be a drift in the FOMC's assessment of the longer-term fed funds rate forecast during the short run of the current economic expansion. The FOMC has consistently lowered its expectations for the longer-term funds rate.

During this cycle, we have also witnessed a consistent drop in the estimates of potential GDP growth by the Congressional Budget Office (CBO), as illustrated in Figure 9.14, largely due to slower labor force growth and a slowdown in productivity growth. Growth estimates

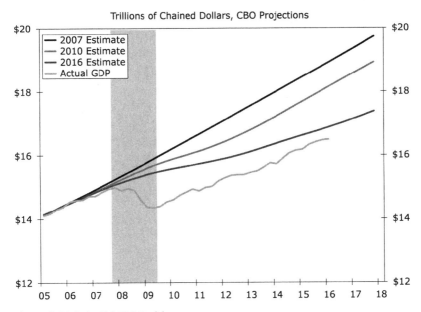

Trillions of Chained Dollars, CBO Projections

Figure 9.14 Potential GDP Revisions
Sources: CBO and U.S. Department of Commerce

have consistently moved toward a 2 percent consensus as opposed to the 3 percent plus that was the standard for many forecasts—both in the private marketplace and among policy makers. Lower potential growth estimates would incentivize firms to borrow less to invest in future production and lower rates would lead households to save more, leading to a lower natural rate of interest.

Downshifting Equilibrium Rates Produces Lower Policy Rates

The persistent downshifting in policy expectations can also be observed in the dot plot (Figure 9.15). For example, the long-run fed funds rate projections by the FOMC began at 4.25 percent, and have consistently been downshifted to the current estimate of 3.25 percent. The global decline in yields indicates that the drift to lower rates is a global pattern and the forces behind these movements are likely global as well. For investors and policy makers, there is no return to the past. We have moved into new territory with new opportunities and risks.

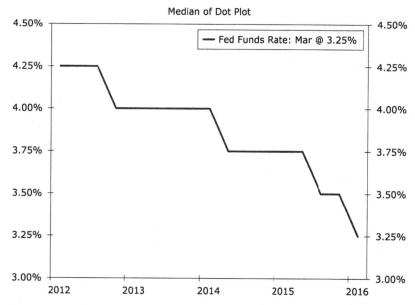

Figure 9.15 FOMC Longer-Term Fed Funds Rate Forecast
Source: Federal Reserve Board

CREDIT AND ADMINISTERED RATES

Interest rates represent the price of credit. The differences in interest rates on different financial instruments (U.S. Treasury and corporate debt for example) or similar instruments (the yield curve) are largely indicative of relative risk. However, what can we say about the behavior of these interest rate differences during the current economic expansion and in an era of administered, not free market-setting interest rates? Moreover, how can we employ these interest rate spreads as a measure of sentiment, and possibly, speculation or credit revulsion over the business cycle when such interest rates are significantly impacted by public policy? For example, one puzzle to resolve is the current low level of sovereign interest rates given the perceived risk due to poor long-term fiscal outlooks for these countries. Could these low rates be a by-product of administered rates along with an upsurge in financial regulation? A second puzzle is the recent weakness in the pace of housing and business investment in the United States, despite low nominal interest rates.

Identifying Trend: The Anchoring Bias

What has been the trend in 5- and 10-year yields since 1968, the start of rising inflation and interest rates in an activist policy era, and are those trends reliable guides for the future? How permanent is permanent? How normal is normal? Figure 9.16 highlights the problem of an anchoring bias for the period since 1968. For both the 2- and 10-year Treasury benchmark yields there are two distinct patterns. First, there is a steady rise in interest rates from 1968 to 1979 and then a distinct downtrend thereafter. This highlights the issue that there have been two different economic regimes and, indeed, we know that since 1979, Paul Volcker's focus on inflation led to a new set of central bank objectives. Second, there is an equally apparent steady decline in nominal interest rates since 1982. These two distinct patterns indicate that neither the 2-year nor 10-year Treasury rate over this period are mean reverting, and treating the 2- and 10-year rates as a coherent series since 1968 is not the correct approach. Yet many analysts will employ the extended period since the 1960s as their sample set when developing

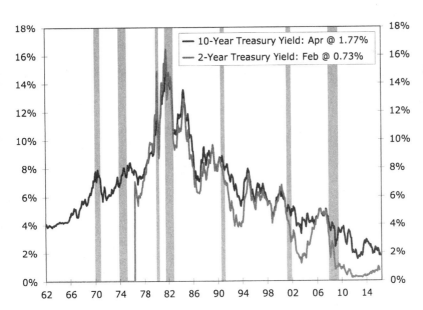

Figure 9.16 U.S. Treasury Yields
Source: Federal Reserve Board

econometric models. In prior work, we have found separately that the 5-year Treasury rate is also not mean reverting.[3]

In Table 9.1, we show the calculations that indicate that the average and standard deviations of interest rates are distinct between the two periods and that the average values of the 5-year and 10-year rates are statistically different. For example, for the 1968–1981 period the average value of the Aa corporate bond was 8.99 percent in the first period and 7.82 percent in the second period.[4] Are these values significantly different such that we can proceed on the assumption that they represent two different interest rate regimes?

One counterintuitive result is that once we compare the means and standard deviations between these two periods, we note that the stability ratio—a series's standard deviation as a percent of its mean— is actually higher in the second period than in the first period. This is true for the four interest rates examined in Table 9.1. The evidence from the stability ratios indicates that despite the recent low level of interest rates, the volatility of interest rates has actually risen in recent years.

We can also test for a structural break in these series by employing a State-Space approach.[5] The results listed in Table 9.2 confirm the structural break. There is clear evidence of a structural break in the level of market interest rates in the fourth quarter of 1982. For example, a break occurred for the Aa corporate bond yield, 5-year Treasury yield, and 10-year Treasury yield, which are all statistically significant at the 0.01 level. The table also shows a second intriguing result: the structural break for the Baa corporate bond occurs in 2008:Q4, just after the collapse of Lehman Brothers.

These results illustrate the important role that intellectual biases can play in investing and economic forecasting. Here, the problem of the anchoring bias appears in two ways with respect to the level of rates.[6]

---

[3] Tests for mean reversion on 2-year Treasury rates in the spirit of this exercise were completed in John Silvia, Azhar Iqbal, Kaylyn Swankoski, Sarah Watt, and Sam Bullard, *Economic and Business Forecasting* (Hoboken, NJ: John Wiley & Sons, 2014), 341–344.

[4] The Aa and Baa corporate bond yields utilized in this analysis represent the Moody's benchmark yields as reported in the Federal Reserve's H.15 tables.

[5] See Silvia et al., 2014, Chapter 7; G. S. Maddala and In-Moo Kim, *Unit Root, Cointegration and Structural Change* (Cambridge, UK: Cambridge University Press, 1998).

[6] See John E. Silvia, *Dynamic Economic Decision Making* (Hoboken, NJ: John Wiley & Sons, 2011), 71–73.

Table 9.1 Bond Yield Statistics

	1968–1981 Average	1982-Present Average	1968–1981 Std. Dev.	1982-Present Std. Dev.	1968–1981 Stability Ratio	1982-Present Stability Ratio
Aa	9.0	7.8	2.15	2.56	23.89	32.73
Baa	9.8	8.6	2.36	2.67	23.99	30.98
5-Year	8.0	5.8	2.32	3.10	28.91	53.67
10-Year	8.0	6.3	2.20	2.84	27.31	45.16

Source: Federal Reserve Board

Table 9.2 Identifying a Structural Break Using the State-Space Approach

Aa Corporate Bond Rate			5-Year Treasury Rate		
Break Date	Type of Break	Coefficient	Break Date	Type of Break	Coefficient
Q4-82	Shift	−2.35*	Q4-82	Shift	−2.51*
Q1-80	Additive	0.96*	Q1-80	Additive	1.37*
Q4-79	Shift	1.20*	Q3-81	Additive	1.05*
Q2-84	Shift	1.14*	Q4-80	Shift	1.80*
Q4-80	Shift	1.10*	Q4-79	Shift	1.29*
Baa Corporate Bond Rate			10-Year Treasury Rate		
Break Date	Type of Break	Coefficient	Break Date	Type of Break	Coefficient
Q4-08	Shift	1.75*	Q4-82	Shift	−2.35*
Q4-82	Shift	−1.53*	Q1-80	Additive	1.28*
Q4-80	Shift	1.36*	Q3-81	Additive	0.83*
Q1-80	Shift	1.30*	Q4-80	Shift	1.26*
Q4-79	Shift	1.32*	Q4-79	Shift	1.20*

Significant at the 0.01 Level

Based on the experience of the early post-WWII period, investors were accustomed to low inflation and were surprised by the blowout of inflation in the late 1970s. Meanwhile, the next generation of bond investors anchored their expectations of inflation on the experience of the late 1970s and failed to anticipate the drop in inflation and interest rates in the 1980s.

As noted earlier, the structural break in corporate bond yields followed the Lehman Brothers collapse. This represents a challenge to interest rate modelers since we must now recognize that since 2008 we are in a different sampling period with a new interest rate regime. This may help explain the problems for many forecasters in accounting for the continued low level of interest rates compared to the historical lineage.

The Dramatic Shift in Real Interest Rates

Real interest rates were consistently below zero during the 1970s and above zero throughout the post-1970 period until the recovery from the 2001 recession (Figure 9.17). These patterns corroborate the view that investors in Treasury debt were consistently surprised by the rise in inflation during the 1970s. Then, during the 1980s, inflation fears

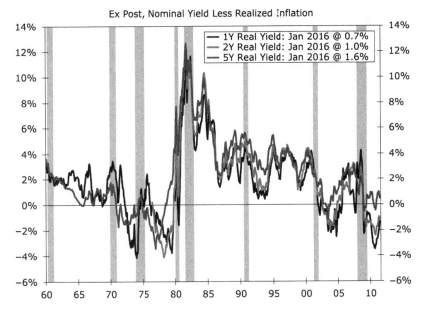

Ex Post, Nominal Yield Less Realized Inflation

— 1Y Real Yield: Jan 2016 @ 0.7%
— 2Y Real Yield: Jan 2016 @ 1.0%
— 5Y Real Yield: Jan 2016 @ 1.6%

Figure 9.17 Real Treasury Yields
Sources: Federal Reserve Board and U.S. Department of Labor

persisted and nominal rates did not completely adjust to the rapid drop in actual inflation from 1982 to 1992. These behaviors imply that investors exhibit a dynamic adjustment process where they gradually learn about the path of policy and policy's implications for inflation. Therefore, real interest rates partially adjust to lower actual inflation.

The current period is also unusual since the conduct of monetary policy is aimed at keeping nominal interest rates very low while promoting a rise in inflation. The net result is that real interest rates remain negative throughout this period. Lowered expectations for economic growth and inflation may reflect, in part, the experience of this recovery but also the impact of higher taxes and underlying changes in labor force growth and productivity.

IMPERFECT INFORMATION AND CREDIT

Problems of dynamic adjustment in response to changes in economic factors reflect the crucial role of information. The problem of incomplete information emphasizes the observation that in the real world, in contrast to the perfectly competitive model assumption, no agent has full information as to the actions of other policy makers, economic agents' budgets, preferences, resources or technologies, plans for the future, and numerous other factors that affect prices in those markets. Given the reality of incomplete information, economic agents are right to be cautious to make dramatic moves in their financial positions. Therefore, there is only a partial adjustment on the part of both lenders and borrowers in any given economic shock. In economics, there is also the issue of incorrect information. Here, the problem revolves around the reality that the information we have on the economy is often based on preliminary samples that are frequently revised in subsequent months and years. Finally, there is no crystal ball into the future, and therefore anticipations of future data and policy actions are often revised even while agents must make long-term plans on the information available today.

Incomplete Information: Regulation and Capital Spending

First, there is the issue of incomplete information—economic agents do not know all the facts and may delay decisions or make different decisions than what would have been made if perfect information was available. This is evident today in the full plate of regulations and capital requirements associated with the Dodd-Frank Act, the Affordable Care Act, and Basel III, since the full set of rules has yet to be spelled out. Moreover, there is the legacy of legal risks from the events of 2004–2009 that continues to leave a sense of caution in financial markets today.

Limits to Financing the Economy

Complete information on policy actions is not available, so we must recognize that current financial markets have significantly more risk embedded in them than commonly perceived. Therefore, lending and investment decisions depend on a broader set of economic and policy factors than commonly associated with those decisions. For example, business investment is commonly modeled as a function of expected final sales, market interest rates, and current cash flow/profitability.

However, in an environment of uncertain tax, regulatory, and credit policy, business firms would be projected to invest less given the higher level of policy uncertainty, as discussed in Chapter 5.

Given the uncertainty of economic policy, the high level of cash on hand at nonfinancial firms and households, as well as the high level of reserves held by private banks, is more understandable. As illustrated by Townsend, there is a significant cost to verification that will impact economic activity.[7]

Imperfect Information: Altered Reality

Second, the case of imperfect information—information that does not perfectly reflect reality—is often the reality facing decision makers in the current environment of administered interest rates. Administered interest rates necessarily represent imperfect information—they do not represent the forces in the marketplace, and like wage-price controls, rent controls, and usury rates, often lead to pricing distortions. These distortions make it exceedingly difficult to make proper risk-reward trade-offs.

In credit, there are the issues of adverse selection, moral hazard, and questions on the quality of bank capital in the United States, Europe, and especially China under the conditions of administered—not market-set—interest rates. Central banks around the globe are influencing short-term interest rates to remain below levels that would be present in an open, private capital market. Moreover, unconventional monetary policies can further distort market pricing.[8] Finally, there are always questions on the quality of corporate profits and market valuations under a regime of administered rates. How can an investor properly assess the benchmark risk-free interest rate, reinvestment risk, or the refinancing risk associated with any financial commitment today, given that interest rates may adjust dramatically once the era of administered rates has ended?

---

[7] Robert Townsend, "Optimal Contracts and Competitive Markets with Costly State Verification," *Journal of Economic Theory* 21 (October 1979): 265–293.

[8] See Richard Fisher, "Fed's Fisher Concerned Credit Spreads Have Narrowed Too Much," Reuters, June 30, 2014; Charles Plosser, "Fed's Plosser: If Economy Improves as Forecast, Current Taper Pace May Be Too Slow," CNBC, May 20, 2014.

Economic variables that we model are presumed to influence, or at least represent, the actual economy. However, imperfect information or unanticipated economic factors drive real-time decisions. Imperfect information on interest rates under the current monetary policy regimes—whether the current level of interest rates or the spread along the yield curve between corporate and Treasury debt—will lead a decision maker to be uncertain as to how much to attribute any interest rate change to either:

1. A change in the relative pricing of financial assets (bonds, cash, or equities),
2. A general decline in the pricing of all assets, or
3. A change as the result of a policy action to alter administered interest rates.

Therefore, this uncertain pricing will lead to a departure from output, credit, and exchange-rate pricing in an open market setting and generate changes in economic behavior that are an increasing function of the distortion and persistence of administered interest rates. For decision makers, the crucial problem is to determine how much of our current macro data may reflect activity that is the result of administered interest rates and would not occur, or in some cases would occur quite differently with different pricing, in an open market setting.

Backlash to Administered Interest Rates: False Information Cannot Deliver True Outcomes

Policy-manipulated prices cannot provide a true gauge of consumer demand nor producer supply in the marketplace. The same is true for administered interest rates. For private economic agents, if there is a sense that the current set of market interest rates, labor costs, or input prices do not accurately reflect the real cost of an economic asset, especially over time, then economic agents will not actively pursue any activity based on imperfect pricing schemes. For example, one lesson of the teaser rates of the past decade is that low interest rates today should rise, and when they do there is significant refinancing risk. Second, temporary tax cuts meant to spur hiring are short term and therefore not an incentive to hire a worker for the long term.

The hiring firm must still assess the return on the worker compared to the cost once the temporary tax credit expires. Temporary tax programs for inputs, such as for energy, will not alter the long-run cost trends, since firms that invest long-term capital cannot do so wisely based on short-term tax breaks.

Administered interest rates, independent from market fundamentals, are most evident in sovereign debt rates in two ways. First, many central banks are buying their own country's debt and holding sovereign debt at levels out of proportion with their historical position (Figure 9.18). Second, increased capital requirements, in the attempt to create financial stability, create a demand for sovereign debt on the part of private financial institutions, which assists in the buying of public debt at the risk of crowding out lending in the private market. This helps explain the continued low level of sovereign debt yields despite the outsized deficit and debt levels in many industrialized and emerging-market countries.

In policy making, the problem of imperfect information arises in two distinct paths. First, while there is one monetary policy, we often

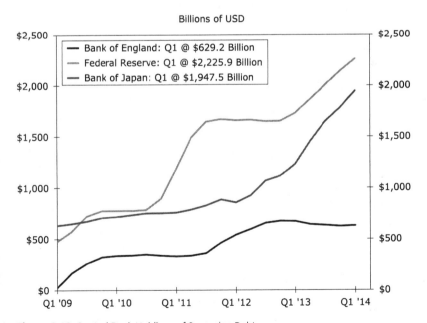

Figure 9.18 Central Bank Holdings of Sovereign Debt
Source: Federal Reserve Board, Bank of Japan, and Bank of England

hear from several different Fed speakers that create different impressions for the direction of policy. Second, the Fed is currently following a broad set of labor market indicators to determine the direction of policy. While this may make good policy, a central bank that follows multiple labor market indicators can send a confusing signal to private-sector investors. This policy-making problem is further complicated by the replacement of the initial unemployment rate guidepost of 6.5 percent by a discussion of a lower guideline and an expansion of labor market indicators. This problem is compounded even further when several different inflation guidelines are offered (core and headline inflation, consumer price index [CPI], and personal consumption expenditures [PCE]). As the adage goes, a man with one clock will know what time it is, but a man who has two clocks is never sure.

Information: Future Uncertain

Information is also dynamic over the business cycle and over time itself. For example, information on the pace of economic growth and employment growth changes over time. This changed perspective leads to alternative or regretted decisions that would have been different if economic agents did indeed have perfect foresight or perfect models of the economy. It is said that in war, battle plans change after the first shot. In recent months, the significant revisions to U.S. GDP have certainly altered perceptions of the economy's momentum and of monetary policy.

In credit markets, we have witnessed how policy benchmarks (such as the unemployment rate) have been rebenchmarked by policy makers at the Fed and the Bank of England, when the target rate was achieved more quickly in their respective countries than was initially forecasted. Moreover, the unemployment rate benchmark in the United States has been replaced with a broader set of labor market conditions due to changing underlying fundamentals, such as the participation rate. Whatever the intention of policy makers by rebenchmarking, the impact on investors and financial asset pricing will be, first, a reassessment of policy goals and, second, less specific guidance on the actions of policy makers. In both cases, information from policy makers is less than perfect in its forward guidance and, therefore, investors' mistakes are bound to occur given the fog of policy making.

During and after the Great Recession, regulatory policy making has altered the information set for investors, creditors, and borrowers. Regulators suffer from the reality that implementing new laws takes time and interpretation. Many firms exhibit a framing bias away from the risk the new rules and regulations introduce, and could put investment and credit decisions on hold in the short term.[9] This bias for risk avoidance could lead to a reduction in the supply of credit, and, thereby, a slower pace of economic growth. Indeed, this outcome came to pass in the current economic recovery as firms adjusted to new regulations like the Dodd-Frank Act, which reversed some common market behavior and standards.

Credit decisions in recent years have also been impacted by court decisions on municipal bankruptcies, corporate bankruptcies, sovereign debt and federal mandates, or simple rewrites of federal/state laws that upset the previously understood relationship between creditor and debtor. Once again, we witness the shift in preferences away from risk taking, resulting in less credit supplied and slower economic growth. Finally, recent years have witnessed shifts in sovereign government commitments to exchange rate regimes and trading agreements as one political party assumes leadership from another in a given nation. Once again, changes in exchange rate regimes or trading relationships will impact credit markets in a way that is outside the traditional fundamentals of economic growth and inflation expectations.

Asymmetric Information—The Reality of Setting Interest Rate Benchmarks

Asymmetric information is a driving force of financial market imperfections and is the product of a marketplace where parties do not have the same information. In the traditional sense, asymmetric information arises when one party to a transaction is better informed on their future actions than the other party.[10] Credit card issuers do not have as clear a picture of the credit quality or the intentions of the credit

---

[9] Silvia, 2011, 111–113.
[10] See Douglas Diamond, "Financial Intermediation and Delegated Monitoring," *Review of Economic Studies* 51 (July 1984): 393–414.

card borrower as the borrowers themselves. While generally associated with private borrowers and lenders, recent years have witnessed significant surprises from public-policy makers that have impacted the realized returns to private investors in public debt. For example, in recent years the true credit quality of sovereign debt in several countries was not well known in the marketplace.

Private investors have an incentive to acquire all relevant information on future economic conditions and policy actions. However, the literature is clear that unanticipated policy actions, not already anticipated actions, will lead to changes in economic activity.[11] Therefore, policy makers have an incentive to surprise the marketplace to generate the desired responses to public policy.

Louis XVI's continued devaluation of the public debt during his reign set the pattern of public policy surprises and reflects the power of the sovereign to alter the rules of the investment game. At first glance, sovereign debt in most countries is considered fairly safe from nominal default. However, the real value of the public debt can be devalued by inflation, currency depreciation, and new taxes on the future returns to public debt. In effect, financial repression by public-policy makers act to keep nominal interest rates low while increasing inflation, such that the real value of the debt continues to decline. For example, in the United States, inflation in much of this recovery has outpaced the level of short-term interest rates such that real returns have been negative for investors at the short end of the yield curve.

Credit Rationing: Role of Nonmarket Factors

Credit rationing represents another imperfection in the financial marketplace that often results from incomplete information—particularly in business and housing finance. When the payoff to the borrower/entrepreneur on some project exceeds a critical level, then the borrower/entrepreneur is able to pay the creditor/investor his expected return. Then, however, the creditor/investor has little incentive to

---

[11] Refet S. Gürkaynak, Brian P. Sack, and Eric T. Swanson, "The Sensitivity of Long-Term Interest Rates to Economic News: Evidence and Implications for Macroeconomic Models," *American Economic Review* 95, no. 1 (2005): 425–436.

monitor the ultimate payoff for the investment by the entrepreneur since she has already received her required return.[12] For example, if a lender makes a loan at 5 percent interest but the project actually returns 12 percent, the lender has little incentive to monitor the returns to the excess return. The lender has made her 5 percent required to return.

In contrast, if the project is not projected to yield the required minimum return of 5 percent, then credit is rationed and lending does not occur at any interest rate such as 6, 8, or 10 percent. Unfortunately, when regulatory policy is changing rapidly or is suspected to change in an uncertain way, regulatory risk will inhibit lending at any interest rate, especially to marginal credits, as witnessed during the early period of the current economic expansion.

Credit rationing leads to discontinuity in the marketplace, which is often the result of nonmarket forces acting to inhibit the proper assessment of risk/reward. This is another example where the lack of a perfectly competitive marketplace engenders interest rates to allocate capital inefficiently.

We also have the example when sovereign debt is rated as Tier 1 capital by regulatory institutions and yet the credit quality of all sovereign debt is noticeably not equal. Arbitrary ratings on sovereign debt lead to narrower spreads than would be assigned in an open, free market, which results in a misallocation of capital in global markets. We witnessed this pattern prior to the 2007–2009 recession. Sovereign debt traded at interest rate levels below what would be achieved in the private marketplace. The pricing of corporate and mortgage debt, which is often priced off Treasury debt rates, would also exhibit signs of mispricing.

Our review, so far, indicates that agency costs arising from asymmetric information raise the cost of external financing and further discourage real economic investment. In addition, financial market imperfections create agency costs that affect investment, altering the impact of anticipated final sales, profitability, and interest rate moves on investment. Policy uncertainty further alters private agents' ability to make judgments on internal/external financial options.

---

[12] David Romer, *Advanced Macroeconomics* (New York: McGraw-Hill, 2006), 421–424.

Information Complications for Policy Effectiveness

These incomplete information issues further complicate the assessment of fiscal, monetary, and regulatory policies on economic growth, inflation, interest rates, and exchange rates. Economic actors will be hesitant to react completely to new policy actions or economic information given the higher degree of uncertainty associated with incomplete information. This gives rise to the dynamic adjustment issues discussed in an earlier chapter. The result, therefore, is that predictions made on the effectiveness of policy actions, with the assumptions of a perfectly competitive marketplace, will not come to fruition in the world of incomplete, incorrect, and uncertain information.

Households and firms are uncertain on the current economic environment and suspected future policy options. Therefore, any good news would only draw a partial reaction, and, hence, economic activity delivers less than the full anticipated outcome to policy initiatives than would otherwise be projected. This has certainly been the case in the United States during the current economic recovery/expansion.

One intriguing note is that many variables that do not affect investment in perfect capital markets matter very much in an imperfect capital market. Average tax rates, idiosyncratic risk, and policy uncertainty enter the picture. The average corporate tax rate, as well as the marginal rate, impact investment by reducing the firms' ability to exploit internal finance. Risk impacts agency costs. Policy uncertainty impacts household and firms' assessments on the anticipated future returns on any contemplated economic activity.

Finally, the combination of dynamic adjustment and incomplete information gives rise to a broader set of possible economic outcomes that would not have been considered within the confines of the perfectly competitive model.

Incorrect Information—The Price of Inaccurate Information

What is the price of making economic decisions based on incorrect information? When we assume perfectly competitive markets with efficient and accurate information, we are idealizing the decision-making environment for households, firms, and investors. Unfortunately, inaccurate information on growth, inflation, and credit quality abound and may lead to decisions and economic outcomes that would not occur if we had perfectly accurate information.

Decision makers must make investments based on their reading of the economic releases that are frequently revised. In fact, the variability of the employment release, arguably the single most important monthly economic release, is notable for the significant revisions that occur in subsequent months. Measures of inflation reflect the well-meaning but arbitrary adjustments for quality changes, as well as a number of implicit price assumptions. Moreover, the existence of administered prices and direct price controls, as well as sales and excise tax changes, will alter perceptions of price trends for many economic agents. Unemployment rates come in several varieties, from U-3 to U-6, presenting the decision maker with numerous alternatives to judging the labor market, each with its own measurement problems.

Our financial system is an indicator of real investment performance and the efficient allocation of capital. However, there are many issues with judging the accuracy of information of individual and corporate credit. The experience of the 2007–2009 recession period drew out the visible flaws in credit ratings for corporations, states, and mortgage securities and denotes that credit quality differences were not accurately reflected in the credit ratings utilized by lenders and investors. Moreover, public-policy makers, through incentives and credits, alter the risk profiles of selected investments. Sometimes the proper risk is not accurately reflected in interest rate spreads. Therefore, the real market risk of a project is not recognized until too late, as we have observed with several municipal issues in recent years.

Over the long run, incorrect signals on the real risk of an investment will lead to the persistent misallocation of capital over time. Questions on the pace of real economic growth, for example, are aimed at several emerging markets today. Inflation may also be understated in many countries, including several advanced nations, since many prices are controlled by governments and accurate comparisons between nations on the pace of inflation are difficult to judge. Moreover, comparisons on real exchange rates and trade competitiveness are also difficult. Government's role in housing policy and the secondary market will cloud the assessment of the real return on housing and mortgage finance. McKinnon provides a starting point to address the relationship between economic growth and financial markets.[13]

Yield Curve Term Premium in an Administered Interest Rate Marketplace

Interest rates on long-term bonds should reflect the expected average of the interest rates on short-term bonds over its lifetime—but what happens when selected parts of the yield curve are manipulated for public policy objectives?

> The committee is prepared to increase or reduce the pace of its asset purchases to ensure that the stance of monetary policy remains appropriate as the outlook for the labor market or inflation changes.
>
> —FOMC Statement, May 1, 2013

A reduction in Fed-provided liquidity would be projected to raise short-term interest rates due to reduced liquidity in the short run and lower long-term interest rates over time as expectations for the pace of growth and inflation would decline. Yet from May to October, the yield curve steepened as 10-year Treasury yields rose relative to 2-year Treasury yields. In an environment where growth and inflation changed very little, there was a clear rise in the term premium for Treasury notes.

> The Committee decided to await more evidence that progress will be sustained before adjusting the pace of its purchases.
>
> —FOMC Statement, October 30, 2013

This halt to the threat of tapering would signal a reversal of a move to tighten policy immediately and thereby generate a flatter yield curve, which indeed is what happened initially, and yet the impact was very short-lived.

> The Committee decided to modestly reduce the pace of its asset purchase.
>
> —FOMC Statement, December 18, 2013

---

[13] Ronald McKinnon, *Money and Capital in Economic Development* (Washington, DC: The Brookings Institution, 1973).

The action to reduce liquidity over time by the FOMC would have been foreseen to flatten the yield curve as short-term rates would increase relative to long-term rates. This is what happened during the December 2013–April 2014 period. There was a clear decline in the term premium in direct contrast to the experience of May 2013–December 2013.

This peculiar period highlights the problem of many interest rate models that solely employ economic factors such as expectations and estimates for growth, inflation, deficits, and the federal funds rate as inputs. In an era of administered interest rates by the monetary authority and forward-looking financial agents, changes in interest rates will reflect changes in sentiment and Fed commentary that are difficult to catch within the traditional modeling process.

Both monetary policy and financial regulatory policy will alter the term premium in the marketplace (as well as spreads between corporate and federal debt, for example) all along the yield curve. As a result, investors cannot be certain of the real, market-setting term premium. Nor can investors be certain of how the market will react when the era of administered interest rates ends.

For example, in theory, a "permanent" increase in money growth eventually increases the short-term nominal interest rate—but investors are unsure about how long "permanent" will last. For example, investors debate today to what extent the Fed will maintain its enlarged balance sheet. The liquidity effect of easier monetary policy has reduced short-term interest rates and assisted in liquidity for the equity and bond markets as well as several emerging-market currencies. However, this effect disappears when "permanent" becomes something less. This impact of less-than-permanent monetary policy ease became evident in the sell-off in bonds and emerging-market currencies in mid-2013.

The Policy Maker's Catch-22—The Dynamic Inconsistency of Current Policy and Implications for Private Decision Makers

One of the catch-22s of policy is that anticipated, well-announced policies have little economic impact upon announcement. Kuttner finds that since 1989, there is no evidence that anticipated monetary policy moves have any impact on interest rates.[14] Therefore, there is a question of whether forward guidance has any impact on markets at all. Moreover, well-telegraphed policies, such as the Fed's tapering program, should also have little to no market impact since that policy is fully anticipated once that policy is announced.

Today, the challenge for policy makers and private-sector decision makers is that a consistent, well-telegraphed monetary policy will not move the markets. Instead, policy must surprise the marketplace to have a market impact. We witnessed this in May 2013, when Chairman Bernanke surprised markets when he indicated a tapering of large-scale asset purchases was in the offing. As a result, interest rates rose rapidly.

Moreover, Kydland and Prescott show that policy makers have an incentive not to stay with a commitment to a consistent low-inflation policy since the additional cost of slightly more inflation is perceived to be very low. Policy makers will therefore pursue an expansionary policy to achieve a greater pace of growth (and lower rate of unemployment).[15] In recent months, we have witnessed a tendency on the part of some U.S. monetary policy makers to allow for the possibility that inflation could drift above the formerly perceived 2 percent target for a while in order to achieve a higher pace of growth and a lower unemployment rate. These recent comments fit the pattern that Kydland and Prescott analyzed, where policy makers would seek a little more growth at the price of a little more inflation, but also at the expense of lowered credibility of a set 2 percent inflation target. For private-sector agents, however, there is also a problem of judging just how much and how long policy makers will accept an inflation rate above the 2 percent target.

Once economic agents anticipate a given inflation target, the policy makers, given discretion, have an incentive to allow just a bit more inflation to achieve just a bit more growth/lower unemployment rate. However, given the long-run neutrality of money, higher inflation will, over time, be met by marginally diminishing improvements in employment

---

[14] Kenneth N. Kuttner, "Monetary Policy Surprises and Interest Rates: Evidence from the Fed Funds Futures Market," *Journal of Monetary Economics* 47 (June 2001): 523–544.
[15] Finn E. Kydland and Edward C. Prescott, "Rules Rather than Discretion: The Inconsistency of Optimal Plans," *Journal of Political Economy* 85 (June 1977): 473–492.

and real growth. In addition, higher inflation also has the advantage of depreciating the real value of federal government debt. This pattern of financial repression, where inflation exceeds the administered level of nominal interest rates, will lower the real value of government debt and thereby lead to a loss of wealth by government bond holders.[16]

This dynamic inconsistency problem persists in many other areas of policy, such as financial regulation, housing, and fiscal policy, where there is an incentive for policy makers to give the appearance of a set of goals in the short run and then renege on those goals to achieve a bit more success in achieving another particular goal. In reality, the public does not know in advance whether policy makers truly share their preferences on inflation and growth—witnessed in the grand debate surrounding the initial creation of the euro and the European Central Bank, where so many Germans were skeptical that their strong anti-inflation preferences would be honored.

For the U.S.-based decision maker today, there is a great deal of uncertainty about the policy makers' trade-off between inflation and growth and, for now, there appears to be an acceptance on the part of policy makers that a little more inflation will be acceptable in order to reduce unemployment, but at the cost of debt depreciation of U.S. sovereign debt. Yet, over time, there is no long-run trade-off between inflation and unemployment.[17] Moreover, there is a worrying pattern in recent years that the unemployment rate gives the appearance of being relatively steady while the rates of inflation in consumer prices and producer prices have started to rise on a year-over-year basis. Although inflation rates may be perceived as low by some, inflation is rising and that change will lead to an uncertain degree of market response in a world of administered interest rates.

Predicting Yields—Multivariate Analysis

As U.S. Treasury yields have remained at historically low levels, it is important to consider whether the tools applied to predict yields have changed. Using historical benchmarks to perform analysis on yields

---

[16] Guillermo Calvo, "On the Time Consistency of Optimal Policy in a Monetary Economy," *Econometrica* 46 (November 1978): 1411–1428.
[17] Romer, 2006, 254–256.

may be misleading, given the permanent shift in the relationship between asset classes since the past recession. This shift can be attributed to changes in the anticipated pace of economic growth and inflation, future tax changes, and changes in the balance of and demand for Treasury debt.

When performing analysis on the yield curve, it may be more practical to look at the direction of change rather than the yield levels compared to historical norms. In addition, looking at the pattern of yield movements in other countries (specifically, the G7 countries) may be a practical tool in understanding movements in the U.S. Treasury yields. In fact, the two-way relationship between global yields and the U.S. Treasury yields implies that changes in U.S. Treasury yields can also have predictive power over global yields.

Do Global Yields Correlate with U.S. Yields?

As investors seek higher returns and safe investments, they may compare government bonds from different countries, typically the world's major economies. This raises some questions: How have global yields been affected by recessions, and more specifically, the Great Recession? Is there a correlation between the average global yield and the U.S. 10-year Treasury yield that might help explain the persistence of continued low Treasury benchmark rates?

To answer this question, we create a "global yield" proxy that is the simple average of the 10-year Treasury bond yields from the G7 countries excluding the United States.[18] To see the impact of the Great Recession on the global yield proxy, we utilize a State-Space approach to test for a structural break (Table 9.3). The results below show that in December 2008—in the midst of the Great Recession—there was a structural break in which global yields saw a downward shift.

Two-Way Causality: U.S. and Global Yields

To test whether global yields are statistically associated with the U.S. 10-year Treasury yield, we utilize the Granger causality test

---

[18] The Group of Seven (G7) consists of Canada, France, Germany, Italy, Japan, the United Kingdom, and the United States.

Table 9.3 Identifying a Structural Break Using the State-Space Approach

Global Yield		
Break Date	Type of Break	Coefficient
Dec-08	Shift	−0.37*
Oct-99	Additive	0.21*
Aug-11	Shift	−0.34*
Jul-03	Shift	0.33*
Oct-96	Shift	−0.32*

*Significant at 1 percent

(Table 9.4).[19] The Granger causality test indicates whether the global yield proxy is a statistically serviceable variable to predict movements in the U.S. 10-year Treasury yields. As shown in Table 9.4, there is two-way causality between U.S. and global yields. This indicates that both global yields and U.S. Treasury yields are statistically applicable in explaining movements in the other. Simply put, changes in the U.S. 10-year yield have an impact on the 10-year yields of other G7 countries, and vice versa.

Given the statistical association between global yields and the U.S. 10-year yield, to what extent should global yields be employed as a predictor in forecasting the U.S. 10-year Treasury yield? To determine

Table 9.4 Granger Causality Test

	Dependent variable	
Regressor	Ten-Year Yield	Global Yield
Ten-Year Yield	NA	0.10*
Global Yield	0.07*	NA

*Significant at 10 percent

---

[19] The Granger causality test identifies whether two (or more) variables statistically cause each other and thereby it is appropriate to say "Granger-causes" instead of "causes." The term *Granger-causes* implies quantifying statistical causality between the variables of interest. See Clive W. J. Granger, "Investigating Causal Relationships by Econometric Models and Cross-Spectral Methods," *Econometrica* 37 (August 1969): 424–438, for more detail.

Table 9.5 Ordinary Least Squares Estimates

10-Year Yield	RMSE	R² Value
Without Global Yield	1.01	0.50
With Global Yield	0.46	0.90

All variables in this model are significant at 1 percent

this, we utilize two different models to estimate future U.S. 10-year Treasury yields, with the results reported in Table 9.5. The first model, labeled "Without Global Yield," utilizes the unemployment rate and inflation (year-over-year change of the PCE deflator) to predict the U.S. 10-year Treasury yield. The first model produces a root mean square error (RMSE) of 1.01, which indicates that the estimated U.S. 10-year Treasury yield is, on average, off by 101 bps from the actual yield.[20]

The second model, labeled "With Global Yield," utilizes the global yield as a predictor along with the unemployment rate and inflation rate. Using the global yield, the model's forecast for the 10-year Treasury yield is, on average, 46 bps away from the actual yield. In other words, including global yields in the model cuts the level of error in half (when compared to the level of error from excluding global yields from a model). Therefore, the global yield can be applied as a useful predictor of the U.S. 10-year Treasury yield.

10-Year Treasury Behavior for Selected Countries

The 10-year Treasury yield's behavior may be different for different countries and here we test the hypothesis using data from a selected list of OECD countries. From Table 9.6, the U.S. 10-year Treasury yield has a structural break in 2008 that is consistent with the Great Recession. However, Canada's and the United Kingdom's 10-year yields did not experience breaks during the Great Recession. Instead, both coun-

---

[20] The important determinants of interest rates are inflation and unemployment rates, and that is why we include these variables in the model.

Table 9.6 Identifying a Structural Break Using the State-Space Approach

U.S. 10-Year Treasury Yields (Not Mean Reverting)		
Break Date	**Type of Break**	**Coefficient**
Sep-87	Additive Outlier	0.655
Nov-08	Level Shift	−0.945
Canada 10-Year Treasury Yields (Not Mean Reverting)		
Break Date	**Type of Break**	**Coefficient**
Mar-94	Level Shift	0.948
Sep-98	Level Shift	−0.719
U.K. 10-Year Treasury Yields (Not Mean Reverting)		
Break Date	**Type of Break**	**Coefficient**
Dec-08	Additive Outlier	−0.685
May-94	Level Shift	0.798

Estimates are significant at 1 percent

tries' 10-year yields experienced breaks during the 1990s (1994 and 1998 for Canada and 1994 for the United Kingdom).

On the other hand, Germany and Singapore's 10-year yields behavior may be consistent with U.S Treasury yields as both countries' yields show a break in 2008 (Table 9.7). The Japanese 10-year yield depicts a break during the 1990s (1990 and 1998), which is in line

Table 9.7 Identifying a Structural Break Using the State-Space Approach

Germany 10-Year Treasury Yields (Not Mean Reverting)		
Break Date	**Type of Break**	**Coefficient**
May-12	Additive Outlier	−0.431
Nov-08	Level Shift	−0.603
Japan 10-Year Treasury Yields (Not Mean Reverting)		
Break Date	**Type of Break**	**Coefficient**
Oct-90	Level Shift	−1.062
Dec-98	Level Shift	0.954
Singapore 10-Year Treasury Yields (Not Mean Reverting)		
Break Date	**Type of Break**	**Coefficient**
May-08	Level Shift	1.016
Jun-13	Level Shift	0.639

Estimates are significant at 1 percent

with the behavior of Canadian and U.K. yields. Therefore, the behavior of the Treasury yield of a country may be different compared to other countries.

Credit Spreads: A Break with History

Traditionally, credit spreads vary over the business cycle. Spreads tend to widen during periods of economic weakness or uncertainty and narrow during periods of economic prosperity. Therefore, periods of optimism can be represented by a tightening in credit spreads, while pessimism is associated with increases in spreads. These patterns reflect the dominance of cyclical forces—not secular change—and yet, secular forces may indeed be the more important driving force in interest rates since 2007.

Tradition may be taking a backseat. For analysts, the challenge is to recognize when credit spreads are at extremes and when such spreads provide a signal of a possible change in the economy, or at least sentiment on the economy. Behind the utilization of any cyclical pattern as a guideline is an implicit assumption that spreads may vary and that they will vary around the same mean value over time and over different cycles. However, how might we assess changes in sentiment as represented by credit spreads if, in fact, the average values and their volatilities vary over time?

Table 9.8 shows that credit spreads between corporate bonds and Treasury bonds have, on average, risen during the post-1982 period. In addition, standard deviations have also risen, while stability ratios have actually declined. The smaller stability ratio for the 1982–present period implies that the volatility of spreads has declined in recent years. How can we measure changes in benchmark credit spreads as a signal of possible change in the economy? Moreover, can we identify a structural change in credit spreads since 1968?

Testing for a structural break in credit spreads is crucial, as a positive finding indicates that a series has changed for a specific time period when compared to its historical norm. A break implies that a benchmark for a series—for example, the average level of volatility for a given period—has shifted compared to historical standards. In this example, we can test to determine if there has been a structural

Table 9.8 Bond Yield Statistics

	1968–1981 Average	1982-Present Average	1968–1981 Std. Dev.	1982-Present Std. Dev.	1968–1981 Stability Ratio	1982-Present Stability Ratio
Aa/5-Year Spread	0.9	1.5	0.38	0.52	40.07	33.69
Aa/10-Year Spread	1.8	2.3	0.56	0.73	31.61	31.52
Baa/5-Year Spread	1.0	2.0	0.56	0.85	56.42	41.73
Bca/10-Year Spread	1.8	2.8	0.71	1.02	39.07	36.34

Source: Bloomberg LP and Federal Reserve Board

break in a credit spread. Given a structural break, it would be misleading to employ a historical benchmark in analysis. Following a break, a benchmark may be higher or lower than the historical average.

We test for a structural break in credit spreads using the State-Space approach, with the results presented in Table 9.9. Using the results from the table, we are able to determine that yield spreads between corporate and Treasury bonds did experience a shift during the past recession (2008:Q4) that was significant at the 1 percent level. For the Aa corporate 5-year spread, there is evidence of a structural break during the Volcker period (1980:Q2) and again in 2008:Q4, the Lehman shock.

Patterns since the Great Recession: Corporate Debt Yields and Equity Earnings—Case against the Central Wisdom of Low Volatility

There may have been a shift in the relationship of returns between asset classes since the Great Recession. Typically, an increase in economic growth is associated with an improvement in earnings and a rise

Table 9.9 Identifying a Structural Break Using the State-Space Approach

Aa/5-Year Spread			Baa/5-Year Spread		
Break Date	Type of Break	Coefficient	Break Date	Type of Break	Coefficient
Q2-80	Shift	1.47*	Q4-08	Shift	2.46*
Q4-08	Shift	1.26*	Q2-80	Shift	1.87*
Q4-81	Shift	1.18*	Q4-81	Shift	1.55*
Q1-08	Shift	1.02*	Q3-09	Shift	−1.37*
Q3-09	Shift	−0.89*	Q4-74	Shift	1.30*
Aa/10-Year Spread			Baa/10-Year Spread		
Break Date	Type of Break	Coefficient	Break Date	Type of Break	Coefficient
Q2-80	Additive	0.79*	Q4-08	Shift	2.22*
Q4-08	Shift	0.99*	Q3-09	Shift	−1.51*
Q3-09	Shift	−0.86*	Q2-80	Additive	1.01*
Q3-81	Additive	−0.43*	Q4-74	Shift	1.04*
Q1-08	Shift	0.59*	Q4-81	Shift	0.96*

*Significant at 1 percent

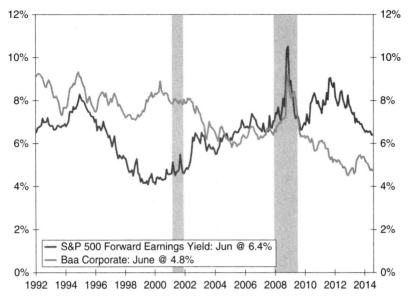

Figure 9.19 Forward Earnings and Corporate Yields
Source: Federal Reserve Board and Bloomberg LP

in interest rates. Alternatively, weak economic growth is associated with weaker earnings and a decline in bond yields. In the expansion of the 1990s, S&P 500 earnings declined along with declining Baa bond yields (Figure 9.19) as would be anticipated. However, in more recent cycles, the pattern has not always held. Earnings yields rose, while Baa yields fell in the early parts of the 2001 and 2009 expansions (2001–2003 and again during the 2009–2013 period). The Aa corporate 10-year spread repeats this pattern. In contrast, the Lehman shock appears the dominant factor in the Baa corporate 5-year spread and Baa 10-year spread. Has there been a change in the relationship between bond yields and the S&P 500 earnings yield? Is there evidence of a structural break in this relationship, particularly since the past recession?

One simple way to identify a possible shift in the relationship is to calculate the mean, standard deviation, and the stability ratio during several economic expansions. The mean for the S&P earnings yield in the most recent period (2007–2014 [Table 9.10]) exceeds the Baa corporate bond yield mean, which is different than in the first three periods. While there appears to be a shift in the mean, is there a change in volatility?

Table 9.10 S&P 500 Earnings Yield and Baa Corporate Bond Yield

Period	S&P 500 Forward Earnings Yield			Baa Corporate Bond Yield		
	Mean	Std. Dev.	Stability Ratio	Mean	Std. Dev.	Stability Ratio
1992–2014	6.55	1.24	18.9	7.11	1.20	16.9
1992–2000	6.28	1.18	18.8	8.09	0.61	7.6
2000–2007	5.77	0.92	15.9	7.12	0.87	12.2
2007–2014	7.55	0.82	10.9	6.06	1.06	17.5

Source: Bloomberg LP and Federal Reserve Board

To gauge how volatility among series may have changed over time, we can compare the stability ratios of different time periods. If the ratios of the recent period are smaller than the past, then we can conclude that volatility has declined over time. As shown in Table 9.10, the mean of the S&P 500 earnings yield was highest in the 2007–2014 period, while its standard deviation and stability ratio were both lower when compared to the other periods.

These data imply that earnings have behaved differently since the start of the Great Recession when compared to the past. The Baa corporate bond yield has the smallest mean along with a fairly large standard deviation, leading to the largest stability ratio for the 2007–2014 period compared to the past two subperiods. That is an indication of different behavior in the Baa series as well. Curiously, with a large stability ratio, this argues against the case that the recent period is one of low volatility. There appears to be confusion between a low mean value of Baa rates and their volatility.

Identifying a Structural Break

We can test for a permanent shift in the behavior of bond yields and the earnings yield by utilizing a State-Space approach. The approach shows possible additive outliers—spikes or temporary shocks—in the S&P 500 earnings yield. The Baa series shows a structural break during 2008 (Table 9.11). Again, the Lehman shock appears the most likely candidate (October 2008).

Table 9.11 Identifying a Structural Break Using the State-Space Approach

S&P 500 Earnings Yield			Baa Corporate Bonds		
Break Date	Type of Break	Coefficient	Break Date	Type of Break	Coefficient
Oct-08	Shift	1.74*	Oct-08	Shift	1.27*
Dec-08	Shift	−1.81*	Dec-08	Shift	−0.80*
Aug-11	Shift	0.95*	May-00	Additive	0.45*
May-10	Shift	0.92*	Jun-09	Shift	−0.41*
Aug-07	Additive	0.64*	Jan-08	Additive	−0.25*

*Significant at 1 percent

Possible explanations for a break in equity earnings and bond earnings are numerous. Included are potential changes in the expected pace of growth and inflation as well as future tax changes. Lowered projections for economic growth and inflation may reflect, in part, the experience of this recovery but also the impact of higher taxes and underlying changes in labor force growth and productivity. Changes in the overall balance of supply and demand of Treasury debt in the post-Lehman era may also have affected yield spreads. New capital requirements, the relative risk of European sovereign debt, and large-scale central bank purchases have increased demand for Treasury debt, while the moderately improved revenue situation of the U.S. federal government has led to lower issuance over the past few years.

CONCLUSION: SHIFT FROM HISTORICAL BENCHMARKS

As U.S. Treasury yields have remained at historically low levels, it is important to consider whether the tools utilized to predict yields have changed. Using historical benchmarks to perform analysis on yields may be misleading given the permanent shift in the relationship between asset classes since the past recession. This shift can be attributed to changes in the expected pace of economic growth and inflation, future tax changes, and changes in the balance of and demand for Treasury debt.

When performing analysis on the yield curve, it may be more productive to look at the direction of change rather than the yield levels compared to historical norms. In addition, looking at the pattern of yield movements in other countries (specifically, the G7 countries) can be exploited in understanding movements in the U.S. Treasury yields. In fact, the two-way relationship between global yields and the U.S. Treasury yields implies that changes in U.S. Treasury yields can also have predictive power over global yields.

CHAPTER 10

Three-Dimensional Checkers

Open Economy, Capital Flows, and Exchange Rates

Since the Great Recession, the importance of global capital flows and foreign economic policy has become increasingly relevant to financial (bond and equity) and real (real estate) asset prices across many countries. In a traditional view, a country's economy may be viewed primarily as a stand-alone subject. That country can grow at a pace determined by internal forces (demographics, economic policies, or regulatory change) unless acted upon by an external force. Economic policy is conducted on primarily a domestic basis. In this way, some analysts would follow the path of Isaac Newton's first law: an individual object will continue to move in a state of constant velocity unless acted upon by an external force. Unfortunately, for the domestic-centric analyst, Newton did not stop there.

NEWTON'S THIRD LAW

Newton's third law, instead, focused on the interactions between different bodies (e.g., the United States and other nations) and that there is no such thing as a unidirectional force, or a force that acts on only one body. The evolution of commentary by the Federal Open Market Committee (FOMC) with respect to "global economic and financial developments" is exhibit number one.[1] Whenever a first body (the U.S. economy) exerts a force on a second body (the global economy), the second body also exerts a force back on the first body. In a manner similar to Newton, and despite the urging of Aristotle, there is no natural state of rest for the economy. Instead, the economy is a continually evolving system. Outside the textbook, there is no obvious set of equilibrium values for growth and inflation that would generate a stable path for asset prices. So begins our journey.

Economic growth, measured by gross domestic product (GDP), is not a fixed equilibrium value, but a series of values along the way. Economics is a study of unbalanced forces acting within this evolving system. Our recognition of these forces includes the partial adjustment of both prices and quantities, the role of expectations and the differential speeds of adjustment for prices, exchange rates, and capital flows

---

[1] See the statement from the September 16–17, 2015, FOMC meeting and how the language on global economic and financial developments evolved over subsequent meetings.

for different countries. Our challenge as decision makers is that often we are so anxious to get the answer that we ignore the path to get there. Yet, it is the path, the distance between equilibrium points, that allows us to answer questions under different circumstances rather than attempting to build a decision strategy that performs under only one set of limited assumptions. Under way here is a closer examination of those assumptions and the workings of the economic model, so that we can appreciate the journey and just how sensitive the projection of economic growth is to the method of analysis.

The Open Economy: A Complex System of Many Moving Parts

For the United States, our economic framework is that of a large, open economy that must include the potential influences of economic and policy changes in foreign countries.[2] Capital mobility and a floating exchange rate are characteristics of our U.S. financial framework. Owing to these two market characteristics and generally market-determined interest rates, we judge our central bank as an independent institution. The central bank is independent not only in the political sense, but also in the economic sense given its ability to set policy without significant institutional constraints such as the legal one-target inflation restrictions as imposed on several central banks such as New Zealand.[3]

Under such a monetary/financial regime, an easing of monetary policy would typically lead to a decline in interest rates and an expansion in economic growth and incomes. Ceteris paribus, we would also suspect, under a flexible exchange rate regime, a weaker dollar and capital outflows from the United States. But all other factors are not constant. This is what makes our economy so dynamic and what excites us in the challenge of economic analysis.

While monetary policy is one factor that influences asset prices, there is also fiscal policy. In recent years, we have witnessed U.S. fiscal policy turn restrictive in terms of the pace of spending growth, which

---

[2] John E. Silvia, *"Dynamic Economic Decision Making"* (Hoboken, NJ: John Wiley & Sons, 2011).
[3] This reflects the work of Robert Mundell and Marcus Fleming on domestic policy under alternative fixed and flexible exchange rates. See Rudiger Dornbusch, *Open Economy Macroeconomics* (New York: Basic Books, 1980), Chapters 10 and 11.

would evoke a decline in aggregate demand, prices, and interest rates, as well as a weaker dollar. That expectation turned out to be only partially correct, as we only saw interest rates decline, while aggregate demand, prices, and the dollar exchange rate have continued to rise. Finally, beyond the patterns of economic policy, there is the underlying flow of economic activity that reflects the factors of labor force growth and productivity gains.

Outside the Frictionless Economic Model

Yet these stylized results are within the context of a perfectly smooth economic system. In reality, we do not have that perfectly functioning system. Instead, our work in this book has consistently emphasized the existence of partial adjustment mechanisms, imperfect information, and the operation of an economy with no real set of "equilibrium" conditions.

Since 2008, easier monetary policy has been the primary means to achieve faster growth in the U.S. economy. This policy has produced lower interest rates and helped provide for the basis of improved economic output. Lower interest rates reduced the burden of financing real estate and raised the valuation of both bond and equity assets. Yet the gains in housing have been less than many anticipated given the decline in interest rates. In part, this has been due to the greater regulatory constraint on lending institutions, which reflects the many factors not accounted for in a perfectly functioning, purely private-sector model. Meanwhile, financial markets, especially the equity market, are said to have climbed a wall of worry. Why?

International capital flows and their impact on asset prices are central to understanding the global framework that we accept would more accurately represent the actual conduct of economic activity and helps explain U.S. equity and fixed-income market behavior.

We focus on several points. First, economic activity reflects the impact of the change in relative forces/prices that mimics Newton's third law—and the choices households and business make in response to changes in those forces. Second, the economy is in constant motion and not at an equilibrium point. There is no Aristotelian natural state here. As a result, even when the domestic U.S. economy may give an appearance of balance, foreign shocks, such as the 2011–2012 euro sovereign debt crisis or the collapse of global oil prices since mid-2014, lead to changes in the domestic economic and financial activity. There is a duality of internal-external economic conditions that moves markets.

Another central theme to the analysis is that economic activity does not fully adjust to a new equilibrium—instead, economic activity reflects a series of partial adjustments given the constraints of imperfect information and the frictions associated with labor and capital. Moreover, as we have previously noted, different economic actors, such as workers and employers, exhibit differential speeds of adjustment for prices and exchange rates and this gives rise to a cyclical pattern in profits.[4] Finally, the role of exchange rate expectations remains critical, especially in the world of financial assets—equity and bond valuations reflect the expected future, not past, returns for these assets.

Looking at the World We Have

Let's return again to our fundamentals of disequilibrium and dynamic and partial adjustment under conditions of imperfect information, and the importance of expectations in the economy. The entire period of 2005 to the present (2016) has been characterized by a sense of disequilibrium in the economy. As the economy was characterized by a housing bubble prior to 2007, a real expansion was followed by an economic bust, a long period of persistent high unemployment, slow recovery in housing starts, and subpar aggregate income growth. Contrary to the perfectly competitive conditions of economic theory, households, and businesses do not have perfect foresight on the effectiveness of monetary/fiscal policy or the underlying pace of the real economy. As a result, households and businesses have made only a partial adjustment to the change in expectations.

In a repeat of the experience of 2002–2004, the initial monetary policy easing post-2008 did not lead to an immediate economic recovery. This led many analysts to question the traditional effectiveness of monetary policy. In addition, fiscal policy was initially extremely

---

[4] John E. Silvia, "Corporate Profits: Reward, Incentive and the Standard of Living," *Wells Fargo Economics*, September 26, 2014.

expansionary with the 2009 stimulus program. However, a significant share of that program was not well directed and much of the program was spread out over time. Again, the impact of economic policy actions was less than anticipated. Finally, there was no perfect information about the potential change in the underlying trend growth of the economy as well as the impact of increased regulatory structures on the financial system. In recent years, the concern about labor force participation and its impact on potential growth has moved to center stage.

Dynamic adjustment is exemplified by the gradual and sometimes stop-and-go movements of households and business decision makers. While the economy improved on many fronts, individuals have been hesitant, as evidenced by the gradual improvement in consumer confidence (Figure 10.1). For businesses, confidence surveys indicate that business sentiment is not back to prerecession levels (Figure 10.2). Both the National Federation of Independent Business (NFIB) and Wells Fargo indices denote a long period of below-average business confidence and only a slow recovery back toward prior heights. Finally,

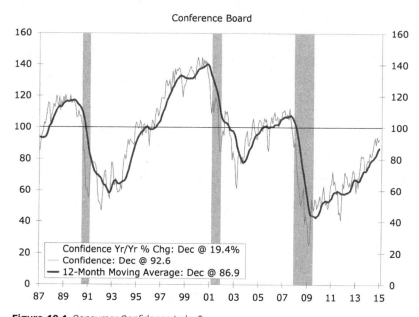

Figure 10.1 Consumer Confidence Index®
Source: The Conference Board, Inc. Reprinted with permission of The Conference Board. For more information, please see www.conference-board.org. Consumer Confidence Index is a registered trademark of The Conference Board, Inc.

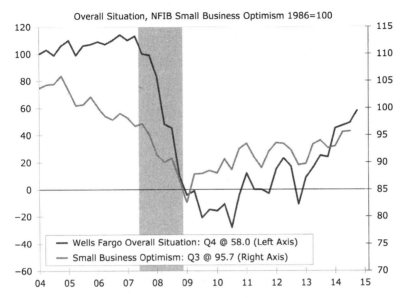

Figure 10.2 Wells Fargo Small Business Survey and NFIB
Sources: NFIB, Gallup, and Wells Fargo Bank, N.A.

policy uncertainty provides a basis for understanding the lack of follow-through effects from fiscal and monetary policy since 2008.

Money and credit expansion by the Federal Reserve did lead to a decline in interest rates and an expansion in income, but these patterns did not immediately lead to the expected real results in the economy. Imbalances persisted, including excess unemployment in the labor market, strong capital inflows in the currency market (despite the low interest rates) and a rising dollar (again despite a lower interest rate regime for short-term securities). In a frictionless model, when interest rates decline we should witness currency outflows and a weaker currency. However, even in a frictionless model we witness capital outflows and exchange rate depreciation if other economies cut interest rates more on a relative basis. Exchange rate depreciation would reduce the relative price of domestic goods, raise the demand for domestic output, and thus national income would expand. This would increase the demand for financial assets (money, equity, and bond assets) and thereby alter their respective values. The relative improvement in the balance of trade via exchange rate depreciation should raise domestic output and employment.

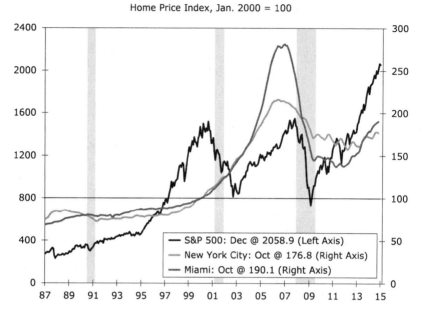

Figure 10.3 S&P Case-Shiller Home Price Index vs. Equity Prices
Sources: Bloomberg LP and S&P CoreLogic Case-Shiller

However, in the United States' case, easier monetary policy was accompanied by lower short-term interest rates as expected, but what was unanticipated were the greater capital inflows and rising currency values. The capital inflows led to rising asset valuations for equities, bonds, and real estate (Figure 10.3).

But in economics, unbalanced forces bring further change—and the seven years following the recession have witnessed a continuous set of unbalanced changes both internally and externally among countries. Whatever depreciation we have witnessed for the euro and Japanese yen has not been accompanied by an economic recovery in each region and has not led to an outperformance of financial assets in each region relative to the United States (Figure 10.4). Initially during the current economic expansion, easier monetary policy in the United States led to lower interest rates, dollar appreciation, stronger capital inflows, and rising asset values for equities, bonds, and real estate. Yet even with the switch to tighter U.S. monetary policy relative to continued easier policy abroad, we have witnessed lower U.S.

Index, Jan. 1990 = 100

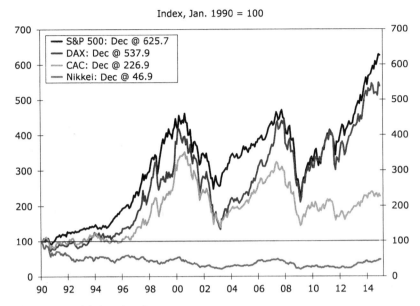

Figure 10.4 Global Equity Prices
Source: Bloomberg LP

long-term rate and rising asset values for both bonds and equities. Positive financial market reactions to both easier and tighter U.S. monetary policy signals the complexity of markets and their reading of economic fundamentals.

INTRODUCING A NEW PRICE TO THE ANALYSIS:
THE ROLE OF EXCHANGE RATES

Today, what makes the global influence on asset prices so different is the rapid change in the relative price of domestic and foreign currencies with significantly different economic policy expectations. The rapid alteration in policy expectations sets up a rapid change in exchange rates given the uncertainty of the pace and character of growth/inflation combinations across nations. These rapid changes and their effects are compounded by the differential speeds of adjustment, with the North American economies picking up speed while European and Japanese economies continue to lag. This creates a tension between expectations for monetary policies, different fiscal policies, interest rates, and patterns of exchange rates in these economies.[5]

Therefore, the exchange rates and expectations of future values become an additional price in the global context along with interest rates and inflation, which influence economic growth.

National growth trends are a function of the interest rate and the real exchange rate, but the role of the exchange rate is often overlooked in terms of its influence on domestic asset prices. Appreciation of the domestic currency would be expected to reduce aggregate demand for domestic goods while a decline in domestic interest rates leads to a positive impact on domestic demand and output. There is an internal-external duality in interest rates and exchange rates where both factors influence, and are influenced by, domestic and foreign developments.

For the European and Japanese situations, currency depreciation and lower interest rates did not lead to asset price increases and the aggregate pace of economic growth remains subpar. In contrast, lower rates and currency appreciation in the U.S. accompanied asset price inflation and continued economic growth. Moreover, U.S. short-term rates on two- and three-year Treasury debt actually rose, yet equity and real estate asset prices, along with the total return on longer-term Treasury and high-grade debt, continued to rise in 2014. Meanwhile, the dollar continued to appreciate as capital flows remained positive. However, we must note that the continued appreciation in the U.S. dollar is not necessarily just a function of capital inflows to the United States alone, but also the large divergence in monetary policy between the Federal Reserve, the European Central Bank, and the Bank of Japan.

To further complicate the issue, domestic U.S. interest rates have not equalized to the global level of interest rates contrary to the theoretical implication that real global interest rates should tend to equalize through capital flows and exchange rates. Instead, recent years have witnessed a persistent gap in real interest rates as well as real economic growth and a rising U.S. dollar.

---

[5] Axel Weber, "Prepare for the Tremors as Europe and America Drift Apart," *Financial Times*, June 2, 2014.

Exchange rate expectations for the future matter a great deal for financial and real asset holders who will react to international differentials in anticipated asset returns adjusted for expected exchange rate movements. This observation reinforces the importance of the principle that asset prices today will react to anticipated future differentials in expected returns and changes in the expected movements in exchange rates as well. Asset markets are in constant disequilibrium as analysts must allow for interest rates, exchange rates, and asset price adjustments whenever either domestic or foreign economies deviate from full employment. During this economic recovery, the linkage of interest rates, exchange rates and capital flows in an integrated world capital market have become a driving influence in the path of asset prices.

Figure 10.5 provides a picture of the volatility of foreign purchases of U.S. securities. Corporate debt was clearly the favorite prior to the Great Recession, but then the flight to quality supported the move to U.S. Treasury debt. Meanwhile, agency and equity debt exhibits

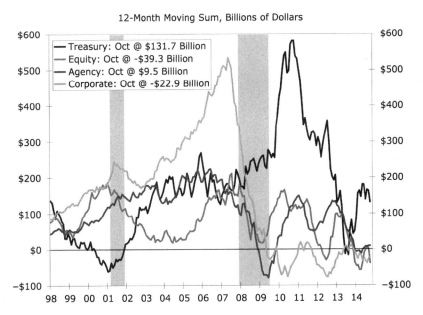

Figure 10.5 Foreign Private Purchases of U.S. Securities
Source: U.S. Department of the Treasury

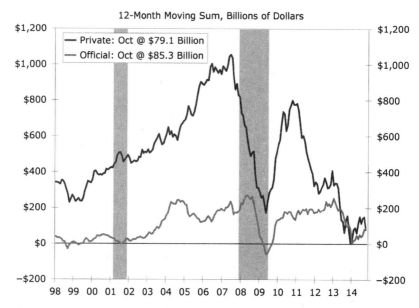

Figure 10.6 Foreign Purchases of U.S. Securities
Source: U.S. Department of the Treasury

separate patterns of volatility. In Figure 10.6, we can see that foreign private purchases of all U.S. securities are highly volatile. This stands in contrast to the relative stability of foreign official purchases, even though it is the volatility of official purchases that receives the lion's share of publicity.

Foreign portfolio holdings of U.S. securities are also a bit surprising. The size of the holdings of long-term debt by Japan and China is expected by many (Figure 10.7). But for all the other jurisdictions, ex-Belgium, the large share of securities held as equity may be surprising. Places such as the Cayman Islands (C.I.), Canada, and the United Kingdom have a greater share of their holdings in equities. The allocations of Switzerland, Luxembourg, and the Middle East are more even.

U.S. capital flows exhibit significant volatility but also a distinct downshift since 2006–2007 and again after 2010 (Figure 10.8). Private portfolio holdings and other private holdings have diminished since 2007.[6]

---

[6] Jay H. Bryson, Nick Bennenbroek, and Zachary Griffiths, "The Structure of U.S. Capital Flows and the Dollar," *Wells Fargo Economics*, May 28, 2014.

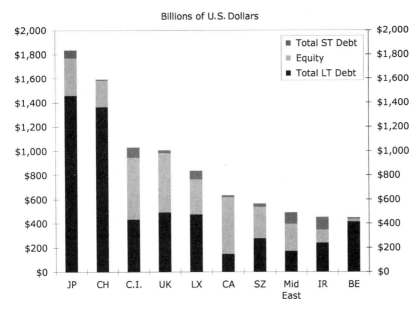

Figure 10.7 Foreign Portfolio Holdings of U.S. Securities
Source: U.S. Department of the Treasury

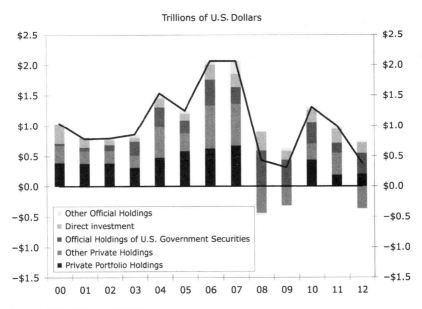

Figure 10.8 U.S. Capital Inflows
Source: U.S. Department of the Treasury

The Rising Visibility of Foreign Economic Policy

Foreign monetary policy has become an increasingly important channel driving U.S. asset prices. Changes in expectations of foreign monetary policy have become a factor on their own, independent of an actual change in policy. Changes in policy expectations act as shocks much the same as any exogenous economic shock such as an oil price spike.

For example, note the recent volatility in expectations of the European Central Bank, where weak responses to easier policy led to increased expectations for further policy easing.[7] In another recent article, foreign investors were portrayed as piling into U.S. Treasury debt due to the "broad demand for safe government debt amid global turmoil and uneven economic growth."[8]

The list of economic shocks includes changing expectations of fiscal policy in the Eurozone, alterations of economic goals in China, and the on again/off again Japan consumption tax along with easing by the Bank of Japan. As evidenced by this litany, foreign economic policy, as well as U.S. domestic economic policy, contains a significant degree of policy uncertainty and these actions, or lack of action, affect not only the pace of economic activity but also the volatility of activity.

Imperfect Capital Mobility—A Constraint to Equilibrium and an Invitation to Volatility

Beyond the actions of public and private policy makers, market structure is also a source of frictions in the economy. Financial regulation and the consequent market structure from such regulation limits the flow of capital into countries and investment into the various possible set of real and financial assets. These frictions reinforce the message that the realities of the marketplace contrast with the models of perfectly smooth-functioning capital markets that drive many predictions of future asset values.

---

[7] Todd Buell and Brian Blackstone, "Weak Demand for Loans Raises Hope for ECB Stimulus," *Wall Street Journal*, December 11, 2014.
[8] Min Zeng, "Foreign Investors Pile Into Bonds," *Wall Street Journal*, December 15, 2014.

To begin, many central banks take actions to alter the market determination of exchange rates. Second, countries differ by their level of sophistication in their capital markets. For example, sovereign debt is a significant portion of private bank assets in Europe and this led to further complications when such sovereign debt was downgraded and asset values deteriorated. This limited the extent of economic recovery in Europe, reinforcing the message that the impact of monetary and fiscal policy actions is limited by the character of the marketplace in which such actions occur. Capital flows are clearly limited in cases, such as China, where the currency is not convertible. In cases such as the United States and Europe, increasing capital requirements for private banks have the result of redirecting funds away from funding private activity to funding public debts. Along these lines, there remains the legacy of legal risk associated with prior action associated with the 2008–2009 Great Recession. In the marketplace, the existence of all these regulatory frictions results in a misallocation of credit away from the allocation that would be determined in the private marketplace and gives rise to dead weight losses in the economy.

Asset price movements reflect the framework of an exceedingly complex, imperfect marketplace. Capital flow frictions, the uncertainty of future policy actions, and differential speeds of adjustment make long-term economic projections, within the context of short-term horizons of the next election, enormously difficult. These limited forecast horizons and heavily discounted future returns would tend to discourage longer-term investment projects. As a result, asset prices would be anticipated to be lower and more volatile in such a context. Moreover, asset prices would not tend to equalize across countries. Interest rate differentials would persist and a less efficient allocation of capital across countries would continue over time.

THREE-DIMENSIONAL CHECKERS ON AN INTERNATIONAL PLAYING FIELD

In an attempt to stimulate the Japanese economy, the Bank of Japan (BOJ) lowered benchmark policy rates on January 26, 2016, but after the immediate reaction, the Japanese yen appreciated versus the dollar, taking the exchange rate to a level commensurate with the period before the BOJ announced increased asset purchases back in October 2014.

Traditionally, lower interest rates, certainly negative rates, would be associated with a weaker currency and yet that is not what happened. A weaker yen would be expected to boost exports and thereby GDP, as well as raise import prices and inflation. However, there was no weaker yen. Instead the value of the yen rose after the BOJ's actions, flat growth continued and prices fell.

Here is a classic example of the complexity of interest rates, exchange rates, and capital flows. Ceteris paribus, those pesky other economic factors have altered the simplistic one-dimensional link from interest rates to the currency. First, owing to its safe haven and funding currency status, the yen improved during periods of uncertainty as was true at the start of this year (Figure 10.9). However, until at least February 11, there was significant concern about China and global equity weakness, a factor that likely supported the

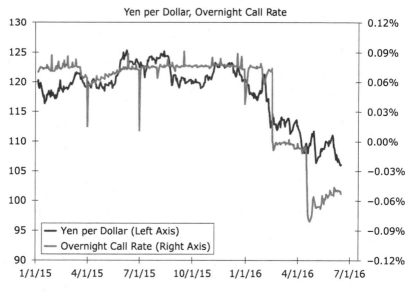

Figure 10.9 Japanese Interest Rates and Currency
Source: Bloomberg LP

yen as a low interest and funding currency. Second, less hawkish comments by the Federal Reserve likely also restrained the U.S. dollar against many currencies, including the yen. Third, the Bank of Japan's easing was a tentative step into negative interest rate territory. The negative rate was set to just –0.10 percent, and applies to only 5 to 10 percent of Japanese banks' cash holdings at the central bank. By contrast, the European Central Bank's –0.40 percent deposit rate applied to approximately 85 percent of European banks' cash holdings. That is, Japan's negative interest rate was less deep and less broad, and may explain why its negative impact on the currency was less consequential. Related to that point, even though Japan's policy rate turned negative, interbank interest rates remained positive. The 1-week Tokyo Interbank Offered Rate (TIBOR) fell, but remained positive (Figure 10.10).

Such are the mysteries of interest rates, exchange rates, and capital flows. In a like manner, the comments by Mario Draghi, head of the European Central Bank, to "do whatever it takes" was followed by an appreciation of the euro against both the British pound and the

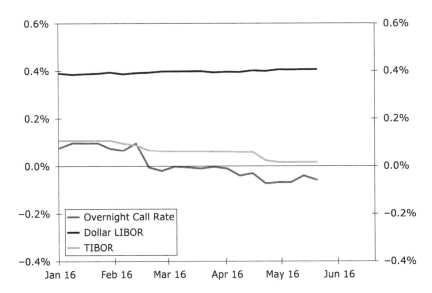

Figure 10.10 Japanese Money Markets
Source: Bloomberg LP

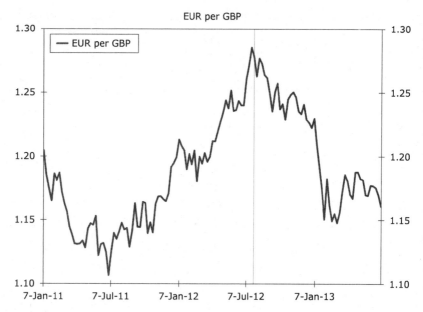

Figure 10.11 European Currencies
Source: Bloomberg LP

U.S. dollar (Figure 10.11).[9] Draghi's pronouncement had two impacts. First, and the most important, was the verbal signal to the market that the currency union would stay together. Second, the prospect of easier monetary policy by Draghi provided a second channel for improved expectations of a better economic performance relative to earlier concerns of recession/deflation. These two channels contributed to the appreciation of the euro relative to earlier pessimistic euro expectations.

A PERFECT MODEL IN AN IMPERFECT WORLD

In any election year, especially 2016, the politics of international economic relations is front and center. Claims of manipulated exchange rates through central bank interest rate changes and directed or limited capital flows are prevalent. Yet, as an alternative, model-based policy prescriptions strike a thoughtful analyst as having limited ability to achieve real world goals given the imperfections in global financial

[9] Mario Draghi as quoted in an Associated Press article, "Draghi Promise to Save Euro Triggers Market Rally," July 12, 2012.

markets as witnessed by both the BOJ and European Central Bank (ECB) interventions.

The daily tensions in the current economic and political environment, both domestic and global, raise the risk factor for decision makers. Discussions revolve around notions of competitive devaluations, concerns about currency and monetary policy manipulation to gain competitive trade advantage in a global economy, and fair, as opposed to free, trade.

Global financial markets provide one interesting backdrop for policy prescriptions in an election year. Yet while the vision is one of perfectly competitive markets, the stuff of real life is awkward, muddled, and far from perfect.

Three Challenges

Our perfect market model faces three challenges. First, information is imperfect, not only for the economic data but particularly for policy maker intentions. A persistent challenge in recent years is that the pace of inflation has actually turned out to be much below policy maker and market expectations, while the impact of policy actions has also delivered real economic growth below expectations.

Second, exchange rate and interest rate adjustments are not instantaneous and often drag out over time. Moreover, dynamic adjustments may also be delayed or diminished by financial and economic regulations that inhibit markets from reacting quickly to initial economic shocks. Therefore, there can be a period of persistent disequilibrium in the marketplace. We will see this below in the Plaza/Louvre examples. Third, price adjustments are far from uniform across sectors and often contradictory to our initial expectations as illustrated by recent exchange rate/interest rate actions.

For decision makers, the importance of these issues is illustrated vividly in the figures below. International revenues for the S&P 500 equities (Figure 10.12) are significant, particularly so for sectors such as information technology, materials, and health care. Therefore, equity market valuations will be impacted by all three challenges relative to economic expectations. We saw earlier the volatility of private capital inflows into U.S. financial assets. The rapid expansion of capital flows

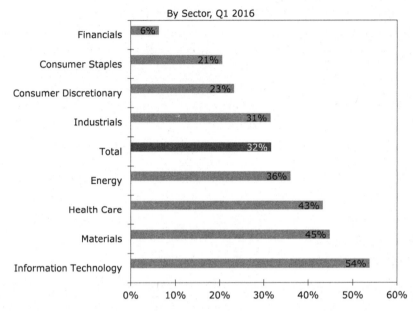

Figure 10.12 Percent of S&P Revenues Earned Abroad
Source: Bloomberg LP

post-2008 was followed by a slowdown and then another increase during the challenges of the euro crisis of 2012. This pattern of financial flows provides a significant impact on the values of U.S. financial assets and once again the ability of domestic firms to finance economic activity.

The experience of the Plaza and Louvre accords of the 1980s provide a glimpse into the challenge of a view of market-determined exchange rates and dynamic adjustment in the marketplace in the context of discrete policy actions. Domestic U.S. producers were unhappy about the large and ongoing current account deficits for the U.S. in the mid-1980s. However, the policy reaction in Washington was not immediate. At the time, exchange rate policy favored leaving currency markets to set exchange rates and was termed *benign neglect*.[10] Yet over time, political pressures overcame market philosophy as benign neglect with respect to dollar's value was dropped in September 1985.

---

[10] "American Economic Policy in the 1980s," *National Bureau of Economic Research Book*, January 1994.

The decision to intervene reflected a change in policy makers' reaction function, in part due to political pressures. Policy makers then adopted a proactive stance. This outcome reflects the evolution of a public-policy agenda that finds market results unfriendly.

To appreciate the implications of our three challenges to market and policy processes, we now turn to the perfect market model and the workings and results implied by such a model.

A Model for Policy—Not the Real World

Our model structure begins with three assumptions. First, the money stock is the driving force for economic activity and is under the control of the monetary authority. Second, there is a floating exchange rate regime. Third, the balance of payments is indeed balanced.

In the case of a small country (one in which the country does not set the benchmark for global interest rates), a monetary expansion is effective in the sense that an expansionary monetary policy raises output. This effective policy operates through two channels. First, the monetary expansion alters the relative price of domestic goods versus foreign goods. Second, the monetary expansion alters the relative interest rates between countries and, in an integrated world, capital markets lead to changes in global rates, exchange rates, and capital flows.

In our model, output is a function of interest rates and real exchange rates. A real depreciation of a currency raises demand for domestic goods as global demand for a country's output rises. Meanwhile, a rise in interest rates leads to a fall in demand and output. Within the monetary sector of the economy, real money demand depends on real income and the rate of interest. To close the model, we require that the domestic rate of interest equals the given rate of interest in the world.

How does our idealized model work? A monetary expansion results in a rise in real money balances since prices are sticky in the short run. This channel highlights the importance of both the dynamic adjustment and price adjustment assumptions. With the rise in real balances, the market adjusts by a fall in interest rates and thereby an expansion of income.

At this point, there is disequilibrium as domestic interest rates are now below global rates, which will produce a capital outflow, a balance of payments deficit, and thereby lead to exchange rate depreciation. In turn, exchange rate depreciation lowers the relative price of domestic goods, leading to an increased demand for domestic production; income grows to restore monetary equilibrium at the world interest rate. The trade balance improves due to the relative decline in the price of domestic goods and consequently imports. The result is a monetary expansion that increases output through improvement in the balance of trade.

In a perfectly competitive economy, we can define internal balance as an economy at full employment in the labor market. For external balance, the balance of payments reflects the influence of the flexible exchange rate structure. The current account balance serves as the target in a free market model—a contrast from the persistent surplus/deficit positions of countries in the current global economy. Under that current system, a country aims neither to borrow nor lend excessively from abroad.

In addition, we have an asset market equilibrium that will be altered when interest rates are not equalized across countries. In this case, there is another dynamic adjustment critical to market prices. As a rule, the differential between interest rates between countries will be offset by anticipation of exchange rate appreciation/depreciation between currencies. Investors are considered to be indifferent between similar securities (denominated in domestic/foreign currency) if the differential in interest rates is exactly offset by the expected exchange rate change.

An interesting result here is that interest rates in the home country are no longer fixed as a change in interest rates abroad implies a change in domestic rates as well. Domestic interest rates are low relative to foreign rates if the market expects an exchange rate appreciation of the domestic currency. In contrast, the domestic interest rates are high relative to foreign rates if the exchange rate is expected to depreciate. This result helps explain the persistent low interest rates in Japan/United States, while the yen/dollar appreciates, and the persistently high interest rates in some emerging markets, such as Brazil, as its exchange rate is expected to depreciate.

Expectations of appreciation/depreciation reflect the difference between the perceived long-run equilibrium rate and current actual exchange rate. In the perfectly competitive model, we have three economic conditions at equilibrium. First, the money supply will equal money demand. Second, interest rates will adjust for depreciation/appreciation and be equated internationally. Finally, expectations will be a function of the discrepancy between the long-run and current exchange rate. For example, if the current exchange rate is above the perceived long-run equilibrium exchange rate, then interest rates will decline. In contrast, if the actual exchange rate is below the long-run exchange rate, then interest rates will rise.

There is also a dynamic aspect to the adjustment process. The rate of adjustment of prices in an economy depends on the structural links in the economy as well as how expectations are formed. For example, the actual rate of depreciation of a currency is proportional to the discrepancy between the long-run equilibrium value of the exchange rate and its current value. The speed of adjustment depends on the responsiveness of real and monetary factors to the change in interest rates.

The perfectly competitive global financial market that frames the vision many observers have of global markets begins with three simple assumptions—all of which are violated daily in the practice of markets and policy decisions.

Sharp adjustments in exchange rates, capital flows, and long-term interest rates are often not set in the marketplace by changes in economic fundamentals but by discrete policy changes at the national level. We now turn to the implications of these violations and how to identify them in empirical work.

Violation of Three Conditions for Perfect Competition

First, there is imperfect information on both the policy and underlying economic model. We have already examined the role of imperfect information in economic factors such as growth, inflation, and consumer spending. There is also imperfect information about the intents of policy makers—what is their policy reaction function?

In 2015 and early 2016, central banks in both the euro area and Japan have engaged in surprise policy actions within a very imperfect global marketplace and produced counterintuitive results for capital flows and inflation. Experience in both the euro and yen situations cited earlier are the product of notably different conditions than what the traditional perfectly competitive model would indicate. The Bank of Japan went to negative rates and yet the yen revalued upward. As for the Swiss National Bank, it altered its reaction function by dropping the peg to the euro and adopting negative interest rates.

Swiss Interest and Exchange Rates: Policy-Maker Shifts and the Lack of Mean Reversion

Interactions between exchange and interest rates for Switzerland illustrate the importance of international factors in determining domestic interest rates. As illustrated in Figure 10.16, the depreciation of the Swiss franc during the 2005–2007 period accompanied the rise of the three-month London Interbank Offered Rate (LIBOR). In contrast, beginning in 2009, the rapid decline in the three-month LIBOR was accompanied by a steady appreciation of the Swiss franc. From mid-2011 to the start of 2015, the Swiss National Bank (SNB) target exchange rate was associated with a steady LIBOR.

At the start of 2015, the SNB decoupled from the target and the Swiss franc immediately appreciated relative to the euro. The shift in policy makers' response function away from an exchange rate target highlights the importance of the third factor—capital flows.

Swiss Delinking and the Lack of Mean Reversion

One recent surprise to the markets was the revaluation of the Swiss franc (CHF) via a delinking to the euro in early 2015. Without any obvious immediate change in economic fundamentals, the SNB likely perceived the ability to maintain the link was not sustainable.

Beginning in 2008, economic fundamentals supported an exchange rate adjustment in favor of a steady Swiss franc appreciation. Yet from 2011 until the end of 2014, the link between the Swiss franc and euro was maintained. However, the underlying economic fundamentals continued to erode the economic rationale for the link. After the delinking in early 2015, the Swiss/euro rose about 10 percent higher by the end of 2015 compared to 2011–2014 levels.

There is also imperfect information in the real economy, as evidenced by the link from exchange rates to trade. The distinction here is between the real versus nominal exchange rates—a distinction lost in public and many professional discussions. The nominal exchange rate states how much of one currency can be traded for a unit of another currency. In contrast, the real exchange rate is a measure of price competitiveness. That is, the real exchange rate measures the prices of goods and services in one country when converted to the prices of goods and services in another country.

The problem of interpretation arises when the prices of goods and services in one country rise relative to the other country and that relative price change is not offset, often by deliberate public policy, by a compensatory change in the nominal exchange rate. In that case, the price competitiveness of the first country erodes relative to the second country. Consequently, the export volumes of the first country tend to decline while its import volumes tend to rise. Nominal exchange rates are the focus of market and decision makers and yet real exchange rates are the drivers of competitiveness and the trade balance.

Imperfect Information and Price/Policy-Maker Discovery

Decision makers face two problems of imperfect information. First, the current indications of nominal interest rates and exchange rates may not reflect market forces and would be distorted by administered interest rates and targeted exchange rates by sovereign authorities. As a result, capital flows between countries are driven by a distorted set of interest rate/exchange rate combinations. Second, the current model for policy making is unclear.

Imperfect information creates problems where market price signals may not reflect the economic tradeoff between alternative investments or exchange rates. Financial markets may also have truly poor information about the policy framework and intentions of policy makers—the market shocks due to the SNB delinking the Swiss franc from the euro, as well as the surprise BOJ move to negative rates in January 2016 and then surprising the markets by not moving at all in April. Even earlier, we contemplate the market disruptions associated with the U.K. withdrawal from the European Exchange Rate Mechanism (ERM) on September 16, 1992.

Imperfect Price Signals

When interest rates and exchange rates do not accurately reflect market forces, there is a misallocation of economic resources. Administered prices, either in the form of interest rates or exchange rates, create uncertainty and instability in the short run and set up the conditions for significant economic crises in the long run. The attempt by both the United States and the United Kingdom in the 1960s to maintain a parity of currencies to gold proved untenable in the face of fundamental changes in the economy.[11]

In the case of interest rates, the attempt by central governments to maintain a set of interest rates below market equilibrium rates sets up the situation referred to as financial repression. When interest rates, particularly short-term rates, are set below market rates, then the return to savers is depressed and thereby results in a redistribution of income away from savers to debtors. In the aftermath of WWII, real interest rates were kept arbitrarily low for both U.S. and U.K. debt, which reduced the real burden of debt for the government at the expense of savers. This program in the United States prompted the Federal Reserve to seek an accord with the Treasury to no longer maintain low interest rates given the emergence of inflationary pressures, the expansion of the Korean War, and concerns about the Fed's own independence.[12]

There are two major problems with policies of administered interest rates that maintain a set of rates below a market-determined set of rates. First, the income transfer from creditors to debtors reduces the incentive to save and provides a greater incentive to take on debt that would be inconsistent under normal economic circumstances. This is particularly true when the debtor is a government with short-run political objectives who discounts the longer-run implications of debt when economic growth may fall short of the required hurdle to repay the debt. Second, low rates also take the form of a tax as negative real rates effectively reduce/liquidate debt and are a transfer of wealth from savers/taxpayers to the government.

---

[11] Michael D. Bordo, Owen F. Humpage, and Anna Schwartz, "U.S. Intervention during the Bretton Woods Era: 1962–1973," NBER working paper No. 16946.

[12] Robert L. Hetzel and Ralph F. Leach, "The Treasury-Fed Accord: A New Narrative Account," *Federal Reserve Bank of Richmond Economic Quarterly* 87, no. 1 (Winter 2001): 33–55.

Imperfect Policy Signals

When information on the reaction function for policy actions is unclear, it sets up uncertainty on the timing and nature of any action. As we have discussed, the Bank of Japan surprised the markets in 2016 by pursuing a move into negative interest rate territory on excess reserves of banks deposited at the BOJ. In response, the yen fell 2 percent against the dollar, thereby reinforcing the linkage between policy, interest rates, and the exchange rate. Yet, in April, the markets were surprised again when the BOJ did not ease again as was widely expected given falling business confidence and deteriorating inflation fundamentals.

Such policy actions that occur in opposition to market expectations result in immediate capital losses/gains as well as raising the risk premium for future policy actions.

In another case of policy uncertainty, Chairman Bernanke raised the possibility in 2013 of withdrawing liquidity from the marketplace—the taper tantrum as illustrated in Figure 10.13—with significant impacts on emerging market interest rates and exchange rates.

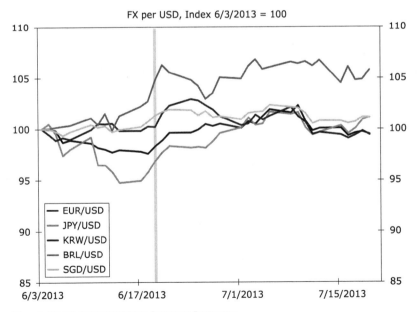

Figure 10.13 Taper Tantrum: Currency Response
Source: Federal Reserve Board

Information about the reaction function of a central bank is a challenge for decision makers. First, is there a clear reaction function? Second, will the central bank follow that reaction function? For the Federal Reserve, the perceived reaction function was some variant of the Taylor rule. However, the introduction of the factor of "global economic and financial developments" has clouded the basis of the original reaction function. For the SNB and the BOJ, the break with the historical reaction function was clear and led to significant repricing of financial assets and risk.

Altering interest rates to achieve exchange rate targeting, as was the tack by the SNB and BOJ, introduces an arbitrary element into asset pricing and confuses the price discovery mechanism in currency and credit/interest rate setting markets. These problems are rendered even more difficult in the case of a nonindependent central bank, which is the tendency in many emerging markets.

Persistent Disequilibrium in Prices and Exchange Rates' Dynamic Adjustment Problem

Things take time—especially in economics. There is a distinct dynamic adjustment following any economic shock or policy initiative. Markets do not adjust instantaneously and therefore, there is a period of disequilibrium as markets move to a new equilibrium.

Portfolio investment in U.S. fixed-income instruments provides a valuable illustration. Purchases of U.S. Treasury, corporate and agency debt continue to fluctuate and give the appearance of constant adjustment toward a desired equilibrium and yet never seem to get there. The volatility of these purchases indicates a constant stream of market/policy surprises and responses. At the global level, the volatility of portfolio investment flows for the United States, United Kingdom, and Canada (Figure 10.14) provides a similar impression of constant motion.

Lags in market responses to policy initiatives are illustrated in Figure 10.15. In this case, the Plaza accord was intended to weaken the dollar versus the Deutschmark and yen. First, the dollar had actually peaked in late 1984/early 1985 prior to the Plaza accord in September 1985. The Louvre accord was intended to stabilize the dollar but that did not occur right away. The dollar continued to decline in value until

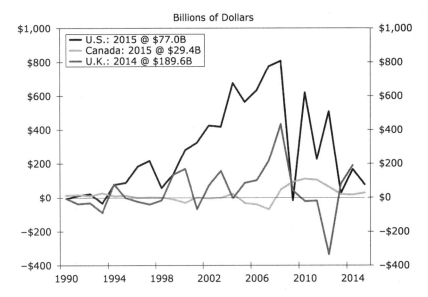

Figure 10.14 Portfolio Investment
Source: International Monetary Fund

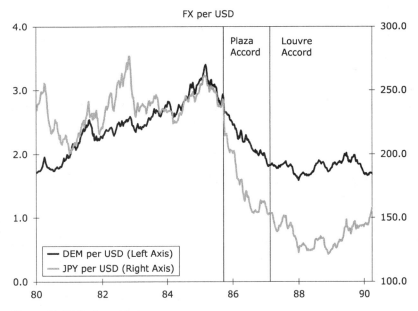

Figure 10.15 Exchange Rates
Source: Federal Reserve Board

early 1988. The Plaza/Louvre experience also illustrates the challenge of overshooting, which is discussed later in this chapter.

A free, competitive market model assumes that any imbalance in trade and capital flows would be resolved by changes in exchange and interest rates. But in the real world, policy makers have incentives to avoid adjustments for domestic political reasons.

Price rigidity gives rise to an incomplete adjustment in the rest of the economic system. When exchange rates/interest rates are out of line, then there is either too much or not enough output/employment in various sectors. Market prices for goods and services are also out of line. The mispricing leads to investment in overpriced sectors and not enough investment in underpriced goods and service sectors. Rigid nominal interest rates/nominal exchange rates lead to inflation/deflation that alters the terms of trade and therefore the balance of imports/exports. This can lead to involuntary unemployment of workers and capital in one country and overemployment in another. This sets up a day of reckoning when the adjustment does occur. This is one of the issues faced by China in 2016 as its exchange rate adjusts and the Chinese authorities attempt to guide a transition from export-oriented goods production to more domestic services production.

Dynamic adjustment—adjustment over time to shocks—particularly the wholesale revaluation or devaluation of a currency is often frustrated by domestic policy for domestic political reasons. Domestic sectors that have benefited from a mispriced currency pay a high price over the long run when the currency barrier breaks down. In the short run, domestic firms are protected from competition by an undervalued currency—but there are two problems. When protected by an undervalued currency, there is an overallocation of both business capital and labor to the protected industry. When the inevitable currency adjustment occurs, then the doors are open to large business failures and structural unemployment. There is also the problem of capital controls, which directly misallocate capital among economic winners and losers.

As illustrated in Tables 10.1 and 10.2, we first look at the behavior of capital flows, both direct (Table 10.1) and portfolio (Table 10.2), for various nations. We want to identify patterns of behavior in a series to decide if these patterns return to equilibrium or whether they are

Table 10.1 Identifying a Structural Break Using the State-Space Approach: Direct Investment

U.S. Direct Investment (Not Mean Reverting)		
Break Date	Type of Break	Coefficient
Dec-08	Level Shift	−1.0
May-00	Additive Outlier	0.43
Aug-11	Level Shift	−0.59
Canada Direct Investment (Not Mean Reverting)		
Break Date	Type of Break	Coefficient
Aug-11	Level Shift	−0.53
U.K. Direct Investment (Not Mean Reverting)		
Break Date	Type of Break	Coefficient
Nov-11	Level Shift	0.98
May-95	Level Shift	−0.94
Singapore Direct Investment (Not Mean Reverting)		
Break Date	Type of Break	Coefficient
Jun-94	Level Shift	1.74
Dec-08	Level Shift	−0.68
Sounth Korea Direct Investment (Not Mean Reverting)		
Break Date	Type of Break	Coefficient
Nov-11	Level Shift	0.98
May-95	Level Shift	−0.94
Japan Direct Investment (Not Mean Reverting)		
Break Date	Type of Break	Coefficient
Jun-94	Level Shift	1.74
Dec-08	Level Shift	−0.68
Nov-99	Level Shift	−0.55

in persistent disequilibrium over time. Our econometric results suggest that the investment behavior (both direct and portfolio) is not mean reverting for all countries. That is, if decision makers believe that capital flows move around a long-run average in their respective countries, then they are incorrect. Furthermore, decisions based on the past averages are misleading and emphasize the issue of incorrect information.

Table 10.2 Identifying a Structural Break Using the State-Space Approach: Portfolio Investment

U.S. Portfolio Investment (Not Mean Reverting)		
Break Date	**Type of Break**	**Coefficient**
Dec-08	Level Shift	−1.0
May-00	Additive Outlier	0.43
Aug-11	Level Shift	−0.59
Canada Portfolio Investment (Not Mean Reverting)		
Break Date	**Type of Break**	**Coefficient**
Aug-11	Level Shift	−0.53
U.K. Portfolio Investment (Not Mean Reverting)		
Break Date	**Type of Break**	**Coefficient**
Nov-11	Level Shift	0.98
May-95	Level Shift	−0.94
Singapore Portfolio Investment (Not Mean Reverting)		
Break Date	**Type of Break**	**Coefficient**
Jun-94	Level Shift	1.74
Dec-08	Level Shift	−0.68
Sounth Korea Portfolio Investment (Not Mean Reverting)		
Break Date	**Type of Break**	**Coefficient**
Nov-11	Level Shift	0.98
May-95	Level Shift	−0.94
Japan Portfolio Investment (Not Mean Reverting)		
Break Date	**Type of Break**	**Coefficient**
Jun-94	Level Shift	1.74
Dec-08	Level Shift	−0.68
Nov-99	Level Shift	−0.55

Incomplete nominal adjustment of exchange rates and interest rates alters the path of capital flows and trade and frustrates the allocation of resources to best uses across the globe. Undervalued currencies tend to protect domestic firms from global competition and allocate too many resources to those firms and generate overemployment. Alternatively, overvalued currencies fail to protect domestic firms and workers and create involuntary unemployment or overemployment. For many nations, these imbalances lead to the political issues today.

During the early Bretton Woods era, the persistent disequilibrium of exchange rates prevented price discovery for both exchange rate and interest rates. The period was characterized by persistent trade deficits (United States and United Kingdom) and surpluses (France) and a steady claim on gold from deficit countries by surplus countries. These flows eventually were resolved by a break in the gold exchange–based system and sharp adjustments in exchange rates and interest rates.[13]

Price Adjustments: Limits by Policy Makers

Policy sets the context—and the risk. When economic policy is not oriented toward flexible, free markets but rather toward interventionist policies (e.g., administered interest or exchange rates, limited capital flows), policy actions increase the risks of sharp breaks in market prices.

Economic outcomes are not simply a reflection of perfectly competitive market forces but the impact of given policy regimes and their alterations. Such policy actions lead to often sharp market adjustments. Most recently we have seen a sharp policy change by the SNB (Figure 10.16).

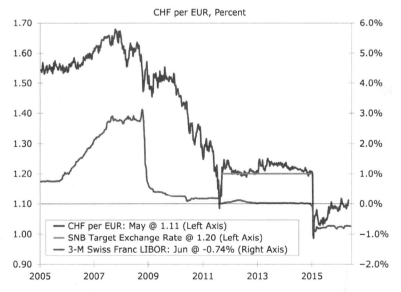

Figure 10.16 Swiss Exchange Rate and LIBOR
Source: Bloomberg LP

---

[13] This period was covered nicely in Bordo, Humpage, and Schwartz, 2011.

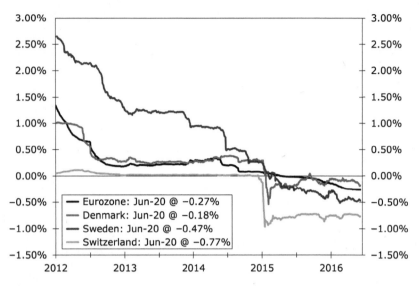

Figure 10.17 Three-Month Interbank Offered Rates
Source: Bloomberg LP

By delinking the Swiss franc from the euro, the SNB has broken patterns for all three economic activities: delinked the exchange rate peg, entered into negative interest rate territory, and altered the incentives of capital flows into the Swiss franc.

Flexible exchange rates and interest rates—jointly determined in the private marketplace—also reflect policy actions. As illustrated in Figure 10.17, the actions of the central banks of Denmark and Sweden to alter their exchange rates also meant altering their interest rates and venturing into the world of negative interest rates.

Here is a clear illustration of the interrelationship between market prices that creates interdependent price movements for exchange and interest rates and also creates a dynamic interplay of exchange rates and interest rates.

In Figure 10.18, the three-month forward exchange rates are illustrated for four cross rates. High interest rate currencies tend to show a depreciating forward curve. Low-rate currencies tend to show an appreciating forward curve, or at least that is what interest rate parity would imply in a frictionless market. For the 2002–2008 period, the three-month-ahead forward rates for the euro/dollar continued to

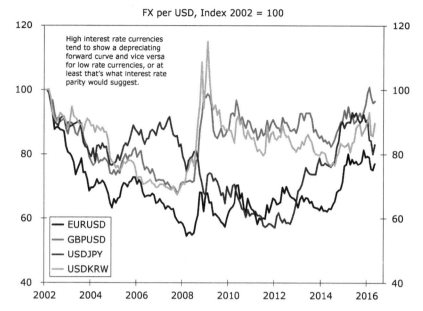

Figure 10.18 Three-Month-Ahead Forward Rates
Source: Bloomberg LP

decline, indicating that euro interest rates would be high relative to U.S. interest rates. After 2008, these expectations changed and U.S. rates were anticipated to rise relative to euro rates.

After the spike in 2008 associated with the global recession, the dollar relative to the yen initially declined but has risen since 2012. Here, then, is an alteration of market expectations. Whereas initially the dollar/yen signaled declining interest rates for the United States, the period since 2012 indicates rising interest rate expectations relative to Japan. A similar pattern occurred for the British pound versus the dollar since early 2014 as well as for the U.S. dollar versus the Korean won.

The interrelationship between market prices and expectations gives rise to the phenomenon of overshooting.[14] When a monetary authority eases policy, under conditions of perfect capital mobility, interest rate differentials are offset by exchange rate movements. Domestic interest rates exceed the global interest rate only if the domestic

---

[14] Rudiger Dornbusch, "Expectations and Exchange Rate Dynamics," *Journal of Political Economy* 84 (December 1976): 1161–1176.

currency is expected to depreciate in real terms at a rate equal to the interest rate differential. When market expectations are introduced the situation is altered.

Now, the initial exchange rate response to an economic surprise is greater than the long-run response. When the central bank eases, the currency initially depreciates, but given the price level, the currency falls below the long-run value. That is, the real exchange rate has not changed since relative prices do not initially adjust. Therefore, the interest rate differential must now equal the anticipated change in the exchange rate. When the current exchange rate is below its long-run equilibrium, then the exchange rate is projected to appreciate over time.

While overshooting may be a short-run phenomenon, we are also interested in permanent change. In Tables 10.3 and 10.4, we focus in on the possibility of a permanent shift in our interest rate regimes for a number of countries. The results are stark. Interest rates are not mean reverting. This presents two problems. First, a shock to the system often implies a permanent shift, not temporary overshooting, in interest rates away from the initial equilibrium. Second, some shocks lead to a shift but not a permanent change in the interest rate regime.

Table 10.3 Identifying a Structural Break Using the State-Space Approach: 10-Year Government Bond Yields

U.S. 10-Year Treasury Yields (Not Mean Reverting)		
Break Date	Type of Break	Coefficient
Sep-87	Additive Outlier	0.655
Nov-08	Level Shift	−0.945
Canada 10-Year Government Bond Yields (Not Mean Reverting)		
Break Date	Type of Break	Coefficient
Mar-94	Level Shift	0.948
Sep-98	Level Shift	−0.719
U.K. 10-Year Government Bond Yields (Not Mean Reverting)		
Break Date	Type of Break	Coefficient
Dec-08	Additive Outlier	−0.685
May-94	Level Shift	0.798

Table 10.4 Identifying a Structural Break Using the State-Space Approach

Germany 10-Year Treasury Yields (Not Mean Reverting)		
Break Date	Type of Break	Coefficient
May-12	Additive Outlier	–0.431
Nov-08	Level Shift	–0.603
Japan 10-Year Treasury Yields (Not Mean Reverting)		
Break Date	Type of Break	Coefficient
Oct-90	Level Shift	–1.062
Dec-98	Level Shift	0.954
Singapore 10-Year Treasury Yields (Not Mean Reverting)		
Break Date	Type of Break	Coefficient
May-08	Level Shift	1.016
Jun-13	Level Shift	0.639

Capital Flows and Treasury Yields in the Post–Great Recession Era

Our global economy is more open today than it has ever been. While this has many positive implications for growth and efficiency, openness also makes decision making more challenging, as private and public policy actions in one part of the world affect private- and public-policy makers' decisions in other regions. In addition, the changing nature of the economic ties between countries requires a continuous reevaluation of the benchmark relationships. That is, the degree of economic interdependency of a country (e.g., the United States) may increase with some countries (after the North American Free Trade Agreement [NAFTA] with Canada and Mexico) and decrease with others (e.g., trade sanctions with Russia or Iran).

In this section, we continue the theme of identifying the interactions of capital flows and their influence on asset prices around the globe. Our goal is to help decision makers characterize the differential behaviors among countries and asset classes in the ever-evolving open world economy.[15]

---

[15] For details see, "The Open U.S. Economy and Newton's Third Law," Wells Fargo Economics Group publication, January 12, 2015.

We characterize U.S. capital inflows behavior using an annual data set for the 1975–2012 period. The Hodrick-Prescott (H-P) filter–based trends for total inflows and direct investment intimate that the pace of capital inflows has slowed down since the early 2000s. In addition, our analysis indicates that the three measures of the global economy that we focus on here (real GDP, inflation, and the current account balance) exhibit different behavior for the post-2007 period compared to the 2002–2007 era.

Is the Post-2007 Economy Structurally Different?

The Great Recession clearly led to a significant shake-up in global financial markets, but did it lead to a structural shift in economic fundamentals? We utilize three different measures of the global economy to address this question: real GDP growth, CPI inflation, and the current account balance. We test real GDP growth rates in the United States, Eurozone, and China, and split the data sets between two periods: 2002–2007 and 2008–2014. To preview, our analysis indicates the average GDP growth rate during 2008–2014 is statistically different from the average growth rate from 2002–2007 for all three countries. Furthermore, the average GDP growth rates of all three countries have shifted downward since 2008: the United States to 1.2 percent from 2.7 percent, the Eurozone to –0.1 percent from 2.0 percent, and China to 8.6 percent from 10 percent. This shift was statistically significant for all three countries in our sample.

Patterns in inflation, as measured by the year-over-year percent change of each country's CPI, exhibit interesting alternative behaviors. The average inflation rates of the United States and the Eurozone from 2008 to 2014 are statistically different from inflation during 2002–2007. For the United States and Eurozone, average CPI inflation shifted downward from 2002–2007 to 2008–2014. However, the average Chinese CPI inflation rates for the pre- and post-2007 periods are statistically indistinguishable.

As a third means of measuring structural change, we examine the current account balances of the United States, Germany (employed as a proxy for Eurozone) and China. The average growth rates of the United States' and Germany's current account balances are statistically different for the post-2007 era compared to the 2002–2007 period. Furthermore, the U.S. current account deficit narrowed and Germany's surplus grew wider. However, the Chinese current account balance is statistically the same, on average, for the post-2007 versus the pre-2007 periods.

Therefore, an analysis of major economic series indicates the global economy may have experienced a structural shift for the post-2007 period compared to the 2002-2007 era for our selected benchmark economic series.

Tracking U.S. Capital Flows: What Has Changed?

The H-P filter–based trends for total capital inflows (Figure 10.19) and direct investment (Figure 10.20) have been moving upward since 1975.[16] However, during the past 10 years, both trends have begun to

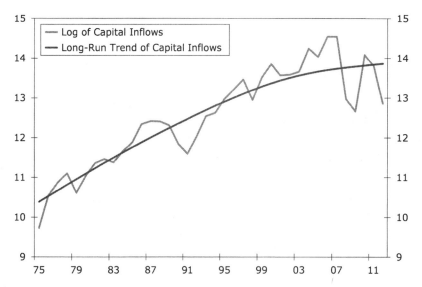

Figure 10.19 Total Capital Inflows into the United States
Source: U.S. Department of Commerce

---

[16] We utilize six different series to characterize U.S. capital inflows and only two of these measures contain all positive values. Thus, we only apply the H-P filter on those two series.

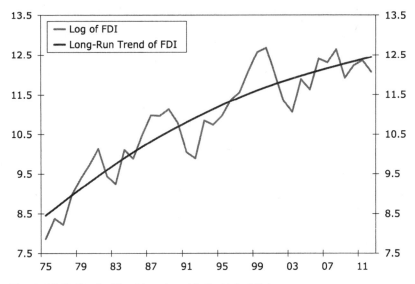

Figure 10.20 Foreign Direct Investment in the United States
Source: U.S. Department of Commerce

show signs of flattening out, hinting that the pace of capital inflows has been slowing since the early 2000s.

The mean, standard deviation, and stability ratio for each series is reported in Table 10.5. In all cases, the stability ratio is greater than 100. Yet a structural break test indicates no evidence of a break for all series except other private holdings, which had a structural break in 2008 (Table 10.6). However, outliers are present in all series, which is consistent with the higher stability ratios of these volatile series. As a means of testing for structural breaks in these series, we conducted Augmented Dickey-Fuller (ADF) tests on each series. The ADF test results indicate all series are mean-reverting. In sum, statistical results indicate the U.S. capital inflows series are largely mean reverting, but there are some volatile periods when the current account series moves away from the mean.[17]

---

[17] ADF test results declare that all series are stationary and mean-reverting. However, since the "Other Private Holdings" series contains a structural break, we therefore characterize the series as not mean-reverting.

Table 10.5 Mean, Standard Deviation, and Stability Ratios

Variable	1975-2012			1975-1989			1990-2012		
	Mean	S.D.	Stability Ratio	Mean	S.D	Stability Ratio	Mean	S.D.	Stability Ratio
Official Portfolio Holdings	−47.30	618.73	−1308.13	−237.84	804.80	−338.37	68.68	454.46	661.67
Direct Investment	24.70	57.22	231.63	36.90	53.62	145.30	17.28	59.22	342.71
Total Inflows	22.64	65.50	289.36	25.56	38.83	151.92	20.85	78.23	375.13
Private Portfolio Holdings	−222.93	1097.72	−492.41	28.69	44.89	156.47	−376.08	1380.50	−367.07
Other Private Holdings	28.22	119.15	422.23	55.77	123.81	221.99	11.45	115.74	1011.04
Other Official Holdings	370.25	2064.20	557.52	866.40	3328.24	384.14	68.24	418.07	612.64

Source: U.S. Department of Commerce

Table 10.6 Identifying a Structural Break Using the State-Space Approach

Official Portfolio Holdings (Mean Reverting)		
Break Date	Type of Break	Coefficient
Jan-86	Additive Outlier	−3010
Jan-90	Additive Outlier	1873
Jan-99	Additive Outlier	−1006
Direct Investment (Mean Reverting)		
Break Date	Type of Break	Coefficient
Jan-93	Additive Outlier	160
Jan-84	Additive Outlier	135
Jan-04	Additive Outlier	121
Total Inflows (Mean Reverting)		
Break Date	Type of Break	Coefficient
Jan-10	Additive Outlier	306
Private Portfolio Holdings (Mean Reverting)		
Break Date	Type of Break	Coefficient
Jan-91	Additive Outlier	−5827
Jan-10	Additive Outlier	−3310
Other Private Holdings (Not Mean Reverting)		
Break Date	Type of Break	Coefficient
Jan-08	Level Shift	−103
Jan-97	Additive Outlier	225
Other Official Holdings (Mean Reverting)		
Break Date	Type of Break	Coefficient
Jan-86	Additive Outlier	12378
Jan-92	Additive Outlier	1355
Jan-95	Additive Outlier	1244

Are Global Sovereign Yields Mean Reverting?

To characterize the global bond market, we utilize four major countries' 10-year sovereign yields: the United States, Germany, Italy, and the United Kingdom. The H-P filter–based trend and log of the U.S. 10-year Treasury yield is plotted in Figure 10.21. The H-P trend moved steadily downward from 1994 to 2012, but has rebounded since then.

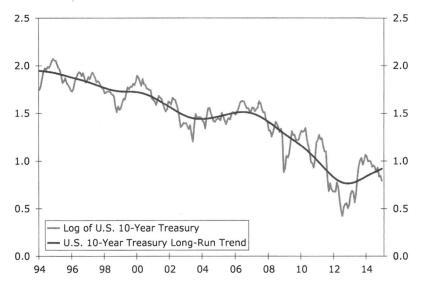

Figure 10.21 H-P Filter–Based Trend of U.S. 10-Year Treasury Yield
Source: Bloomberg LP

The uptick in the trend is consistent with the ending of quantitative easing (QE) programs by the Federal Reserve Board.

Trends for Germany (Figure 10.22) and Italy (Figure 10.23) have also generally been downward since 1994. In contrast to the United

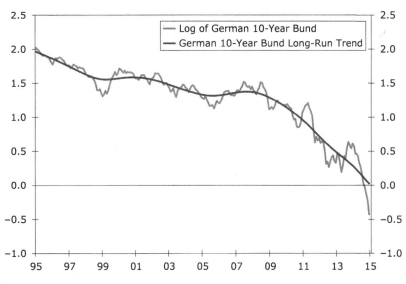

Figure 10.22 H-P Filter–Based Trend of German 10-Year Bund Yield
Source: Bloomberg LP

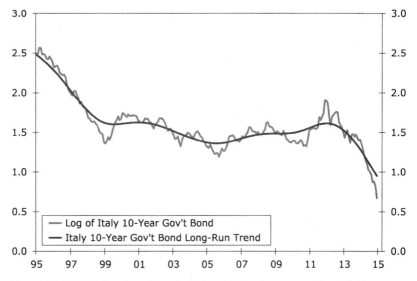

Figure 10.23 H-P Filter–Based Trend of Italian 10-Year Government Bond Yield
Source: Bloomberg LP

States, both countries' trends have plunged in the past few years, which may signal that investors foresee that current expansionary monetary policy may continue in the near future and the economic recovery will continue to be disappointing. The downward trends of the German and Italian sovereign yields are consistent with the announcement of QE from the ECB. The trend in the U.K. 10-year gilt yield (Figure 10.24) has a pattern consistent with the U.S. Treasury trend, bottoming out in 2013 and moving upward in 2014. Overall, the H-P filter analysis shows the global Treasury market has a mixed trend, as two major markets (United States and United Kingdom) were trending toward higher rates while the other two (Germany and Italy) were anticipating further stimulus, which kept rates low.

The mean, standard deviation, and stability ratio for each country's sovereign yields are reported in Table 10.7. For all four countries, the stability ratios are less than 50, which indicates sovereign yields were notably stable during the complete sample period (1994–2014) and subsamples. In the final step, we determine whether measures of global Treasury market are mean reverting (Table 10.8). All four

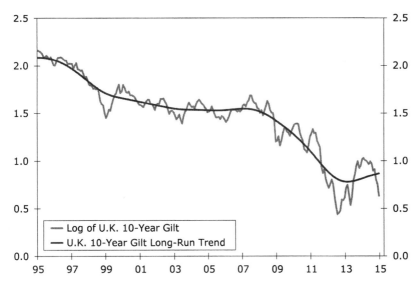

Figure 10.24 H-P filter–based Trend of U.K. 10-Year Gilt Yield
Source: Bloomberg LP

sovereign yields experienced structural breaks and are nonstationary, indicating these series are not mean reverting. Thus, investors should not assume sovereign yields in these nations will return to any sort of long-run average.

The Volatility of Foreign Purchases of U.S. Securities

Investors purchase securities from different countries for any number of reasons, for example, to achieve better returns or to diversify their portfolios. That creates opportunities for a country to sell securities not only to domestic investors but also to foreigners. Foreigners, both in the private sector and in the government sector, buy hundreds of billions of dollars' worth of U.S. securities every year, on average.

Here, we utilize foreign private purchases of U.S. Treasuries, equities and agency/corporate debt to represent foreign purchases of U.S. securities.[18] In addition, we include total private and official

---

[18] We apply the H-P filter on a log of a time series, since if a series contains negative values, then that would restrict the H-P filter application. All measures of foreign purchases of the U.S. securities include negative values, and thereby we are unable to utilize the H-P filter for these series.

Table 10.7 Standard Deviation and Stability Ratio for Country Treasury Yields

Variable	1994–2014			2000–2014			1994–1999		
	Mean	S.D.	Stability Ratio	Mean	S.D.	Stability Ratio	Mean	S.D.	Stability Ratio
U.S. 10-Yr	4.51	1.53	34.00	3.82	1.17	30.76	6.23	0.79	12.67
Germany 10-Yr	4.06	1.58	38.96	3.43	1.24	36.19	5.74	1.09	19.04
Italy 10-Yr	5.38	2.26	41.94	4.45	0.78	17.43	7.88	2.95	37.42
U.K. 10-Yr	4.82	1.77	36.69	3.99	1.13	28.30	6.92	1.28	18.55

Source: Bloomberg LP

Table 10.8 Identifying a Structural Break Using the State-Space Approach

U.S. 10-Year Treasury (Not Mean Reverting)		
Break Date	**Type of Break**	**Coefficient**
Dec-08	Level Shift	−1.0
May-00	Additive Outlier	0.43
Aug-11	Level Shift	−0.59
German 10-Year Bund (Not Mean Reverting)		
Break Date	**Type of Break**	**Coefficient**
Aug-11	Level Shift	−0.53
Italian 10-Year Gov't Bond (Not Mean Reverting)		
Break Date	**Type of Break**	**Coefficient**
Nov-11	Level Shift	0.98
May-95	Level Shift	−0.94
U.K. 10-Year Gilt (Not Mean Reverting)		
Break Date	**Type of Break**	**Coefficient**
Jun-94	Level Shift	1.74
Dec-08	Level Shift	−0.68
Nov-99	Level Shift	−0.55

(government) purchases of U.S. Treasury debt. The mean, standard deviation and stability ratio for each series is shown in Table 10.9. One noticeable observation is that all measures of foreign purchases are highly volatile, as each series' standard deviation is significantly larger than its mean. The smallest stability ratio is 448, which indicates the standard deviation is more than four times greater than the mean.

Structural break tests for these series indicate no evidence of a break in any measure of foreign purchases (Table 10.10). There are, however, outliers in all series, which is consistent with the higher stability ratio values of these volatile series. The ADF test results indicate all series are mean reverting. In sum, statistical results intimate the foreign purchases of U.S. securities are mean reverting, but there are some volatile periods when the series moves away from the mean. We speculate that these outliers represent periods of global panic

Table 10.9 Mean, Standard Deviation, and Stability Ratio for Each Series

Variable	1990–2014			2000–2014			1990–1999		
	Mean	S.D.	Stability Ratio	Mean	S.D.	Stability Ratio	Mean	S.D.	Stability Ratio
Agency (YoY)	159.10	1751.57	1100.90	22.34	672.87	3011.41	363.10	2633.54	725.29
Equity (YoY)	568.75	5592.19	983.24	557.11	5895.08	1058.15	586.11	5131.33	875.49
Treasury (YoY)	221.89	1421.91	640.83	276.26	1710.99	619.34	140.78	820.40	582.75
Corporate (YoY)	242.47	2778.16	1145.78	−13.11	253.89	−1935.91	623.71	4357.37	698.62
Official (YoY)	306.59	1624.03	529.70	362.86	1934.32	533.08	222.67	998.13	448.26
Private (YoY)	114.73	2775.71	2419.24	85.11	3564.49	4188.20	158.93	534.29	336.18

Source: U.S. Department of Commerce

Table 10.10 Identifying a Structural Break Using the State-Space Approach

Agency (YoY) (Mean Reverting)		
Break Date	**Type of Break**	**Coefficient**
Sep-99	Additive Outlier	28620
Mar-09	Additive Outlier	−6699
Feb-08	Additive Outlier	4662
Equity (YoY) (Mean Reverting)		
Break Date	**Type of Break**	**Coefficient**
Apr-13	Additive Outlier	78679
Sep-97	Additive Outlier	55561
Aug-99	Additive Outlier	8218
Treasury (YoY) (Mean Reverting)		
Break Date	**Type of Break**	**Coefficient**
Nov-09	Additive Outlier	20399
Jun-92	Additive Outlier	7891
Jun-02	Additive Outlier	6032
Corporate (YoY) (Mean Reverting)		
Break Date	**Type of Break**	**Coefficient**
Feb-92	Additive Outlier	42740
Jul-94	Additive Outlier	20830
Mar-91	Additive Outlier	5084
Offical (YoY) (Mean Reverting)		
Break Date	**Type of Break**	**Coefficient**
Aug-02	Additive Outlier	21389
Nov-13	Additive Outlier	12286
Jun-94	Additive Outlier	7071
Private (YoY) (Mean Reverting)		
Break Date	**Type of Break**	**Coefficient**
Sep-02	Additive Outlier	34376
Jun-13	Additive Outlier	−32276
Jan-10	Additive Outlier	5736

(i.e., Asian Financial Crisis, Tech Bubble, Great Recession, Double Dip Recession in Eurozone, etc.), although with annual data it is difficult to nail down a specific cause for large inflows or outflows.

CONCLUDING REMARKS: FUTURE LOOKS DIFFERENT

In sum, the Great Recession drove significant structural shifts in a number of economic and financial variables. Specifically, our three benchmark indicators of global economic performance (real GDP, inflation, and the current account balance) have exhibited different behaviors in the post–Great Recession era relative to the 2002–2007 era. Financial indicators have also experienced important shifts as well. Interestingly, 10-year yields in the United States, United Kingdom, Germany, and Italy experienced structural breaks and are not mean reverting. Thus, investors should not assume that economic and financial conditions will necessarily return to the way they were prior to the Great Recession; instead, the future looks to be uncharted territory.

CHAPTER 11

Assessing Economic Policy in an Imperfect Economy

No battle plan survives contact with the enemy.

—Helmuth von Moltke

So it is also true for economic policy, for while economic policy is perfect in the lab, assessing the effect of economic policy in the field of economic battle is a very different story. Since the Great Recession, many policy initiatives have been tried but none have delivered on growth and inflation as predicted by policy makers.

Although economic policy initiatives are treated as exogenous in economic models, the effectiveness of these policies in action still faces the constraints of the real economy as well as the many feedback loops and unintended consequences that upset the best laid plans of the generals.

Four types of economic policy—fiscal, monetary, regulatory, and trade—are all constrained by the limits of our knowledge in dealing with the three deviations from perfectly competitive market conditions we have previously highlighted in our work. Imperfect information, dynamic adjustment, and unequal price movements all act to deliver economic outcomes that differ from the initial battle plan.

In addition, policy makers are faced with conflicts among policies. The effectiveness of fiscal and monetary policy may be constrained by the exchange rate/capital flows policy adopted by their native nation as well as other nations.[1] Second, exchange rate policy is itself controlled by the impossible trinity that constrains central banks to pursue only two of the following three options: a fixed exchange rate, free capital flow, and sovereign monetary policy.[2]

Trade policy also confronts the difficult trade-off between domestic and international economic impacts and the disparate impact of trade

---

[1] Robert Mundell, "Capital Mobility and Stabilization Policy under Fixed and Flexible Exchange Rates," *Canadian Journal of Economic and Political Science* 29, no. 4 (1963): 475–485; Marcus Fleming, "Domestic Financial Policies under Fixed and Floating Exchange Rates," *IMF Staff Papers* 9 (1962): 369–379.

[2] Maurice Obstfeld and Alan M. Taylor, "The Trilemma in History: Tradeoffs among Exchange Rates, Monetary Policies and Capital Mobility in the Long Run," NBER working paper 5960, March 1997.

between producers and consumers and industrial winners and losers with the inevitable political constraints/trade-offs in bringing any trade policy to life. Finally, one conflict apparent in the current economic expansion is that current regulatory policy aims to reduce risk to borrowers and lenders in the credit market while monetary policy is attempting to expand the economy by incentivizing risk taking.

GENERALIZED POLICY MODEL

Economic policy, as in any battle plan, is conducted with a goal of reaching a target based upon the instruments available as well as the quality of information available in public and private sector indicators. Policy therefore includes targets, instruments, and indicators. We immediately recognize the problems in conducting policy in the post–Great Recession era. First, for monetary policy, the target of achieving 2 percent inflation has been hampered by the real-side excess supply of capital, labor, and goods on the global scale. As such, the expansion of high-powered money in the domestic economy has not produced the anticipated pace of growth or inflation. As for instruments, the effectiveness of zero-interest-rate policies and the expansion of central bank balance sheets may have avoided a worse outcome during 2007–2009, yet these policies certainly have not achieved the projected 2 percent inflation pickup nor the promised economic growth acceleration in the United States, Japan, euro area, and the United Kingdom in the period since the recession.

In a similar vein, the fiscal expansion of 2009 in the United States and the years of fiscal spending in Japan have not returned the economies to the anticipated 3 percent plus real growth path. Whatever the instruments of fiscal policy, the economic model of the economy has changed such that such fiscal expansions were offset by more cautious behavior by both households and businesses. Meanwhile, in the euro area, the move to fiscal restraint reflected the view that the long-run goal of policy required the ability to pay public debts and thereby offered no room for the luxury of a fiscal expansion. Fiscal policy is also hampered, in ways not witnessed before, by the demographics of aging populations in Japan, Europe, and the United States, which may lead to rising future long-run debt burdens that offset the ability of governments to conduct short-run fiscal stimulus. Using the tax code to influence household and business spending also has run afoul of crony capitalism where what might appear as fiscal stimulus simply directs public spending into areas that add very little value to the economic pie. Here, of course, are the example of bridges to nowhere and subsidized public ventures that are economically inefficient.

Regulatory and trade policy suffer from the same problems of crony capitalism and special provisions. Both policy areas are often riddled with special exemptions or drawn-out timetables such that the stimulus or constraint provided does not deliver on the economic benefits predicted. Economic policy acts within a political world and as such the political process doles out favors to constituents, and these favors diminish the effectiveness of the promised economic stimulus/constraint.

Monetary Policy: Target Achieved So Let's Ignore It

Since the mid-1990s, the pace of inflation, as measured by the PCE deflator, has averaged less than 2 percent. Therefore, monetary policy has succeeded in lowering inflation and keeping inflation low over time. In addition, inflation expectations appear to have been stable in recent years. But let's not let success go unpunished. Kydland and Prescott bring up the problem that policy makers are unable to commit themselves to low-inflation policy since they are also pursuing a second goal of economic growth/employment and so the marginal cost of additional inflation is perceived to be low and therefore policy makers pursue expansionary policies to push output/employment temporarily above potential. This is exactly the policy position in mid-2016 as the unemployment rate has fallen below 5 percent while economic growth for 2016 is projected to come in at potential—2 percent. Yet, the Federal Open Market Committee (FOMC) continues to pursue expansionary monetary policy despite rising labor compensation and unit labor costs. Given the lack of a long-run trade-off of unemployment and inflation, the expectation is that in the period ahead we get higher inflation without any increase in output.[3]

---

[3] Finn E. Kydland and Edward C. Prescott, "Rules Rather than Discretion: The Inconsistency of Optimal Plans," *Journal of Political Economy* 85 (June 1977): 473–492.

For the case of monetary policy, there are hints that the model of the economy has changed and that policy suffers under the weight of imperfect information on labor market structure. The FOMC places great emphasis on the labor market but we can identify two problems. First, as illustrated in Figure 11.1, the responsiveness of wages to a decline in the unemployment rate has been muted in this cycle relative to the prior three cycles (1980s, 1990s, and 2000s). Unfortunately, this muted response has opened up the door to greater FOMC policy easing in the Kydland-Prescott mold since further easing beyond full employment appears to represent very little risk of further inflation with the reward of greater employment/output. Second, as illustrated in Figure 11.2, the outward shift in the Beveridge curve represented a higher unemployment rate for workers at any given vacancy rate reported by employers. The efficiency of allocating labor has deteriorated in this cycle. This structural change in the labor market creates a policy problem since the unemployment rate is a key policy target metric, and yet the rate does not represent the same efficient level of labor resources as in the past.

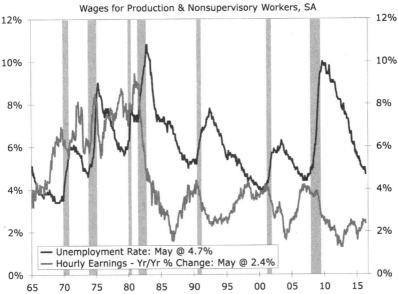

Figure 11.1 Unemployment and Wage Rates
Source: U.S. Department of Labor

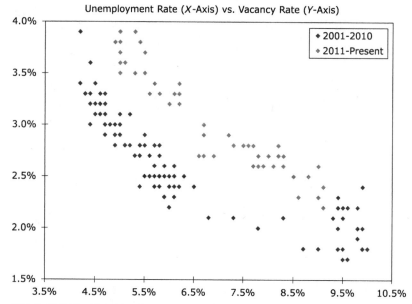

Figure 11.2 The Beveridge Curve
Source: U.S. Department of Labor

Fiscal Policy: Multiple Conflicts for Targets and Instruments

Conflict in fiscal policy pervades both the target setting and the exercise of instruments in setting policy. One target for fiscal policy is to improve patterns of economic growth, and a second, in the Keynesian tradition, is to achieve budget balance over time or at least not issue debt that cannot be serviced if/when the pace of growth were to slow. Unfortunately, in the cases of Greece, Argentina, and Puerto Rico in recent years, this last target is sometimes missed. Yet fiscal policy is also targeted to provide short-run stimulus to the economy. This leads to the conflict that short-run stimulus creates a longer-run debt problem. As evidenced by Greece, Portugal, and Argentina, the overhang of debt prevents any short-run fiscal stimulus. This long-run negative feedback to short-run fiscal stimulus creates a regime change in fiscal policy. Economic weakness, under conventional conditions, would lead to pro-cyclical fiscal stimulus of additional spending/tax cuts. However, for Europe, post the Great Recession, the response to economic weakness was fiscal restraint, not stimulus. Such regime changes create increased uncertainty on the part of households and businesses and thereby add to the downward forces on the economy.

Regulation—Trade-Offs Inherent between Risk and Reward

For regulators, the measurable policy goals are far less clear than they are for monetary and fiscal policy. As often stated, the goal of regulatory policy, for financial markets for example, is the avoidance of the last financial crisis. Meanwhile, the measure of the impact of rules and regulatory guidance in terms of benefit/cost analysis can be very flexible given the probabilities of and measure of costs/benefits that are often not immediately apparent. This is indeed a classic example of decision making under conditions of imperfect information. Moreover, there is an inherent bias on the part of regulators. Regulators wish to minimize possible problems on their watch, while regulators do not reap the rewards of economic profit and risk taking. So regulators seek to minimize risk and tilt to greater restraint at the cost of a bit less innovation and economic growth. The limited amount of credit financing in the current cycle is a result of caution on the part of regulators seeking to avoid a repeat of the bubble that occurred in front of the Great Recession.

Trade—Balance-of-Trade Interests and the Promotion of Economic Growth

Trade policy is generally aimed at promoting economic growth and jobs in the economy. While the goal is clear, the challenge is that the instrument, trade agreements, carries disparate impacts among producers and consumers. Meanwhile, besides the flow of goods and services, many nations face the challenge of allowing for capital flows that help/hinder finance trade deficits/surpluses but also influence the pattern of exchange rate changes over the economic cycle.

As for the target of trade policy, besides growth, there is a question to what extent public policy is aimed at achieving a balance on trade or whether there is a goal to run a continued trade surplus in a manner to boost domestic production/jobs to favor export-led growth. In contrast, the post-WWII approach of the United States aimed to run current account deficits to support economic growth and rebuilding Europe.[4] Here is an example of the role of foreign policy objectives that supported the case for current account deficits but also led to a conflict with the policy framework set by Bretton Woods, especially as U.S. inflation rose in the late 1960s and early 1970s.

RULES AND REPUTATION: BEYOND ECONOMIC BENCHMARKS

Policy actions alone are never enough. Successful policy over time requires decision makers to address the issues of rules and reputation. Rules for the conduct of policy cannot account for all unexpected circumstances as was obvious for the Great Recession period of 2007–2009. Second, policy conduct is often framed in consideration of the reputation of policy makers.

In the post-WWII period, there have been two economic periods where the rules no longer fit the problems. For the 1970s, the emergence of stagflation provided a challenge to conventional economic policy at the time. Supply-side shocks (oil embargoes, drought) led to new economic conditions that did not fit the mold of problems that could be addressed by the conventional policy remedies at the time. This led to the reaffirmation of microeconomic principles in labor and goods markets and the focus on the role of expectations in setting economic behavior.[5] In the second case, the Great Recession led to a new set of unconventional monetary policies and several new regulatory initiatives that were developed to deal with the new set of financial/liquidity problems. These periods demonstrate the problem on setting down a set of policy rules that quickly become obsolete in periods of difficult economic outcomes where these conventional policies simply no longer work. Currently, the continuing deflation in Japan appears immutable to conventional policy actions. Continued slow growth, negative interest

---

[4] Michael D. Bordo, Owen F. Humpage, and Anna Schwartz, "U.S. Intervention during the Bretton Woods Era: 1962–1973," NBER working paper No. 16946.
[5] Robert E. Lucas Jr., "Expectations and the Neutrality of Money," *Journal of Economic Theory* 4 (April 1972): 103–124.

rates in Europe, and the slow slide into deflation all call for a new set of thoughts on the actions needed by both public- and private-sector actors. Finally, the challenges of poor productivity and weakening labor force participation in the United States also appear to be outside the reach of conventional macroeconomic monetary/fiscal policy.

Finally, the pursuit of conventional policies has led to one example of unconventional, and we trust, an unintended result—that of financial repression. Both government debt and household savings are denominated in nominal dollars. Therefore, unanticipated inflation, or at least a pace of inflation greater than the pace of inflation discounted in the marketplace, acts as a tax on creditors while lowering the burden for debtors. Therefore, there is an incentive by central governments to pursue economic policies to allow inflation to exceed the nominal, low, returns on savings and government debt and thereby reduce the real burden of the debt—financial repression.[6] In this case, conventional policies, in the context of unconventional situations, do indeed lead to enormously unconventional, and we would argue, counterproductive incentives to discourage saving and encourage debt finance.

Policy makers thrive on their reputation.[7] We can posit that there are two types of policy makers and the public does not know in advance which type is currently in office. This is very much the pattern when we judge incoming Federal Reserve chairs or heads of regulatory agencies or even Supreme Court justices. The first type of policy maker is one that shares the public preferences on output and inflation. For example, members of the German Bundesbank would share the preferences of the German public in favor of low inflation. A second type of policy maker may not share the public's preferences and only cares about one factor—low inflation, balanced budgets, no repeats of the recent credit crisis, fair trade deals. Commonly, we refer to policy makers as hawks or doves, depending on their leanings. Of course, the hawk/dove policy maker certainly faces many public opponents who do not share their single-minded purpose.

---

[6] Guillermo Calvo, "On the Time Consistency of Optimal Policy in a Monetary Economy," *Econometrica* 46 (November 1978): 1411–1428.

[7] David Backus and John Drifill, "Inflation and Reputation," *American Economic Review* 75 (June 1985): 530–538; Robert J. Barro, "Reputation in a Model of Monetary Policy with Incomplete Information," *Journal of Monetary Economics* 17 (January 1986): 3–20.

Second, reputation also is framed by the policy maker's horizon. For U.S. monetary policy, the current focus is on achieving 2 percent inflation over time. For fiscal policy, there is a focus on balancing the budget, or at least assessing the federal budget stance, over the next 10 years. For regulators, there is a focus on no more bank/financial crisis although, realistically, financial crises are a repeating part of economic history. Trade agreements aim to improve economic growth and jobs for both partners to the agreement to take advantage of perceived competitive advantage, although they are often also protecting certain politically favored industries/workers. Of course, each policy, despite its singular focus, also impacts incentives for risk/reward, growth, and employment. Fiscal policy, especially on entitlement issues, also presents intergenerational conflicts—retiree subsidies at the cost of the working population contributions. Moreover, the focus on preserving current entitlements represents a challenge to the long-run financial viability of those same entitlements.

Our problem of imperfect information becomes paramount when we contemplate that economic decisions today by households and businesses reflect their anticipation of policy-maker behavior and their long-run commitment to the goals that policy makers assert as their commitment. We now turn to these expectations and the issue of imperfect information.

CONFRONTING OUR THREE MARKET IMPERFECTIONS

Policy proposals are framed on the drawing board but must work in the quite imperfect world of the real economy.

Measuring and modeling the economy remains an imperfect activity. Moreover, the lack of recognition of imperfect information has had a dramatic impact on judging the state of the economy and even more so on assessing the effectiveness of proposed policies.

Economic growth stands as the first of five critical values that define good due diligence in decision making for both public economic policy and private strategic planning.[8] However, the potential pace of

---

[8] The other four include inflation, interest rates, the exchange rate, and corporate profits, which round out the list of usual suspects.

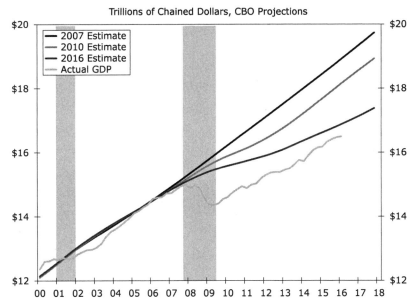

Figure 11.3 Potential GDP Revisions
Sources: Congressional Budget Office and U.S. Department of Commerce

economic growth is not known but rather must be estimated as a critical step in establishing a reasonable path for decisions based on the economy. Yet, as illustrated in Figure 11.3, the estimates of potential growth by the Congressional Budget Office, a standard benchmark in the market, have regularly been lowered in recent years.

Behind the continued lowering of the potential gross domestic product (GDP) estimates has been the disappointment in the performance of the fundamentals. Two supports for growth have both signaled significantly different behavior during this cycle, and as illustrated earlier in the book, the statistical testing for structural breaks in both series provide evidence for such structural breaks.

As illustrated in Figure 11.4, labor force participation has declined for prime age workers—not just the total population—over the past 10 years. While the explanations for such a downswing in both series may be debated, the challenge for decision makers is that we are living in an era of lower labor force participation, and thereby economic growth. Second, as illustrated in Figure 11.5, productivity gains have been exceedingly weak this economic expansion. Moreover, the pace of

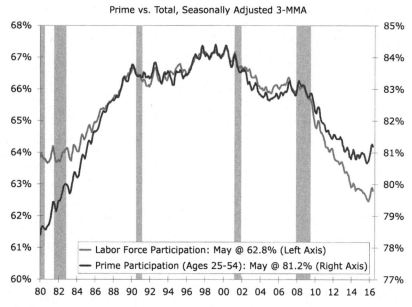

Figure 11.4 Labor Force Participation Rate
Source: U.S. Department of Labor

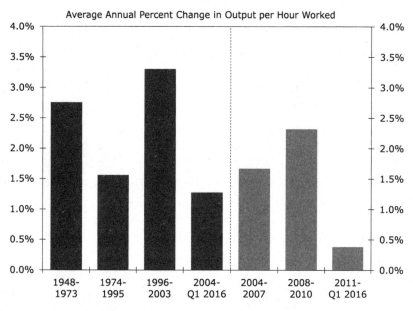

Figure 11.5 Nonfarm Labor Productivity
Source: U.S. Department of Labor

productivity gains during the post-WWII period has been volatile and thereby difficult to rely upon by decision makers when making long-run estimates of economic growth.

Moreover, the distribution of gains from economic growth during the current cycle has deviated from policy maker expectations and the patterns of the last two economic expansions. These gains have diminished in size for each quintile as illustrated in Figure 11.6. The gray bars illustrate the experience of the past two cycles while the much lower black bars are the current cycle. Income growth this cycle fares poorly compared to the prior cycles. Second, income growth has grown more disparate compared to prior cycle as also illustrated in Figure 11.6. There are not two Americas but three Americas. The top two quintiles, on a relative basis, have done fairly well, and even the bottom quintile has experienced some modest improvement. However, the second and third quintiles have experienced little improvement. The distribution of gains has been disappointing for all quintiles but especially for the second and third quintiles.

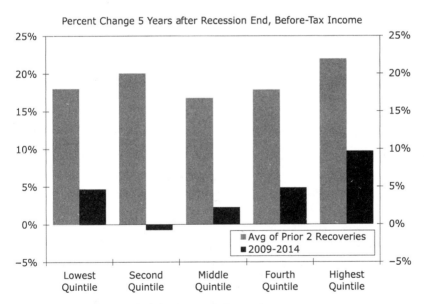

Figure 11.6 Income Growth during Economic Recoveries
Source: U.S. Department of Labor

Imperfect Information on Policy

As illustrated in the current recovery/expansion period, the reaction functions for both monetary and fiscal policy remain uncertain and thereby provide imperfect information to decisions makers. What exactly drives policy? We first consider monetary policy.

In part, the modest pace of growth relative to prior economic expansions provided the feedback on earlier economic policy and has prompted a change in policy focus. For monetary policy, the targets of stronger growth and higher inflation remain elusive. Initially, the model for the conduct of monetary policy was approximated by the Taylor rule that focused on the deviations of employment and inflation from their targets. However, the pace of improvement toward inflation and faster than anticipated declines in the unemployment rate indicated a structural break in the unemployment/inflation trade-off as evidenced by the shift outward in the Beveridge curve that we earlier illustrated. As a result, the FOMC continued to downshift its projections of the fed funds rate despite the decline in the unemployment rate to, and recently below, many assessments of full employment.

As for inflation, once again the pattern of below FOMC forecast inflation results in the United States, along with the continued disappointment on inflation in Japan and Europe, has prompted the FOMC to reduce its tolerance to continued easing in the face of evidence of the reduced responsiveness of inflation to economic growth. Finally, the FOMC reaction function has recently incorporated the factor of "global economic and financial developments" without relaying clear benchmarks for measuring such developments to decision makers.

As for the actual benchmarks to guide policy, we begin with Figure 11.7, which illustrates the actual behavior of inflation over the past 20 years. Since 1994, inflation has actually averaged a bit less than the FOMC's 2 percent target, connoting that there is a clear break in the drivers/model of inflation from the Phillips curve model thinking that was derived in the pre-1982 period and yet remains a focus of current policy.

Moreover, contrary to claims of policy makers, inflation expectations are not well anchored. Over the past three years, inflation expectations have steadily declined as illustrated in Figure 11.8. This decline

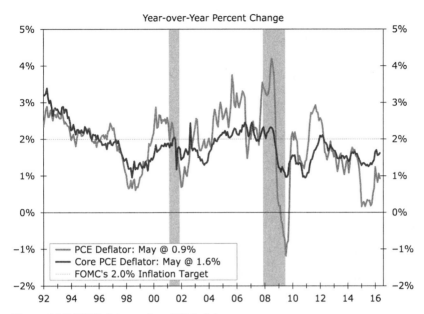

Figure 11.7 PCE Deflator vs. Core PCE Deflator
Source: U.S. Department of Commerce

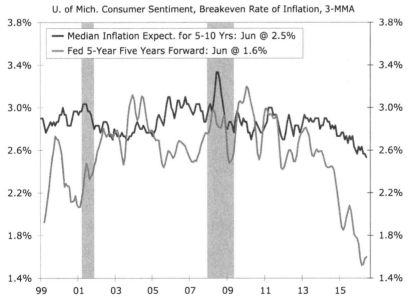

Figure 11.8 Median Inflation Expectations 5 to 10 Years Ahead
Sources: Bloomberg LP and Federal Reserve Board

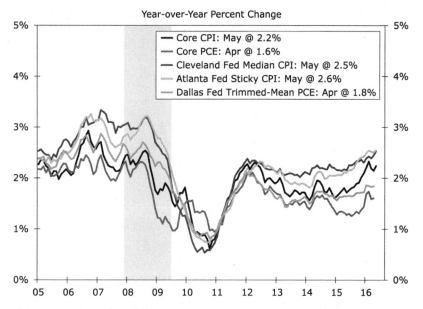

Figure 11.9 Alternative Inflation Measures
Sources: U.S. Department of Labor, U.S. Department of Commerce, and Federal Reserve System

is consistent with the decline in the 10–2-year Treasury yield curve but also contrary to the anticipated pattern that continued declines in the unemployment rate would be accompanied by rising inflation and inflation expectations. The decline in expectations indicates that the FOMC's attempt to raise inflation finds no vote of confidence in the marketplace.

Mixed signals on inflation are further revealed in Figure 11.9 when we examine alternative inflation measures from several sources that indicate that despite the message of inflation expectations, actual inflation is creeping up—yet at a pace that is barely recognizable by the markets and certainly not fast enough for the FOMC to ponder raising the funds rate at a faster pace or even the pace the FOMC had anticipated in its earlier versions of the dot plot. Figure 11.9 provides an excellent picture of the measurement problem of inflation and another example of imperfect information facing both the private market agents and public policy makers.

As a result, the dot plot provided by the FOMC has regularly shifted downward as illustrated in Figure 11.10. This downward shift hints

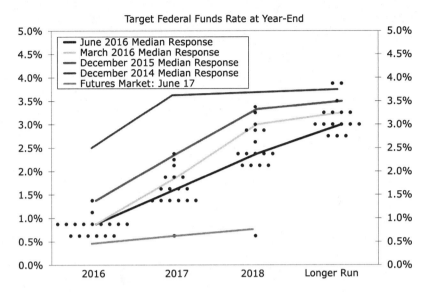

Figure 11.10 Appropriate Pace of Policy Firming
Source: Federal Reserve Board and Bloomberg LP

that the FOMC has consistently overestimated the path of the funds rate, which, in turn, reflects the imperfect information facing both the FOMC and private decision makers with respect to both the reliability of the inflation/policy model and the information that forms the basis of estimating such models for decision making.

Dynamic Adjustment: Change Takes Time

Things take time—especially in economics. Dynamic adjustment concerns bring into focus three considerations. First, policy changes and exogenous shocks demand time to adjust as the old equilibrium is shattered and markets take time to gather and process information to discover a new equilibrium.

Second, economic change seldom is allowed to take effect before a second change is imposed. Particularly in recent years, the turnover in political positions in the U.S. Congress every two years has shifted the preferences and expectations on policy actions and thereby the imperative for economic adjustment. One reason that economic change seldom plays out is that the election cycle is shorter than the economic cycle. Beginning with the Reagan tax program, many fiscal policy programs are phased in and therefore many of the impacts of policy take place over time and, moreover, are often reversed as time passes.

Third, for many programs, such as Dodd-Frank and the Affordable Care Act, the provisions of the program are not clear when the law is passed and administrators are in a learn-as-you-go-along mode so that, in the case of Dodd-Frank, all the provisions are not worked out even seven years later. Regulatory policy, as in fiscal policy, suffers from long periods of adjustment to actual and continual modifications of tax law/regulations over time.

For economic policy, there are three properties of the lag structure—recognition, implementation, impact. For monetary and fiscal policy, especially in the context of countercyclical policy, recognizing the drift into economic weakness or economic boom phases is difficult. First, even when these phases are recognized, implementing policy is difficult given policy actions require agreement among a number of constituents. Second, the impact of policy can be a drawn-out affair as we have witnessed historically for monetary policy and more recently for regulatory policy. Finally, in many ways, countercyclical policy has been abandoned given that the implementation lags are so long that implementing policy ends up being pro-cyclical rather than countercyclical.

In addition, economic policy also has long-run impacts that are often overlooked in the short run in an effort to get something done. In some ways, this is the product of the law of unintended consequences. For current monetary policy, there are concerns that the regime of low interest rates has altered the pricing of risk and interfered with the need to restructure and allow the failure of many economically inefficient companies that are using inexpensive financial capital in an inefficient way.

For fiscal policy, the focus on short-run stimulus as a policy guideline has shifted to concerns about long-run growth as a guideline. Spending is focused on items such as infrastructure spending. Meanwhile, trade-offs are now being framed as choices between generations and no longer stimulus/restraint over the current economic cycle. For entitlement programs such as Social Security, the political payoff for more generous benefits today does not accurately account for the costs over the long run. As indicated by the 2016 Social Security and Medicare trustees report, the long-run outlook for both accounts indicates both are headed for insolvency.[9] In addition, the 10-year horizon benchmark for assessing the fiscal impact of many federal programs may not be enough to properly account for all the long-run impacts.

Dynamic adjustment in federal spending due to demographics is also represented by the Congressional Budget Office in Figure 11.11. Here the steady rise in mandatory spending is especially clear. In addition, the CBO also projects that mandatory spending on interest expense will also rise in the years ahead, thereby further crowding any domestic discretionary spending.[10]

Dynamic adjustment is also the result of constant changes in marginal tax rates over time as illustrated below in Figure 11.12. For households, the variability of the U.S. top marginal income tax rate renders an incentive to alter the timing of income realization and work/leisure decisions.

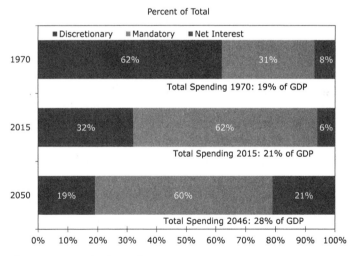

Figure 11.11 Federal Spending
Source: Congressional Budget Office

---

[9] The 2016 Annual Report of the Board of Trustees OASDI Trustees Report estimates that trust fund reserves will be depleted by 2034.
[10] Updated Budget Projections: 2016 to 2026, Congressional Budget Office, March 2016.

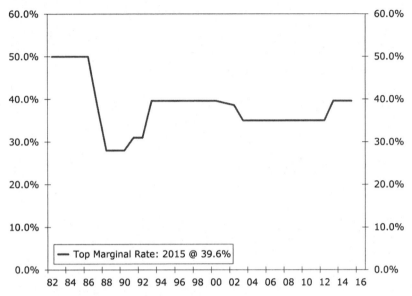

Figure 11.12 U.S. Top Household Marginal Tax Rate
Source: U.S. Department of the Treasury

Regulatory Policy: Minimize Risk but Also Reward?

Regulatory policy alters the after-tax rate of return for many activities while also altering the balance of risk and reward. Incentives matter. Since the initiation of Dodd-Frank, there has been a sequence of discussions and subsequent increases in bank capital requirements. As a result, there has been steady downward pressure on the expected rate of return on bank capital and thereby further restraint in the pace of bank credit growth this cycle.

For regulators, the incentive is clear: seek to minimize risk for professional reputation—"not on my watch." Yet for the overall economy the cost of restrictive regulation is the loss of income and jobs on the rest of the economy. Restrictive regulatory policy in the short run is not met with an elastic supply of credit. Short-run adjustments in the supply of credit function is limited but over time the supply function of the economy becomes more elastic—classic microeconomics. As institutions work around the rules or as new institutions grow to deal with credit within the new rules, the long-run supply of credit becomes more elastic.

There are long-term costs to regulatory overreach as well where the supply of goods and credit simply disappears. The Nye Committee investigations into military armament practices in WWI led firms such as DuPont to drop out of the business and for many other firms to severely limit their commitment to military production. The long-run cost was the limited production capability for American firms to meet the demand in the period leading up to WWII.[11]

Regulation alters the risk/reward trade-off in doing any economic activity. In the short run, there are sunk costs given fixed physical capital and lifetime human capital skills. Over time, capital and labor can adjust but this adjustment is exactly the dynamic response we have examined and, moreover, the elasticity of response will differ by economic sectors. In this U.S. election year (2016), the forward guidance on both regulation and trade policy will reflect different visions of the future for policy and different directions for the economy.

Credit is one example of the dynamic adjustment of consumers and lenders to the new regulatory regime post Dodd-Frank. As illustrated in Figure 11.13, the response in the consumer credit market has been

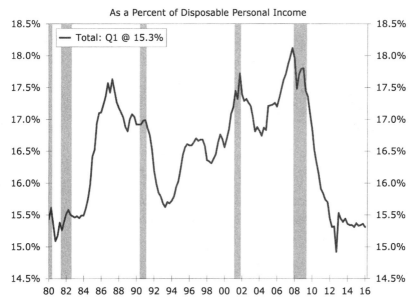

Figure 11.13 Financial Obligations Ratio Total
Source: Federal Reserve Board

---

[11] Arthur Herman, *Freedom's Forge: How American Business Produced Victory in WWII* (New York: Random House, July 2013).

fairly dramatic. The financial obligations ratio, as published by the Federal Reserve, estimates the ratio of debt payments to disposable income for households. The ratio, which accounts for both homeowners and renters, reflects the big change on both the supply and demand for credit. The result since the Great Recession has been a dramatic decline in the financial obligations ratio. During the post–Great Recession era there has been a rethink on the demand and supply of credit.

Dynamic financial adjustments take on a cyclical character as illustrated by the behavior of corporate profit margins (Figure 11.14). These adjustments reflect the evolution of the cost of labor, productivity, and unit labor costs over the economic cycle. As illustrated in Figure 11.15, nonfarm unit labor costs rise in each economic expansion (1998–2000, 2006–2007), and we see the same pattern now in 2014–2016. For each cycle, labor compensation tends to rise as the cycle matures. In addition, productivity tends to decline such

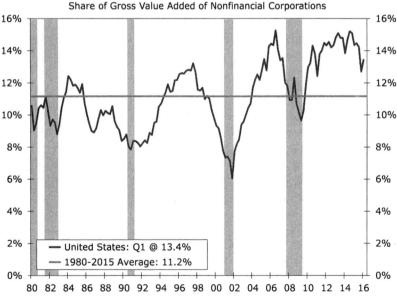

Figure 11.14 Nonfinancial Domestic Profits
Source: U.S. Department of Commerce

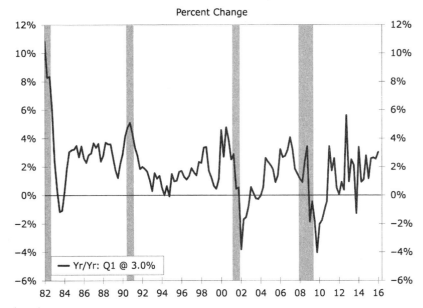

Figure 11.15 Nonfarm Sector Unit Labor Costs
Source: U.S. Department of Labor

that, net, unit labor costs rise, and that puts a squeeze on corporate profits.

Trade policy often reflects the broader macro view of competitive advantage. However, on the individual country level, trade policy reflects a complex/conflicting set of competing industry/consumer interests that lead to a very different set of economic outcomes than would have been predicted by reliance upon a perfectly competitive market framework. Hence, the issues of imperfect information and dynamic adjustment play into all trade policy actions. Moreover, the tariff/quota systems of many trade agreements signal that prices are often set at levels that lead to a misallocation of real and financial resources across countries. In the current economic expansion, there has been a distinct downshift in the pace of economic growth of global trade (Figure 11.16). This signals a possible ominous structural shift in the pace of global trade and thereby an economic barrier to growth by trade in many emerging markets.

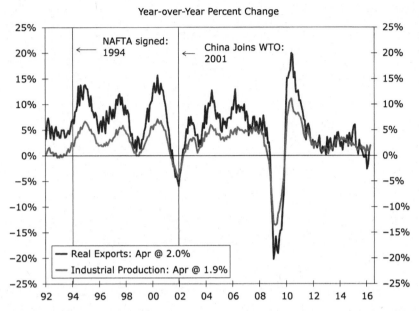

Figure 11.16 Global Trade Indicators
Source: Netherlands Bureau for Economic Policy Analysis

Price Adjustment: Lower for Longer

Probably the most notable price adjustment over the long run has been the downshift from the 1970s to a pace of sub–2 percent growth since the advent of the North American Free Trade Agreement (NAFTA), as illustrated in Figure 11.17. Globalization has benefited consumers by keeping global pressures on prices in the United States under wraps for over 20 years.

Meanwhile, over the short run, we have witnessed a persistent difference between commodity prices, often in traded goods, and service prices, often in nontradable goods (Figure 11.18). Commodities are also often relatively undifferentiated products, more often traded globally, and therefore price competition in commodity markets is intense. In contrast, services are often portrayed as differentiated and less traded globally, thereby allowing service providers to retain some degree of pricing power.

For markets, price adjustments come in many forms. Price changes alter incentives and therefore economic behavior. Yet many of these

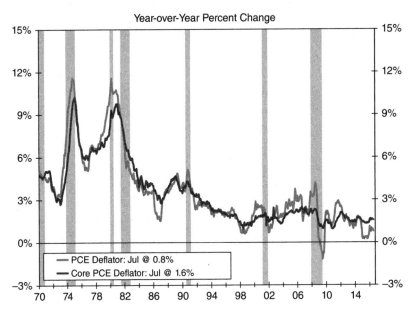

Figure 11.17 PCE Deflator vs. Core PCE Deflator
Source: U.S. Department of Commerce

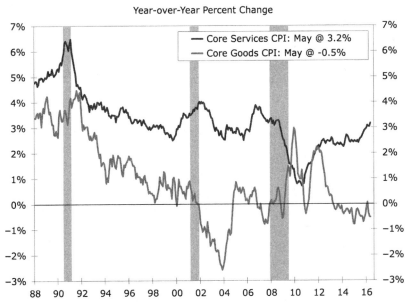

Figure 11.18 Core Goods vs. Core Services CPI
Source: U.S. Department of Labor

price changes are not recognized as price changes, and we therefore highlight them here to emphasize the theme that policy changes are often price changes and therefore impact incentives and economic activity.

For example, monetary policy will alter the price of credit and the difference between credit allocation/investments along the yield curve. Monetary policy, by altering the pace of inflation, alters the time value of money and thereby decisions on the timing to engage in any economic activity. Fiscal policy alters the price of the labor/leisure decision for households while also altering the after-tax rate of return on investment by businesses. Regulation alters the expected rate of return and the regulatory risk assessment in any business/individual economic activity.

Trade policy alters the relative prices of imported and exported goods and thereby alters the real exchange rate and the terms of trade for an economy. For example, in Figure 11.19, the sharp adjustment by policy makers in the four countries represented of the nominal exchange rate abruptly altered the effective exchange rate and thereby the trade and capital flows between the host country and its trading partners. In Figure 11.20, the emergence of China into the World Trade Organization made a sharp change in the trajectory of commodity prices.

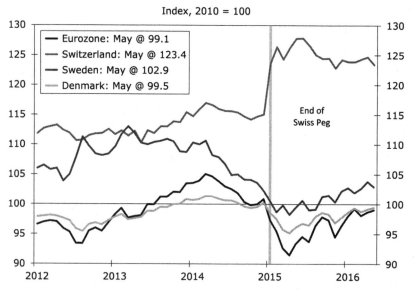

Figure 11.19 Nominal Effective Exchange Rates
Source: Bank for International Settlements

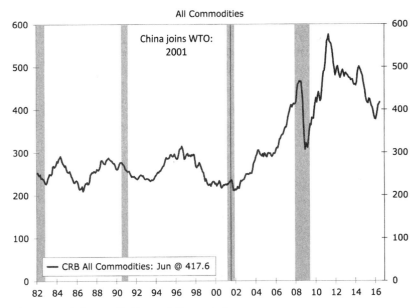

Figure 11.20 Commodity Research Bureau Index
Source: Commodity Research Bureau

Alterations in the price of credit as a reflection of monetary policy actions are represented in Figures 11.21 and 11.22. Changes in the price of credit are often not thought of in the same way as a change in real goods prices and thereby incentives. Yet the changes illustrated in Figures 11.21 and 11.22 certainly impacted incentives and economic activity. The continued drop in the three-month interbank offered rates signaled an easing of policy by central banks in an effort to lower the price of credit and encourage household and business spending. Meanwhile, the bailing-in of private creditors in Portugal to the failure of Novo Banco by Portuguese regulators led to a sharp increase in the risk adjusted price of credit in Europe for all banking institutions.

Finally, the concerns on risk-reward from a monetary policy maker are evident in Figure 11.23. Chair Yellen commented on her concerns about the risk involved in high-yield debt issues. Since that concern was expressed, the risk spread over Treasury benchmarks rose thereby discouraging, at the margin, further investments with high-yield financing.

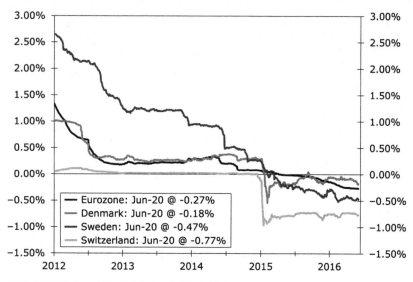

Figure 11.21 Three-Month Interbank Offered Rates
Source: Bloomberg LP

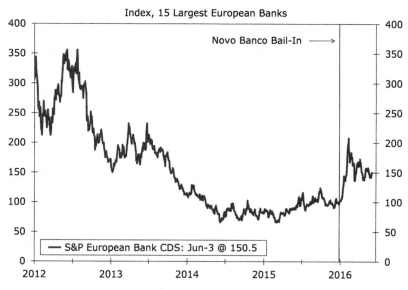

Figure 11.22 S&P European Banks Select 15 CDS Index
Source: Bloomberg LP

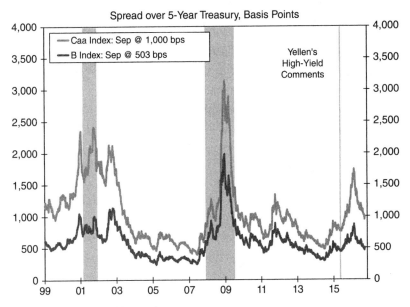

Figure 11.23 High-Yield Spreads
Source: Bloomberg LP

ECONOMIC POLICY IN THE CONTEXT OF AN IMPERFECT ECONOMY

Economic policy does not operate in a vacuum of a perfectly competitive economy of full and complete information and instantaneous adjustment. On the contrary, the economy is imperfect and, moreover, all policy works within the political goals and institutional constraints of a society. Our effort in this chapter is to place economic decision makers in a more practical context of contemporary economic behavior. While typical economic commentary focuses on the action in fiscal and monetary policy, we have also illustrated that regulatory and trade policy suffer from the same constraints in an imperfect economy.

Second, we have focused on the behavior of benchmark economic variables that are the object of policy makers but whose behavior differs under conditions of an imperfect economy from the perfect economy models under which most policy making designs are conducted. In the modern post-1982 era, the role of globalization has altered the behavior of growth, inflation, interest rates, and exchange rates in our economic models. Moreover, the process of globalization has opened up the range of possibilities for corporate revenues/profits. Indeed, over 30 percent of S&P 500 companies' profits are now earned abroad.

In economics, it is the unusual, the imperfect, that provides the clues about the way forward—stagnation in the 1970s, tax policy and deregulation in the 1980s, and the financial crisis and subsequent reforms over the past 10 years. Yet, in empirical work, economists are too frequently guided by a number of uncritical assumptions on how the world works. First, as economists, we must recognize and discourage straw man arguments that improperly identify the false choices in economic decisions or portray the outcomes of such decisions only in the context of an idealized economic model. Second, we must be more critical of arguments that fail to recognize the assumption—or violation—of ceteris paribus when the outcomes of economic decisions are quite different when those ceteris paribus assumptions do not apply. Finally, we must be more critical of the simplistic views of perfect information and efficient markets. Economic outcomes rarely come about as seamlessly as predicted by theories and models. To phrase the philosophy of Captain Barbossa, economic rules are more like guidelines rather than rules.[12]

---

[12] *Pirates of the Caribbean*, Walt Disney Pictures, 2003.

About the Authors

JOHN E. SILVIA

John Silvia is managing director and the chief economist for Wells Fargo. Prior to his current position, John worked on Capitol Hill as senior economist for the U.S. Senate Joint Economic Committee and chief economist for the U.S. Senate Banking, Housing, and Urban Affairs Committee. Before that, he was chief economist of Kemper Funds and managing director of Scudder Kemper Investments, Inc. John was formerly president and a director of the National Association for Business Economics (NABE) and was former president of the Charlotte Economics Club. He has also served on economic advisory committees for the Federal Reserve Bank of Cleveland, the Federal Reserve Bank of Chicago, and the Public Securities Association.

John was awarded a NABE Fellow Certificate of Recognition in 2011 for outstanding contributions to the Business Economics Profession and Leadership among Business Economists to the Nation. For the second time in three years, he was awarded the best overall forecast by the Federal Reserve Bank of Chicago, as well as the best unemployment rate forecast for 2011. John has been awarded the Adolph Abramson award for the best article in economics published in *Business Economics* for a given year. John holds BA and PhD degrees in economics from Northeastern University in Boston and has a master's degree in economics from Brown University. John's book *Dynamic Economic Decision Making* was published by Wiley in August 2011. John's co-authored book, *Economic and Business Forecasting: Analyzing and Interpreting Econometric Results*, was published by Wiley in March 2014.

AZHAR IQBAL

Azhar Iqbal is a director and econometrician at Wells Fargo, responsible for providing quantitative analysis to the Economics group and modeling and forecasting of macro and financial variables. He is based in Charlotte, North Carolina.

Before joining Wells Fargo in 2007, he was an economist and course instructor at the University of Karachi in Pakistan. He has also worked as an economist on funded projects at the United Nations.

Azhar has three master's degrees. He earned his master's degree in economic forecasting from the University at Albany, State University of New York. He also has master's degrees in applied economics from the University of Karachi, and in econometrics and mathematics from the University of the Punjab in Lahore, Pakistan.

Azhar won the 2012 and 2014 NABE Contributed Paper Award as well as the 2010 Edmund A. Mennis Contributed Paper Award for best papers from the National Association of Business Economics (NABE). A strong supporter of education, Azhar teaches a graduate course, Advanced Business and Economic Forecasting, at the University of North Carolina at Charlotte. Azhar's co-authored book, *Economic and Business Forecasting: Analyzing and Interpreting Econometric Results*, was published by Wiley in March 2014.

His interests focus on forecasting, time series, panel data, and macroeconomics. Azhar has presented research papers at the American Economic Association, Econometric Society meetings, the Panel Data Conference, and other international conferences. He has published over two dozen papers in the *Canadian Journal of Economics, Global Economy Journal, Business Economics, Journal of Business Forecasting*, and others refereed journals.

SARAH WATT HOUSE

Sarah House is an economist with Wells Fargo Securities. She received her BA in economics and political economy from Tulane University and her MSc from the London School of Economics. Sarah is a member of the National Association of Business Economics and Charlotte Economics Club.

Index